PERT AND CPM

Program Evolution and Review Technique and Critical Path Method

Dr. P.N. Modi

B.E., M.E., Ph.D
Former Professor of Civil Engineering,
M.R. Engineering College, (Now M.N.I.T), Jaipur.
Formerly Principal, Kautilya Institute of Technology and Engineering, Jaipur

Rajeev Modi

Chartered Accountant

Sanjeev Modi

Chartered Accountant

STANDARD BOOK HOUSE

unit of: **RAJSONS PUBLICATIONS PVT. LTD.**

1705-A, Nai Sarak, PB.No. 1074, Delhi-110006 Ph.: +91-(011)-23265506
Show Room: 4262/3, First Lane, G-Floor, Gali Punjabian, Ansari Road, Darya Ganj, New Delhi-110002 Ph.: +91-(011) 43751128 Tel Fax : +91-(011)43551185, Fax: +91-(011)-23250212

E-mail: sbh10@hotmail.com www.standardbookhouse.in

Published by:
RAJINDER KUMAR JAIN
Standard Book House
Unit of: Rajsons Publications Pvt. Ltd.
1705-A, Nai Sarak, Delhi - 110006
Post Box: 1074
Ph.: +91-(011)-23265506 Fax: +91-(011)-23250212

Showroom:
4262/3, First Lane, G-Floor, Gali Punjabian
Ansari Road, Darya Ganj
New Delhi-110002
Ph.: +91-(011)-43751128, +91-(011)-43551185
E-mail: sbhl0@ hotmail.com
Web: www.standardbookhouse.in

First Published	:	1991
Second Edition	:	1998
Third Edition	:	2002
Fourth Edition	:	2007
Fifth Edition	:	2012
Sixth Edition	:	2017

Price: **₹ 220.00**

ISBN: 978-81-89401-25-2

Typeset by:
C.S.M.S. Computers, Delhi.

Printed by:
R.K. Print Media Company, New Delhi

Preface to the Sixth Edition

In this edition the book has been thoroughly revised and enlarged. A large number of Additional Multiple Choice Questions have been added.

Authors thank all the learned Professors as well as the students of the various universities for their appreciation of the book. The authors also thank their Publishers Shri Rajinder Kumar Jain and Shri Sandeep Jain for bringing out the book with very nice get-up.

Sep. 2016

P.N. Modi
Rajeev Modi , Sanjeev Modi

Preface to the First Edition

The book presents the basic concepts of the project management techniques namely PERT and CPM. It is primarily meant for the students studying in various universities for their first degree course in Engineering, Commerce and Manage-ment. The book will also be useful for the students taking professional examina-tions of the Cost and Works Accountants, Chartered Accountants and the Institution of Engineers. The inservicc personnel working in various projects would also find the book quite useful. In the treatment of the subjectemphasis has been laid to present it in a simple language so thai il may be easily understood by thereaders. The text isprofusely illuslrated with diagrams. All importaniconcepis are illustrated with worked examples. A large number of problems have also been given at the end of each chapter. In order to facilitate proper understanding of thc various terms a glossary has been given in an appendix at the end of the book. Also a large number of multiple choice questions are given in another appendix. The application of linear programming for finding the critical path in any network is also given in another appendix. Thus the book will be useful for the various competitive examinations such as Engineering Services and ICS examinations.

The authors are thankful to Shri Chiranji Lal for preparing the excellent diagrams. The full cooperation and understanding of our publishers Shri Ranjinder Kumar Jain and Shri Sandeep Jain is thankfully acknowledged.

P.N. Modi

December, 1990

Rajeev Modi Sanjeev Modi

Contents

1

Chapter

Project Management

1.1 INTRODUCTION

A project is a scheme or a proposal of something intended to be constructed or devised. A large number of projects, such as, construction of a dam, building of a new factory, installation of a power plant etc., are being implemented in our country under the various Five-Year Plan Programmes. Each project involves a number of activities or jobs (or tasks or functions) which are interrelated in some manner and all of these should be completed in order to complete the project. For the execution of a project the three basic things required are (i) men, (ii) material and (iii) money. Several countries are rich in natural resources so that for any project the required material is available in ample quantity, but they do not possess the required technical know-how as well as money. On the other hand there are several countries which are exceedingly poor in natural resources but are technically quite advanced and possess highly talented and skilled man-power as well as ample funds for undertaking any project. However, even with scarce resources projects may be successfully implemented with proper management. Each project, whether big or small, has three basic requirements as mentioned below :

(i) The project should be completed without any delay.

(ii) The project should use available man-power and other resources as sparingly as possible.

(iii) The project should involve minimum investment as far as possible.

The project management helps to fulfill the above requirements. The project management involves the following three phases :

(i) Project planning

(ii) Project scheduling

(iii) Project controlling.

Out of the above noted three phases of project management the first two phases are accomplished before the commencement of the actual project. The third phase comes into operation during the execution of the project and its aim is to recognize the bottle-necks in the execution of the project and to adopt the measures to eliminate the same so that the project is completed as per schedule.

1.2 PROJECT PLANNING

Project planning forms a very important part of project management. The planning of a project involves specifying the objectives of the project, listing the various activities or jobs (or tasks) to be carried out, determining the gross requirements of the various materials, equipment and man-power, preparing estimates of costs of the various items of the project and determining the durations of the various activities for satisfactory completion of the project.

In the process of project planning the following eight steps are involved:

(i) *Define* the objectives of the project in definite words.

(ii) *Establish* the goals and the intermediate stages to attain the final targets.

(iii) *Develop* the means of achieving the goals i.e., activities.

(iv) *Evaluate* the organizations resource—financial, managerial and operational—to carry out the various activities and to determine what is feasible and what is not feasible.

(v) *Determine* the individual courses of action as well as alternatives that will allow the accomplishment of the desired goals.

(vi) *Test* for the consistency with the general policy of the nation as a whole.

(vii) *Choose* an alternative which is not only consistent with its goals and concept but also one that can be accomplished with the evaluated resources.

(viii) *Decide* on the final plan.

During the planning phase it is essential to have a detailed information of all the operations or activities which would be required to be carried out before the project would be completed. Further the sequence of the various activities as well as their logical inter-relationship should be established.

The implementation of a project requires the use of various kinds of resources which may be classified as follows:

(a) Man power resources

(b) Equipment resources or Plant and Machinery resources

(c) Financial resources

(d) Material resources

(e) Space resources

(f) Time resources

The man power resources consist of skilled craftsman such as carpenter, turner, fitter, etc., unskilled labour, supervisory personnel and also top management. The equipment resources consist of plant and machinery such as dragline, power shovel, concrete batching and mixing plant, etc., to be used in work. The financial resources comprise the money required to be paid for the work and hence these are also known as controlling resources. The material resources include all the material such as cement, sand, coarse aggregate, steel, etc., that are used in the construction work of the project. The space resources include the total working space available for carrying out the various activities of the project. In some cases the available working space may be limited which would put restriction on the various activities of the project. The time resources include the total time available for the completion of the project. Again in some cases the time available for the completion of the project may be limited on account of certain factors. As such both the space and time may be constraining resources in some cases.

Almost in all the projects the resources constitute the starting point and hence their evaluation should be undertaken during the planning phase, before proceeding for the scheduling phase of the project.

1.3 PROJECT SCHEDULING

Scheduling may be defined as the process of laying out the various activities of the project in a time sequence in which they are to be performed and computing the requirements of resources needed at each stage of the project along with the expected time for completion of each activity. In other words scheduling is the process of assigning the starting and finishing dates for each of the activities of the project in such a way that the entire project proceeds in a logical sequence and in an orderly and systematic manner. The entire process of project scheduling, therefore, involves consideration of a number of combinations of *activity, sequence, resource* and *time* for any piece of work in relation to defined *objective* and *constraints.* Thus a project schedule should contain :

- list of *activities* to be completed ;
- chosen *sequence* in which these *activities* are to be taken up;
- chosen *date* and *time* for start and completion of each *activity* ; and
- approved list of *resources* required date by date for completion of the activities.

The project scheduling involves the following four steps.

(i) Listing the various activities to be completed and fixing their priorities i.e., indicating the order of their execution.

(ii) Preparing time table assigning start and completion dates to each activity.

(iii) Allocating the available resources in such a manner that as far as possible optimum utilisation of resources is ensured.

(iv) Considering the various constraints on account of availability of limited resources.

1.4 PROJECT CONTROLLING

Whereas the first two phases of project management viz., Planning and Scheduling of project are undertaken before the actual project starts, the controlling phase is undertaken during the actual execution of the project. The project controlling is the fundamental managerial function which involves reviewing the difference between the schedule and the actual performance once the project has begun. The analysis and correction of this difference forms the basic aspect of control.

In general for any project the following three types of controls are required to be enforced.

(1) Time control

(2) Cost control

(3) Quality control

Time control refers to the adherence to the time target as per the schedule. Cost control refers to the adherence to the cost targets as per the original estimates. Quality control refers to the adherence to the specifications laid for quality standards. There are several operational problems on account of which it may not be possible to achieve the time and cost targets. Some of the causes of delay leading to overruns in time or non-fulfilment of the time targets of a project may be lack of access to site, late drawings, incomplete drawings, changes or modifications in some of the works resulting in rework, unfavourable weather conditions, shortage of resources, late delivery of material, certain organisational problems, etc. Further the delay in the completion of the project may also lead to overruns in cost or non-fulfilment of the cost targets of a project. The quality control may, however, be achieved for almost all the projects. In order to accomplish quality control the following steps need be adopted.

(i) Formation of norms for quality of various items.

(ii) Checking the quality by tests.

(iii) Minor checks at site and major checks at the various laboratories,

(iv) Establishing of operational staff.

The process of project control, however, requires full involvement of all the sections of management, including the scheduler in setting the targets, resource allocation, implementation and control. The various steps involved in the accomplishment of project controlling are as follows.

(1) The various standards or targets should be established.

(2) The progress of the various activities of the project should be judged against the targets set.

(3) The deviations if any from the targets should be identified. Also the various operational problems should be identified.

(4) The correcting measures to rectify the deviations from the plan should be suggested. This will, however, involve the identification of all the problems and decision making.

1.5 PROJECT MONITORING AND CONTROL

Monitoring is a process of comparing the actuals with the planned and identifying the variance. Thus monitoring necessarily requires pre-planning because what is not planned cannot be monitored. Monitoring identifies causes for variances, generates feasible corrective actions and evaluates effects of corrective action taken from time to time. Also it issues warning signals to the concerned personnels who are responsible for taking control action. Monitoring may generate feasible corrective actions but itself cannot take actions. Thus it has more advisory function rather than controlling. Monitoring and control together are comparable to a thermostat which detects excess of temperature and automatically cuts off when it is in excess.

1.6 PROJECT MONITORING AND INFORMATION CELL

The work of planning and monitoring starts from the date the project is conceived and it lasts throughout the period till the project is commissioned. The work involved in this is of such a nature that it requires the use of several management techniques besides the technical know-how of the project. It, therefore, requires personnel who possess management background and thorough knowledge of technology of the project. Moreover, for effective monitoring it is essential to develop an information system. As such a separate cell of personnel termed as *'Monitoring and Information Cell'* is usually formed for this purpose. For a large project this cell may be headed by a person of the rank of chief engineer. The cell would provide information to the management for decision making. The function of the monitoring and information cell is, therefore, like a 'watch dog' which has to give a warning signal, the moment anything unexpected happens. Based on the signal the executive agency which is authorised to take corrective action is supposed to act. If no use is made of signals received from the monitoring cell the effectiveness and the purpose of the monitoring cell gets lost. However, if executive agency does not act readily or pays no attention to the suggestion of the cell, it has to prevail upon the appropriate authorities by pursuation, compulsion or any other appropriate method to make the executive agency to take the action as proposed by the cell. Thus although monitoring cell is not authorised to take actions, it should be able to shape the decisions by virtue of its knowledge and leadership.

1.7 DECISION-MAKING IN PROJECT MANAGEMENT

A decision is the end of the process of deliberation (or the act of considering the reasons for and against any thing). It involves a conscious choice or selection of one alternative from among a group of two or more alternatives. The management must, however, organize in such a manner that the process of deliberations is conscious, planned and appropriate and the decision is taken in time as a result of such deliberation at appropriate levels. A good decision-making involves the following four sequential steps :

(1) diagnosis of the problem,

(2) search for, and identification of, alternative solutions,

(3) evaluation of alternative solutions, and

(4) selection and implementation of the best alternative.

The decision-making exercise must start not with a decision, but with the problem for which the decision is needed. Thus the first job in decision-making is to find the real problem and to define it. The diagnosis of problem must be followed by a search for solution or alternative solutions and the considerations of how the problem can be solved and the options available. Out of the several alternatives it is essential to evaluate them before one can choose the best out of these. This may be successfully done through operations research which involves certain mathematical techniques such as linear programming.

1.8 PROJECT LIFE CYCLE OR PROJECT CYCLE

The various phases involved in the life of a project and which constitute the project cycle may be grouped under the three heads as discussed below.

1.8.1 Pre-Project Execution Stage or Pre-Investment Stage

It includes the following items :

(1) Project identification.

(2) Feasibility of project.

(3) Preparation of project report.

(4) Project appraisal.

(5) Investment decision.

(6) Project approval or sanction by the concerned ministry or organisation.

1.8.2 Project Activisation Stage or Investment Stage

It includes the following items :

(1) Project organisation and activation.

(2) Project planning and scheduling.

(3) Detailed engineering.

(4) Contracting.

(5) Execution

(6) Monitoring and controlling.

(7) Completion and commissioning.

1.8.3 Project Operation Stage or Post-Investment Stage

It includes the following items :

(1) Operation and maintenance.

(2) Project stabilisation.

(3) Project evaluation.

(4) Operational controls.

(5) Technological innovations.

A large size national level project is normally identified by the executive department in consultation with the State and Central planning agency. After the identification of the project the next step is preparation of feasibility report. This is done by the executive department and submitted to the funding agency for approval. If approved, the executive department proceeds with the preparation of the Detailed Project Report (DPR). It includes detailed analysis of project in respect of technical feasibility, economic, financial, cost benefit analysis, and managerial aspects of the project. The funding agency would also like to assess the ability of the executive department to execute and control the operation. The DPR is then evaluated by the funding agency. This is termed as 'Project Appraisal'. At this stage decision is taken whether to invest in the project or not

After the green signal to go ahead with the project is received the executive department begins the implementation of the project. During implementation of a project there may be several stages such as setting up of project organisation, detailed engineering, contracting and execution. Huge capital and other resources are then applied on the project and it is carried through to the commissioning stage. This requires detailed scheduling and monitoring to achieve the targetted completion of the project. After the project is commissioned, some time is allowed for stabilising its operation. The 'Project Completion Report' is then prepared which forms a guide for similar projects in future.

1.9 BASIC TOOLS AND TECHNIQUES OF PROJECT MANAGEMENT

The various tools and techniques of project management may be grouped under the following two heads.

(1) Bar charts, Milestone charts and Velocity diagrams

(2) Network techniques

1.9.1 Bar charts, Milestone Charts and Velocity Diagrams

Bar charts are the pictorial representation in two dimensions of a project For drawing these charts the project is subdivided into a number of manageable units or activities which are shown on one dimension or axis and the durations assigned to these activities are shown on the other dimension or axis. Milestone charts are the modified and improved versions of bar charts. The difference between these two charts being that while the bar charts represent activities, the milestone charts represent the events which mark either the beginning or the end of an activity. Velocity diagrams are useful for representing the activities which require a series of crews working in a given sequence.

1.9.2 Network Techniques

A network (or network diagram or network model) is a symbolic representation of the essential characteristics of a project analysed by network techniques. The most widely used network techniques are PERT and CPM. Each of these techniques are briefly described below.

1. PERT. PERT stands for *Program Evaluation and Review Technique.* It uses event oriented network in which successive events are joined by arrows. PERT is preferred for those projects or operations which are of non-repetitive nature or for those projects in which time for various activities cannot be precisely determined. Similarly research and development projects also come in this category. In such projects or operations management cannot be guided by the past experience and hence these are referred to as *once-through* projects or operations. For example, the project of *launching a satellite* involves the work which has been never done before. For such a project since the range of possible technical problem is immense, the estimates of time required to complete the various activities are made purely as guess-work. Moreover, for each activity in the network of such projects estimate is made not only of the *most probable time* required to complete the activity but also of the maximum time required to complete the activity (i.e., pessimistic estimate) and the minimum time required for the completion of the activity (i.e., optimistic estimate).

2. CPM. CPM stands for *Critical Path Method.* It uses activity oriented network which consists of a number of well recognised jobs or activities. In a CPM network each activity is represented by an arrow and the junctions between the activities represent the events. CPM is generally used for repetitive type projects, or for those projects for which fairly accurate estimate of time for completion of each activity can be made and for which cost estimates can be made with fair degree of accuracy. For example CPM is useful for construction projects for which both time and costs can be estimated fairly accurately in advance. Thus unlike PERT, CPM does not make use of probabilistic activity times ; it is a "deterministic" rather than a "probabilistic" model. However, it does not mean that CPM does not allow for variations in activity times. It does allow for variations in acitivity times, not as a result of random factors (bad luck or good luck) but as the planned and expected outcome of resource assignments.

1.10 ROLE OF NETWORK TECHNIQUES-PERT/CPM IN PROJECT MANAGEMENT

There are several reasons for the possible slippages in projects, such as incomplete detailing of projects, inadequate preliminary investigations, spiralling prices of materials, etc., which may cause overruns in time and cost. The causes of overruns in time and cost are generally classified as controllable and uncontrollable. The detailed study of several projects have shown that most of the causes of time and cost overruns are controllable and by the use of PERT/CPM some savings in these overruns are possible.

The projects of today are of fairly large size and are characterised by high level technology. Several specialised disciplines are involved in them, which call for participation of multiple agencies at various points of time. Their functions are interdependent. Moreover, for the supply of several things like cement, steel, equipments, etc., many outside agencies are involved. For new and complex projects as these, the simple technique of bar chart for planning, scheduling and monitoring does not suffice as it falls short of the requirement. The technique of network analysis such as PERT/CPM on the other hand provides a new systems approach to the management of such projects. These techniques have been used for a number of projects and they have proved to be extremely beneficial and effective in closing the gap between promise and performance. It is being realised that answer to the problem of slippages in project does not lie merely in providing extra resources but lies more in their effective scheduling and monitoring by PERT/CPM.

Various funding agencies for the developmental works such as International Bank for Reconstruction and Development (IBRD) have recognised the importance of these management techniques in the implementation of development projects. As such they have been prescribing their usage to the various development organisations who seek their assistance all over the world.

Government of India has also been prescribing the use of PERT/CPM in schemes/projects of all kinds. Message of scheduling and monitoring by PERT/CPM is being given since 1976–77 through a large number of training programmes sponsored by the Department of Personnel and Administrative Reforms, Home Ministry, Government of India and conducted by various institutes all over the country. Bureau of Public Enterprises has long back in 1970, issued guidelines for public sector corporations on the application of network techniques PERT/CPM. Further the Sixth Five-Year Plan, (1980–85) document states that after determining the exact date of physical start up of the projects, a PERT network should be drawn up for such schemes/projects, no matter in what discipline such a scheme or project exists.

REVIEW QUESTIONS

1.1 What is a project? What are the different phases of project management? Discuss each phase briefly.

1.2 What is meant by project monitoring and control?

1.3 Discuss briefly the significance of monitoring and information cell for a project.

1.4 Write short notes on (i) project planning, (ii) project scheduling, (iii) project controlling, (iv) project life cycle, (v) decision making in project management, (vi) basic tools of project management.

1.5 Define PERT and CPM. Discuss briefly the role of PERT and CPM in project management.

1.6 What do you understand by controlling resources and constraining resources? Explain with examples.

1.7 Describe briefly what is meant by CPM and PERT.

1.8 In what major ways does a CPM network differ from a PERT network?

2

Chapter

Bar Charts, Milestone Charts and Velocity Diagrams

2.1 INTRODUCTION

A project invariably consists of a number of activities or jobs which needs to be accomplished in a definite sequence for the successful completion of the project in a specified time schedule. The bar charts, milestone charts and velocity diagrams are pictorial representation of the various activities of a project. These charts show the various activities to be done and the time required for their completion. A detailed discussion of the bar charts, milestone charts and velocity diagrams has been given in the subsequent sections.

2.2 BAR CHARTS

Bar charts, which are also popularly known as Gantt charts, were developed by H.L. Gantt in the year 1900 during his work on production control. In the earlier times the bar charts were applied for planning and control of jobbing production (i.e., small projects involving job works) and are still found useful in many production control offices for minor job work projects which are not of complex nature. However, for complex projects these have been replaced by PERT and CPM networks which are more sophisticated techniques of project management.

A bar chart consists of two coordinate axes, one (the horizontal axis) representing the time elapsed and the other (the vertical axis) representing the activities or jobs to be performed. The activities or jobs are represented in the form of bars (Fig. 2.1) which are parallel to the horizontal axis. Each bar represents one specific activity or job of the project. The beginning and end of each bar represent the time of start and time of finish of that activity or job and hence the length of bar indicates the time required for the completion of that activity or job. Generally in any project some activities or jobs can be taken up concurrently and some will have to be completed before others can begin. As such in a bar chart of a project, some of the bars run parallel or overlap each other time-wise (these correspond to concurrent activities or jobs) and some run serially with one bar beginning after another bar ends (these correspond to an activity or job that succeeds a preceding activity or job).

Figure 2.1 shows a bar chart of a project which has five distinct activities or jobs viz., *I, J, K, L* and *M* to be performed for the completion of the project. Each of these activities have been represented by bars parallel to the horizontal axis. The time durations required for the completion of these activities *I, J, K, L* and *M* are 3, 4, 4, 5 and 6 weeks respectively. From the chart the following observations may be made.

(i) Activities *I* and *J* start at the same time and proceed concurrently or in parallel, though they take different time periods for their completion.

(ii) Activity *K* starts before the completion of activities *I* and *J*.

(iii) Activity *L* starts only when activity *I* is completed.

(iv) Activity *M* starts only after the completion of activity *K*.

(v) Bars representing activities *I* and *L*, and *K* and *M* run serially.

(vi) End of activity *M* indicates the completion of the project.

(vii) The total duration of the project is 12 weeks.

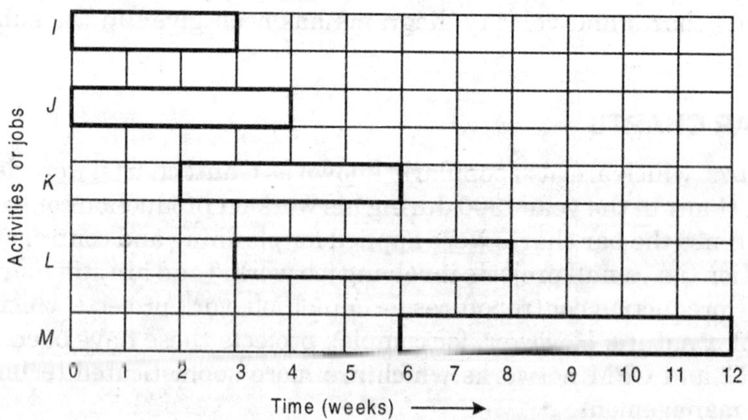

Fig. 2.1 *Bar chart of a project.*

A specific project of manufacturing and installing a Pelton turbine is considered. This project consists of the following activities.

Activity	*Description*	*Time for completion (in weeks)*
A	Preparing patterns for casting the Pelton wheel assembly	6
B	Preparing the moulds	4
C	Casting and cleaning operation	2
D	Machining of wheel assembly	6
E	Assembling the wheel parts	1
F	Fixing the wheel	4
G	Concreting work	16
H	Preparing casing for the wheel	5
I	Fixing of casing	2
J	Making generator parts	10
K	Assembling the generator parts	8
L	Installing the generator	6
M	Connecting the generator with the turbine and testing	8

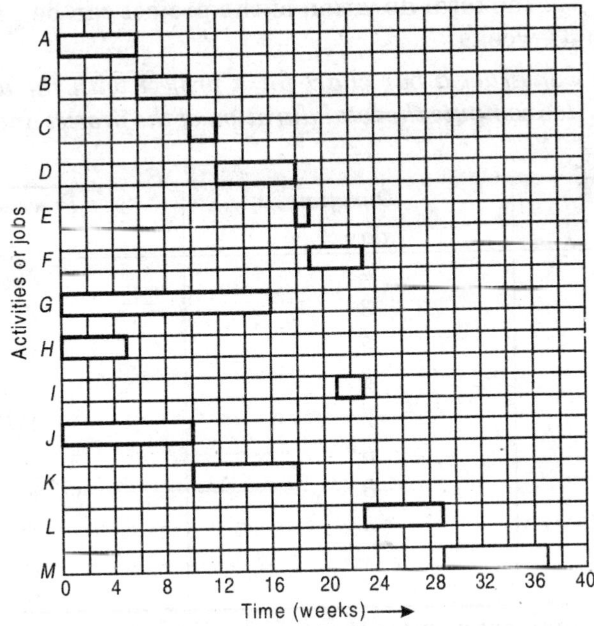

Fig. 2.2 *Bar chart of a project of manufacturing and installing a Pelton wheel turbine.*

Figure 2.2 shows the bar chart for the above noted turbine project. It may be seen that activities *A, G, H* and *J* can start at the same time. This is so because the work of making generator parts (activity *J*) can be started even if patterns for casting the Pelton wheel parts (activity *A*) have not been prepared or casing (activity *H*) is incomplete. Similarly the concreting work (activity *G*) can be started even if patterns for casting the Pelton wheel parts (activity *A*) are incomplete or casing for the wheel (activity *G*) has not been prepared. On the other hand activities *B, C, D, E, F, I, K, L* and *M* are dependent on certain other activities. For example the work of preparing the moulds (activity *B*) can be taken up only when the patterns for casting the Pelton wheel (activity *A*) have been completed. Similarly the work of fixing of wheel (activity *F*) cannot be taken up unless the wheel parts have been assembled (activity *E*). Further fixing of casing (activity*I*) cannot be taken up immediately after the preparation of the casing (activity *H*) as fixing of casing will be taken up along with fixing of wheel (activity *F*). Thus as shown in Fig. 2.2 activities *F* and *I* proceed concurrently or in parallel. Similarly the work of installation of generator (activity *L*) cannot be taken up immediately after assembling the generator (activity *K*) as one will have to wait till fixing the wheel (activity *F*). Therefore activity *L* can be started only after the completion of activity *F* and not after activity *K*, which is clearly depicted in the bar chart of the project.

From Fig. 2.2 the total duration of the project can be computed which works out to 37 weeks.

Example 2.1 *Construct a bar chart for a project with the activity data as noted below. Also compute the total duration of the project and its completion date.*

Activity	*Duration (days)*	*Preceded by*
A	4	*None*
B	3	*A*
C	5	*B*
D	4	*None*
E	7	*B,D*
F	6	*D*
G	8	*E*
H	5	*F*
I	4	*H*
J	3	*G, I*

The date of commencement of the project is 10th October, 2011 and Sundays are observed as holidays

Solution The bar chart of the project with the given activity data is as shown in Fig. 2.3. The total duration of the project is 29 days including 4 Sundays. The project will be completed on 7th November, 2011,

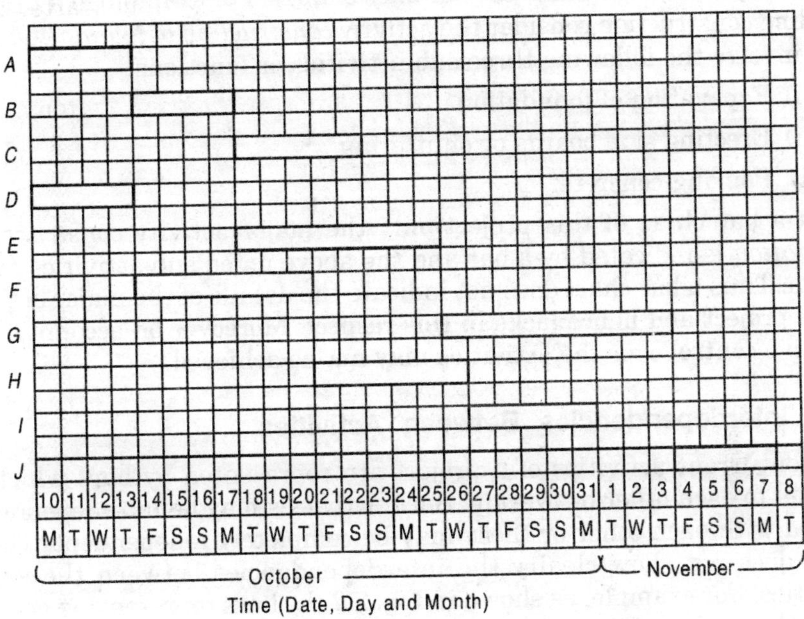

Fig. 2.3 *Bar chart for the Example 2.1*

2.3 STEPS FOR THE CONSTRUCTION OF A BAR CHART

The various steps involved in the construction of a bar chart of a project are as follows:

(i) Identify the various activities or jobs which will be required to be accomplished.

(ii) Arrange the various activities in the order in which they may be taken up. Identify the activities which are independent of the other activities. Also identify the activities which will precede or follow other activity (or activities).

(iii) Estimate the time required for the completion of each of the activities.

(iv) Represent the various activities in the bar chart by horizontal bars at their relative positions.

2.4 LIMITATIONS OF BAR CHARTS

The bar charts have certain limitations as described below.

2.4.1 Lack of Degree of Details

On a bar chart generally only major activities of a project are shown. A major activity, however, involves several sub-activities or functions, but all of these are not shown on the chart because if too many activities are separately shown the bar chart becomes clumsy. For example in a project of building construction consider the activity *construction of foundation* which may involve the following three sub-activities or functions.

(i) Excavation of foundation

(ii) Erecting side boards or shuttering

(iii) Pouring concrete.

On a bar chart of this project only the major activity *construction of foundation* is indicated by a bar and the above noted sub-activities are not shown. Thus a bar chart does not indicate the details of the major activities of the project and hence lacks in this respect. Moreover on account of this, effective control over the activities may not be achieved.

2.4.2 Interdependencies Between Activities

The concurrent activities of a project are represented by bars which run parallel to each other or overlap. Such activities may be interdependent or related with each other or these may be completely independent. The bar chart does not show clealry the interdependencies between the various activities. For example, as shown in Fig. 2.2 the bars representing activities *A*, *G*, *H* and *J* run parallel, thereby indicating that these activities can be taken up concurrently, but these four activities are completely independent in this case. However, two parallel or overlapping bars need not always stand for independent activities as shown in the following example.

In a project of building construction the construction of foundation may be assumed to involve excavation of foundation, erecting side boards or shuttering and pouring concrete. The time required for the completion of each of these three sub-activities are indicated below.

A. Excavating foundation	24 weeks
B. Erecting side boards or shuttering	18 weeks
C. Pouring concrete	21 weeks

All these sub-activities are interdependent and if scheduled serially or in strict sequence the total time taken for the completion of the activity will be 63 weeks. However, these sub-activities may be scheduled for overlapping times to reduce the time of completion of the activity. Thus the erection of side boards or shuttering can start after say one-half of the foundation excavation has been completed. Similarly, the pouring of concrete can start, say, 6 weeks after the erection of side boards or shuttering. The bar chart for these sub-activities will be as shown in Fig. 2.4, from which the time for the completion of the activity will be 39 weeks. According to this plan of working the side board erectors will have 6 weeks of work after the excavation job is over, and 9 weeks of concrete pouring job will be left after the erection of side boards is completed. However, if due to certain unexpected difficulties the excavation of foundation is delayed by a few weeks, how will this affect the job erection of side boards or the concrete pouring job, is not revealed by the bar chart.

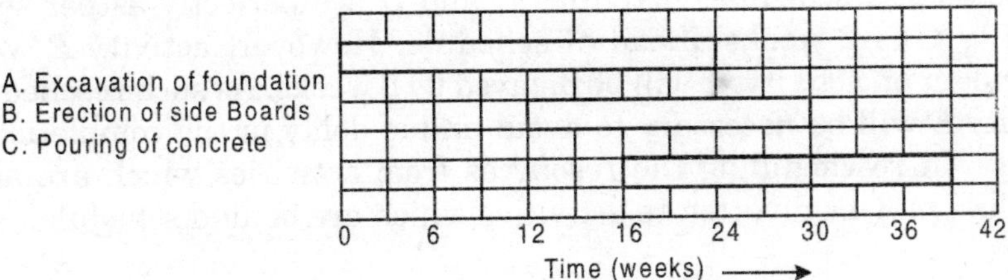

Fig. 2.4 *Bar chart for construction of foundation.*

2.4.3 Review of Project Progress

For revising the progress of a project at any instant of time it is absolutely necessary to know the amount of work in progress or jobs completed. The information about the progress of a project helps to make necessary changes in the working plans by rescheduling the remaining activities so that proper control may be enforced on the project. A bar chart does not show the progress of work

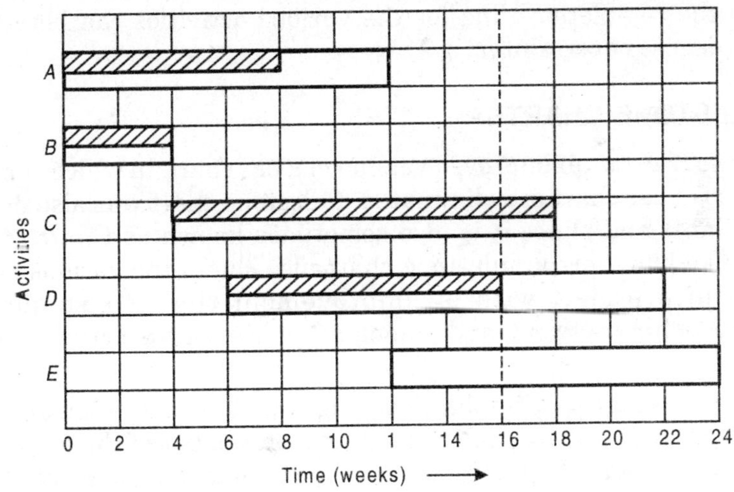

Fig. 2.5 *Bar chart showing progress of activities.*

and hence it cannot be used as a control device. However, a conventional bar chart can be modified to give information about the progress of a project made at any instant of time. This can be done by showing the progress of each activity by hatched lines along the bar of the corresponding activity. Generally hatching is done in the top half width of the bar only as shown in Fig. 2.5.

For example the progress made after a lapse of 16 weeks since a project started is marked on the bar chart of the project as shown in Fig. 2.5. The time required for the completion of activity *A* is 12 weeks, but during 16 weeks only 8 weeks work has been done. This means that activity *A* is 8 weeks behind schedule. Activities *B* and *D* are perfectly as per schedule. Activity *C* is 2 weeks ahead of schedule. However, activity *E*, which is dependent on activity *A*, will be delayed by 8 weeks. As such rescheduling of activity *E* will be necessary to avoid undue delay in the completion of the project. In rescheduling the resources from activities which are ahead of schedule may be diverted to activities which are behind schedule.

2.4.4 Time Uncertainties

One of the most important limitations of the bar chart is its inability to reflect the uncertainty in estimation of the time required for the completion of the various activities. Such uncertainties may exist in space satellite launching projects or other complex projects which are largely characterized by extensive research, development and technological progress. Due to uncertainties in the estimation of time duration of various activities, rescheduling of some of the activities will be necessary which is however, not reflected in a bar chart. As such bar charts are useful for only small conventional projects, especially construction and manufacturing projects in which the completion time for the various activities can be estimated with fair degree of certainty.

2.5 MILESTONE CHARTS

A *milestone chart* is an improved version of a bar chart, in which some of the limitations of bar chart are eliminated. Milestone chart was also developed by H.L. Gantt and hence it is also sometimes known as *Gantt Milestone Chart*. Alike bar chart a milestone chart also shows the various activities involved in a project with an improvement that it also shows the interrelationships between and among all phases of the activities and the project.

Milestones are the specific phases or stages or key events of a main activity, which are represented by circles or squares on the bar of the main activity and are marked serially. Figure 2.6 (a) shows a bar chart of a project which involves four tasks or activities or jobs, viz., task *I*, task *J*, task *K* and task *L*, and Fig. 2.6 (b) shows the corresponding milestone chart. It may be seen that in a milestone chart the long-time activities or jobs or tasks are identified in terms of specific events or milestones, which are plotted against the time scale indicating their accomplishments by specified times. Each bar in a milestone chart again represents an activity or job or task and all the bars taken together represent the entire project.

A milestone chart shows relationship between the milestones within the same activity or job or task. It may be seen from Fig. 2.6 (b) that milestone 2 cannot be started until milestone 1 has been accomplished. Similarly milestone 9 cannot be taken up until milestone 8 has been completed. Thus as compared to bar chart better control can be achieved with the help of a milestone chart, but it still possesses the same deficiency that it does not depict the interdependencies between the various tasks or the relationship between the milestones of different tasks. For example milestone chart does not show whether milestone 6 of task *K* can be started before completion of milestone 2 of task *I* or milestone 4 and 5 of task *J*. This deficiency of milestone chart has led to the development of network which is described in section 2.7.

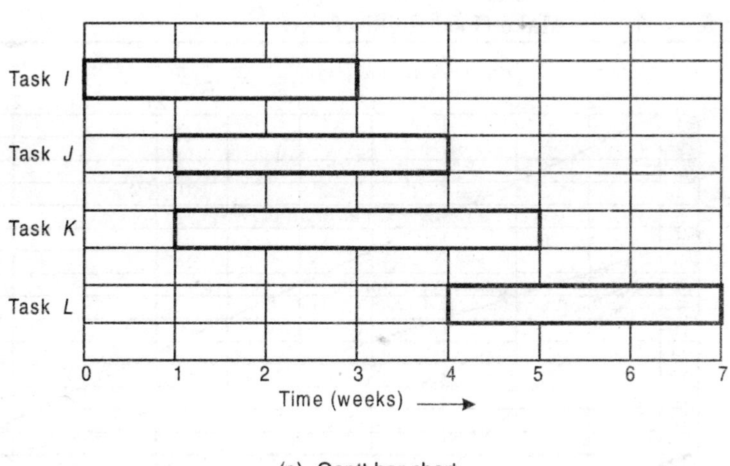

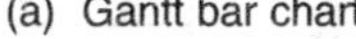

(a) Gantt bar chart

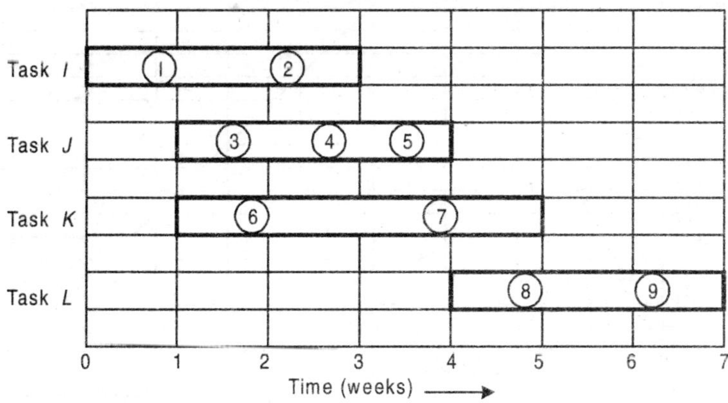

(b) Gant milestone chart

Fig. 2.6 *Bar chart and corresponding milestone chart.*

2.6 VELOCITY DIAGRAMS

In several projects the various activities or jobs requires a series of crews working in a given sequence. In such cases the schedule which displays the interaction of the various crews may be represented by a velocity diagram (Fig. 2.7). For example, a pipeline laying project may be considered to involve five crews which are capable of the production as indicated below.

Crew No.	*Task*	*Speed km/week*
1	Clear Right-of-way (ROW)	2
2	Excavate Trench	3
3	Weld and Set Pipe	1
4	Backfill Trench	4
5	Make Good Right-of-way	5

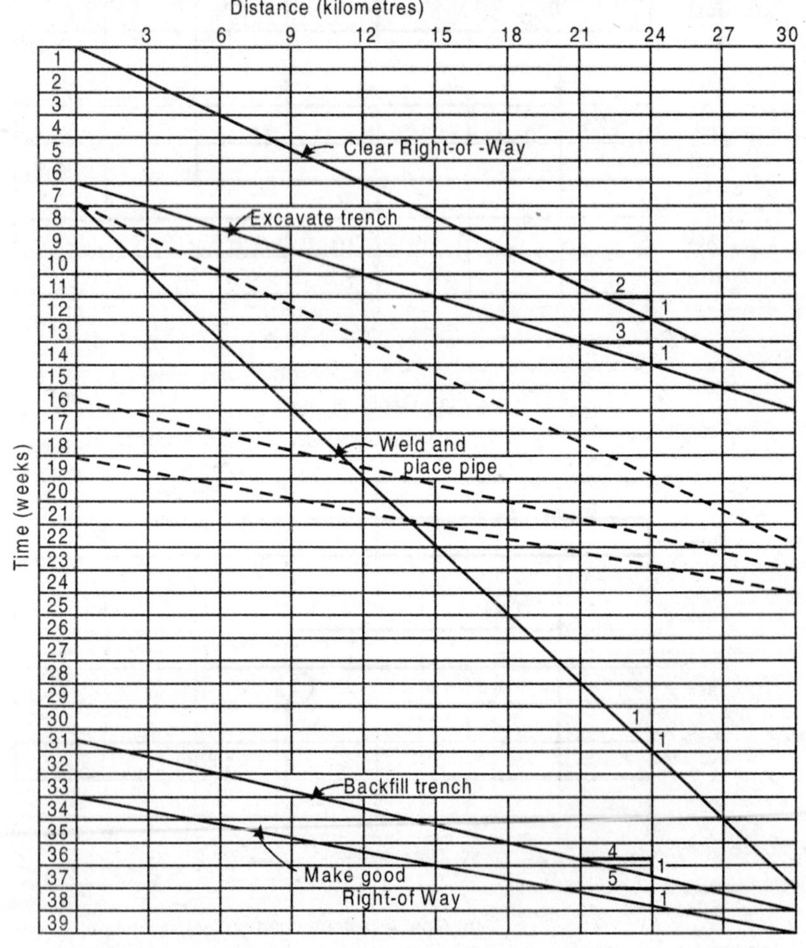

Fig. 2.7 *Velocity diagram for a pipeline laying project.*

A 30 kilometre pipeline is being planned with the aid of a velocity diagram. The progress of a crew on such a diagram is represented by a sloping line. The first crew which clear the right-of-way (ROW) can accomplish 2 km each week. Thus a line having a run of 2 km each week would represent the progress of this crew which may start the work immediately (Fig. 2.7). The second crew which excavate the trench can advance 3 km each week. If this crew was to start shortly after the first crew the trenching would soon be proceeding before the right-of-way has been cleared. This is not acceptable so a line of the appropriate slope can be started (say 1 week) after the right-of-way has been cleared. The welding and setting of the pipe may start in the seventh week i.e., one week after the excavating of trench has started. This procedure is continued until the project is completed in 39 weeks.

It is clear that the major portion of the time is consumed by the welding and setting operation. This schedule may, however, be improved by providing an additional welding crew. The effect of doubling the welding rate can easily be seen as the run of the slope would be increased from 1 km to 2 km each week. The resulting change shown by dotted lines on the same diagram indicates a completion time 24 weeks.

2.7 DEVELOPMENT OF NETWORK

The CPM/PERT network is an improvement over Gantt's milestone chart in a way that the CPM/PERT network illustrated the interrelationships between and among all the milestones in an entire project. The CPM/PERT network may be developed from Gantt's milestone chart in the following four transitional steps.

First step

The horizontal bars representing activities or jobs or tasks in a milestone chart are removed and the interrelationships between milestones within each specific activity are represented by arrows as shown in Fig. 2.8.

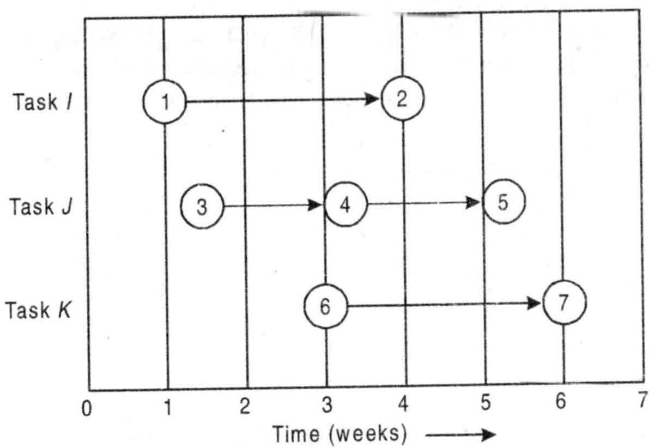

Fig. 2.8 *Illustration of first transitional step for the development of CPM/PERT network.*

Second step

The milestones of different tasks or activities are interrelated by arrows as shown in Fig. 2.9. This is the major advantage of CPM/PERT network over Gantt's milestone charts. It may be seen from Fig. 2.9 that milestone 4 can be started soon after the completion of milestone 3 and one need not wait until completion of milestone 2. Similarly milestone 6 can be taken up soon after completion of milestone 3, without waiting for the completion of milestones 4 and 5.

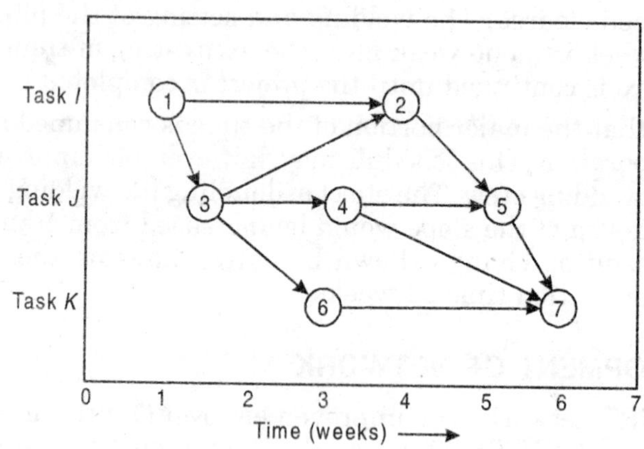

Fig. 2.9 *Interelationship between milestones of different tasks.*

Third step

Since all the milestones have been interrelated by arrows there is no need to designate each task or activity separately. Therefore the term task or activity, represented along the vertical axis in the Gantt's bar or milestone charts, is omitted in the network (Fig. 2.9).

Fourth step

The horizontal time scale is also omitted in the network because the times between the milestones are indicated on the arrows between them as shown in Fig. 2.10. The times on the arrows are normally expressed in weeks. For

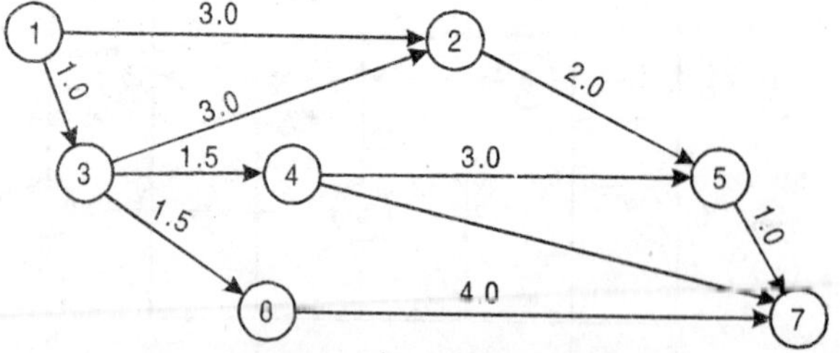

Fig. 2.10 *CPM/PERT network.*

example arrow between milestones 4 and 5 has 3 upon it which indcates that it will take 3 weeks time to reach from milestone 4 to milestone 5.

2.8 CPM/PERT NETWORKS

The CPM/PERT networks have two basic elements. These are the *event* and the *activity*. The event is a specific accomplishment that occurs at a definite point of time and the activity is the work required to accomplish a specific event. In the network events are represented by circles and the event numbers are indicated in the circles. The activities are represented by arrows joining two circles. Figure 2.11 illustrates how the events are joined by activities. The events are numbered to identify them. These events represent a definite point in time; event 1 represents the point in time 'work started' and event 4 represents the point in time 'work finished'. The arrows connecting these events therefore represent the time required to plan and do the actual work.

There are several projects for which the time required to complete the various stages of a project may be arrived at with certainty—such as building a house or a bridge across a river—because in these cases there has been some experience in handling similar projects. On the other hand there are certain projects for which time requirements may not be arrived at with certainty, e.g., developing a new ballistic missile, because these types of projects are unique in nature and there has been little or no experience in

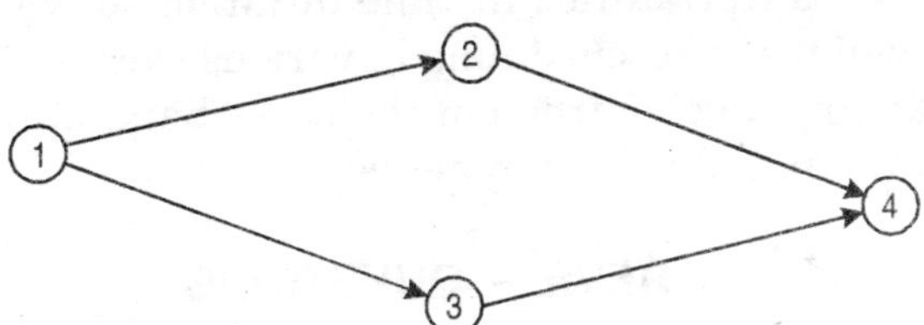

Fig. 2.11 *Events connected by arrows.*

handling such types of projects. CPM is used for those projects for which time estimates can be made with certainty while PERT is used for those projects for which time cannot be estimated with certainty. Further CPM emphasizes the relationship between applying additional resources to shorten the duration of various activities in a project and the increased cost of these additional resources. PERT incorporates uncertainty as to completion time of various jobs in a project model and hence it is used in research and development projects.

2.9 ADVANTAGES OF NETWORK OVER MILESTONE CHART

Some of the major advantages of network over milestone chart are as follows.

1. Interrelationships Among all Milestones. The network indicates the interrelationships among all the milestones but the milestone chart does not show the interrelationship among its milestones. Thus a milestone chart does not indicate that which milestone of a certain task should precede or follow the milestones of other tasks. On the other hand in a network all the milestones (or events) are interrelated (with the arrows) and therefore one can easily see that which milestone depends on the other.

2. No Need of Dividing the Project into Tasks. In a network the project is not required to be divided into tasks because the project is viewed as an integrated whole and hence the designation of task becomes superfluous.

3. Individual Time Value in Place of Common Time Scale. In a network individual time values are given for each of the activities whereas in a milestone chart a common time scale is given for all the activities. Thus the milestone charts do not indicate the time required in between two milestones or events which makes rescheduling difficult.

4. Use in Highly Complicated Project. Network can be used for highly complicated projects consisting of numerous activities but milestone charts cannot be used for such projects.

5. Incorporation of Time Uncertainties. The milestone chart does not reflect the uncertainty in the time durations estimated for various activities. Such uncertainties may be there in modern day space system programmes or other complex projects which involve research and development. The uncertainties in time durations of various activities of these projects will make rescheduling of various events a necessary part of the project planning and control. On the other hand uncertainties in time estimates are well taken care of in network.

REVIEW QUESTIONS

2.1 What is a bar chart? Narrate the various steps for constructing a bar chart.

2.2 What is the difference between bar chart and milestone chart?

2.3 "The developers of network improved on Gantt's milestone chart and modified it in order to illustrate interrelationships between and among all the milestones in an entire project". Comment.

2.4 What are the limitations of bar charts?

2.5 What are the major advantages of network over milestone chart?

2.6 Draw a bar chart with the help of following data

Task 1	5 days
Task 2	3 days
Task 3	7 days
Task 4	2 days
Task 5	4 days
Task 6	7 days

Tasks 1 and 4 will be started together. Task 2 shall start after completion of task 3 and task 3 shall take place after task 1. Tasks 5 and 6 will be taken up together but only after accomplishing task 3.

2.7 Distinguish between CPM and PERT. Give four examples in support of your answer.

2.8 Define 'milestones' and differentiate between a bar chart and a Gantt milestone chart. Illustrate your answer with the aid of suitable diagrams.

2.9 In what specific ways are milestone charts superior to bar charts? How is a network superior to a milestone chart?

2.10 Explain clearly the difference between an activity and an event.

3

Chapter

Fundamentals of Network

3.1 INTRODUCTION

The network (or network model) is a symbolic representation of the essential characteristics of a project analysed either with PERT or CPM. The use of network for project planning and scheduling involves (a) identification of independent activities or jobs and (b) determination of order of precedence of these activities. The order of precedence means the order in which the activities have to be completed before the others can be started. A network is a flow diagram or a graph which portrays each of these activities and the relation among the preceding and succeeding activities. The beginning and end of each of these activities constitute *events* of the project. In a network diagram an activity is represented by an arrow and event is represented by a circle which is referred to as node. The nodes are also sometimes represented by other regular geometrical figures such as square, rectangle, oval etc. The foregoing discussion is illustrated with the help of an example of Pipeline construction as shown in Table 3.1. The first column shows the alphabets identifying the activities involved in this project which are listed in the second column of Table 3.1. The third column shows the beginning and ending events of each activity. The fourth column shows the time needed for each activity.

TABLE 3.1 *Description of activities in pipeline construction*

Activity identification	*Activity description*	*Alternate events*	*Time needed to perform the activities (weeks)*
1	2	3	4
A	Conduct survey	1–2	2

Contd.

Table 3.1 Contd.

Activity identification	*Activity description*	*Alternate events*	*Time needed to perform the activities (weeks)*
1	2	3	4
B	Layout pipes at site	2–3	1
C	Marking for digging	2–4	1
D	Dig trench	4–3	6
E	Lay pipes in trenches and connect	3–5	4
F	Cover pipes with earth and tamp down	5–6	4

In respect of the Table 3.1 a network diagram may be drawn which is shown in Fig. 3.1. As would be noticed from the network diagram, activities have been shown by arrows leading from one circle to another which denote the events. The activity *A* in this project viz., conduct survey, starts at event 1 and ends at event 2. From the ending event of activity *a* (i.e., 2) two different activities *B* and *C* viz., Layout pipes at site and Marking for digging start

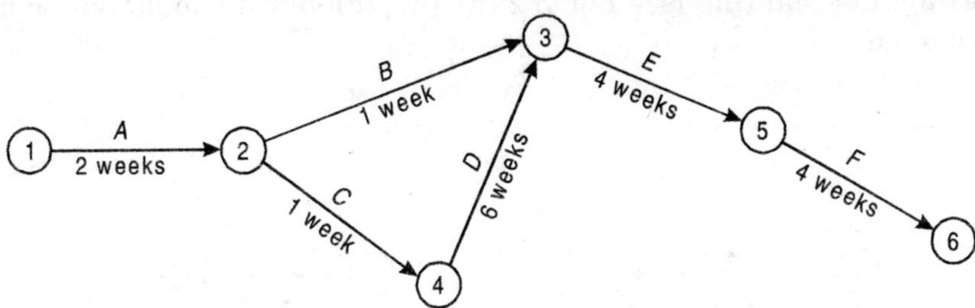

Fig. 3.1 *Network diagram of pipeline construction.*

concurrently. Both these activities (i.e., *B* and *C*) will be started only when activity *A* has been accomplished and therefore activities *B* and *C* are called successor or succeeding activities of activity *A* and activity *A* is called immediate predecessor or preceding activity of activities *B* and *C*. Similarly activity *E* viz., Lay pipes in trenches and connect can start only when the activities *B* and *D* viz., Layout pipes at site and Dig trench have been completed. Thus activities *B* and *D* are predecessor activities of activity *E* and activity *e* is successor activity of activities *B* and *D*.

As stated earlier an activity starts at one circle and ends at another. Thus as shown in Fig. 3.1 activity *A* initiates at circle 1 and terminates at circle 2. Since a pair of circles connected by an arrow represent a single job or activity, it follows that the activity *A* is also alternatively identified by (1, 2) or (1–2), where the number before comma or desh refers to the circle at which activity *A* has initiated and the number after the comma or dash refers to the circle at which activity *A* has terminated.

From the foregoing discussion it is evident that there are two elements of a network viz., *Activities* and *Events*. Both these elements are discussed in detail in the following sections.

3.2 ACTIVITY

An activity is the actual work or task performed to complete a specific event. An activity requires time and resources such as manpower, material, space etc., for its completion and it has definite start and finish time. For example, in the case of construction of a canal : marking the site for excavation, excavating the earth, building side banks, fixing bricks at the bottom and sides of the canal etc., are considered as activities.

The activities, in a network diagram, are represented by arrows which are usually drawn from left to right. Each arrow is joined by two circles—one at its tail end and the other at its head. The tail end of an arrow indicates the starting point of the activity and the head of the arrow denotes the completion of the activity. The arrow is not a vector and also its length does not represent the magnitude of work involved in an activity or time required for its completion. Further the arrow need not be drawn to scale and it may be straight or slanting [see Fig. 3 2 (a), (b) , (c)] but it should not be broken and curved.

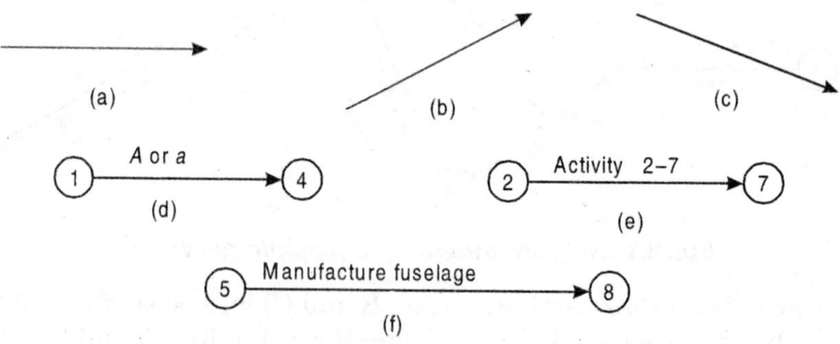

Fig. 3.2 *Representation and identification of activities.*

The activities can be identified in any of the following three ways:

(i) Activity can be denoted by capital or small alphabet as shown in Fig. 3.2 (d).

(ii) An activity can be identified by writing the numbers of two events connected by an arrow (or activity). Thus as shown in Fig. 3.2 (e) the activity connecting events 2 and 7, is designated as activity (2,7) or (2 7).

(iii) An activity can be identified by writing a short description of the actual performance of task over the arrow. Thus as shown in Fig. 3.2 (f) the activity joining events 5 and 8 is described by writing on the arrow '*Manufacture fuselage*'.

3.3 INTER-RELATIONSHIPS AMONG ACTIVITIES

A project consists of several activities and almost all the activities depend on other activities. Due to interdependency there exists inter-relationships among the various activities, on the basis of which the various activities may be classified as (i) Predecessor activities, (ii) Successor activities and (iii) Concurrent or Parallel activities. Each of these activities are described below.

(i) Predecessor Activities. A *predecessor activity* is the one which should be completed before the next activity or job could be taken up. For example engine of an airplane cannot be fixed unless and until the fuselage has been manufactured. Thus in this case 'manufacturing of fuselage' is a predecessor activity in relation to 'fixing of engines to airplane'. It is essential to fix up the order in which various activities shall be taken up for their accomplishment and thus, to sort out all the activities which will precede other activities. It may, however, be noted that the very first activity is exceptional since it is not preceded by any other activity. Further an activity that is required to be accomplished immediately before another activity could be started is called *immediate predecessor activity.* As shown in Fig. 3.3 activities *a, b, c* and *d* are *predecessor activities* to activity *e*, and activity *d* is *immediate predecessor activity* to activity *e*.

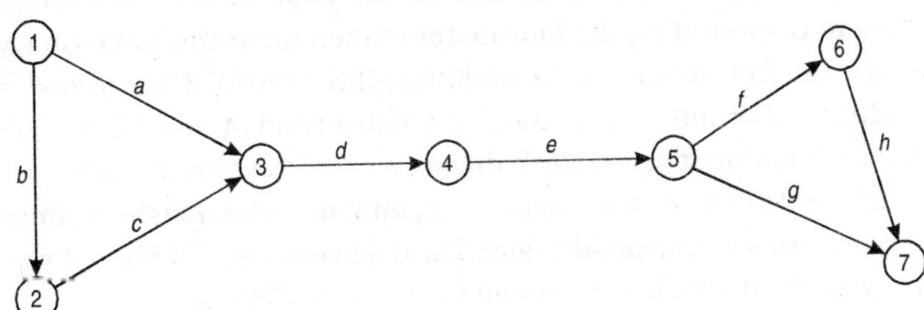

Fig. 3.3 *Predecessor and Successor activities.*

(ii) Successor Activities. A *successor activity* is the one which can be started only after the completion of the other activity. As shown in Fig. 3.3 activities *d, e, f, g* and *h* are *successor activities* to activity *a*. Similarly activities *c, d, e, f, g* and *h* are *successor activities* to activity *b*. Further an activity is called an *immediate successor activity* to another activity if it may be started immediately after the completion of that activity. Thus as shown in Fig. 3.3 activities *f* and *g* are *immediate successor activities* to activity *e*. Similarly activity *e* is immediate successor activity to activity *d*.

(iii) Concurrent Activities or Parallel Activities. The activities which can be undertaken simultaneously and independently are known as *concurrent activities* or *parallel activities.* This would be possible when the completion of one activity does not depend on the start and finish of the other activity. For example, in a project of pipeline construction (see Table 3.1) the activities 'layout pipes at site' and 'marking for digging' can be taken up at the same time. In this case even if due to some reason the activity 'layout pipes at site' is delayed, it will not affect in anyway the other activity 'marking for digging' or *vice versa.* Further as shown in Fig. 3.3 activities *a* and *b* are concurrent or parallel activities. Similarly activities *a* and *c*, *g* and *h*, and *f and g* are also concurrent or parallel activities.

The following example is taken to further illustrate the dependency relationship among the various activities. In manufacture of electric motors, besides other activities, there are four major activities viz., (1) Machining of stator and rotor, (2) Winding of stator and rotor, (3) Assembling all the parts and (4) Testing. It is assumed that a batch of four electric motors is manufactured. Instead of first machining the bodies and rotors of all the four electric motors and then completing the winding, assembling all the parts and testing all the four motors in sequence, in the first instance the machining of the body and rotor of one of the motors is taken up and as and when its machining is completed it is taken up for winding and the machining of the second motor is taken up and so on. Thus in this case the various activities in respect of all the four motors taken up at the same time will be (1) testing the first motor; (2) assembling all the parts of the second motor ; (3) winding stator and rotor of the third motor ; and (4) machining the parts of the fourth motor. The network diagram of this example is shown in Fig. 3.4 which is drawn on the basis of dependency relationships among the various activities as indicated below. The dashed arrows in Fig. 3.4 represent dummy activities which are defined in the next section.

Activity	*Immediate Predecessor*	*Activity*	*Immediate Predecessor*
M_1	–	W_1	M_1
M_2	M_1	W_2	M_2, W_1
M_3	M_2	W_3	M_3, W_2
M_4	M_3	W_4	M_4, W_3
A_1	W_1	T_1	A_1
A_2	W_2, A_1	T_2	A_2, T_1
A_3	W_3, A_2	T_3	A_3, T_2
A_4	W_4, A_3	T_4	A_4, T_3

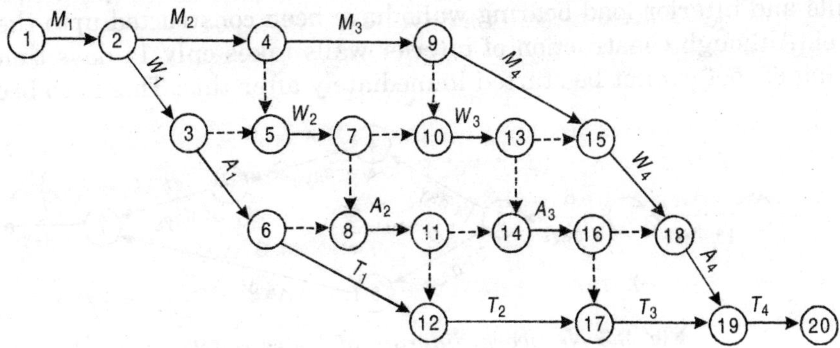

Fig. 3.4 *Network diagram for manufacture of electric motors.*

3.4 DUMMY ACTIVITIES (OR ZERO TIME ACTIVITIES)

An activity that takes no time or resources whatsoever is called *dummy activity* or *zero time activity*. It is an assumed activity which is represented by dashed arrow. When events are connected by activities to show their interdependency, often one may come across a situation where a certain event j cannot be completed until another event i has been accomplished but the activity connecting the events i and j (to indicate the constraint of i upon j) does not involve any time or use of resources. In such a case the two events are connected by a dummy activity. Although it may seem unrealistic that an activity consumes no time or resources but the following illustration would indicate that this can happen and indeed must happen in certain cases.

Consider the various steps involved in building a house as given in Table 3.2. The network of this project would be as shown in Fig. 3.5. In this case

TABLE 3.2 *Steps in construction of a house*

Job Identification	*Job Description*	*Time to Perform Job*
A	Excavate foundation	14 days
B	Pour foundation concrete	7 days
C	Construct interior walls	14 days
D	Construct outside walls	21 days
E	Lay roof	7 days
F	Fix doors and windows	14 days
G	Hang ceiling fans	7 days
H	Inaugurate	1 day

activity 5–4 or *E* is a *dummy activity* because this does not require any time whatsoever. The dummy activity has been inserted in the network diagram

because of the fact that the roof cannot be laid unless and until the outside walls and interior load bearing walls have been constructed upto the roof level. Although construction of interior walls takes only 14 days time but laying of roof cannot be started immediately after this. This is so because

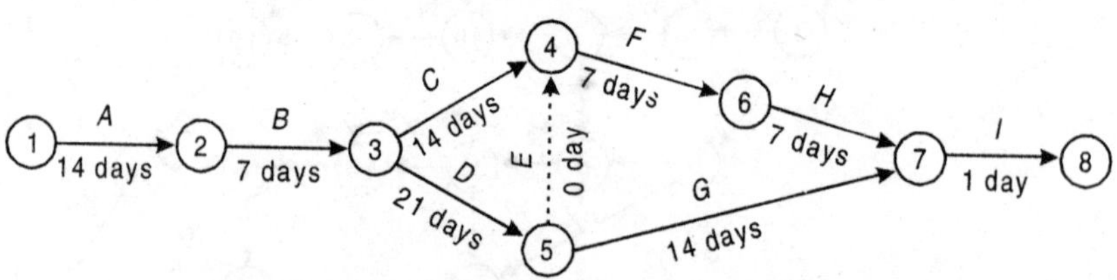

Fig. 3.5 *Net work diagram of house construction.*

construction of outside walls will take 21 days time and therefore one will have to wait for 7 days after the interior walls have been raised upto the roof level before the roof can be laid. Thus activity *F* can be started only after activities *C* and *D* (or events 4 and 5) have been completed. This fact is clearly indicated by the dummy activity *E* or 5–4 as shown in Fig. 3.5. With the introduction of the dummy activity the various activities may be formally listed as given in Table 3.3.

TABLE 3.3 *Formal listing of activities in the project of construction of house*

Job Identification	*Job Description*	*Immediate Predecessors*	*Time to Perform job*
A	Excavate foundation	—	14 days
B	Pour foundation concrete	*A*	7 days
C	Construct interior walls	*B*	14 days
D	Construct outside walls	*B*	21 days
E	Zero-time activity	*D*	—
F	Lay roof	*C, E*	7 days
G	Fix doors and windows	*D*	14 days
H	Hang ceiling fans	*F*	7 days
I	Inaugurate	*G. H*	1 day

For the same case the network diagrams are redrawn as shown in Figs. 3.6 and 3.7 to illustrate the usefulness of *dummy activity*. The network diagram shown in Fig. 3.6 has been drawn without the *dummy activity*.

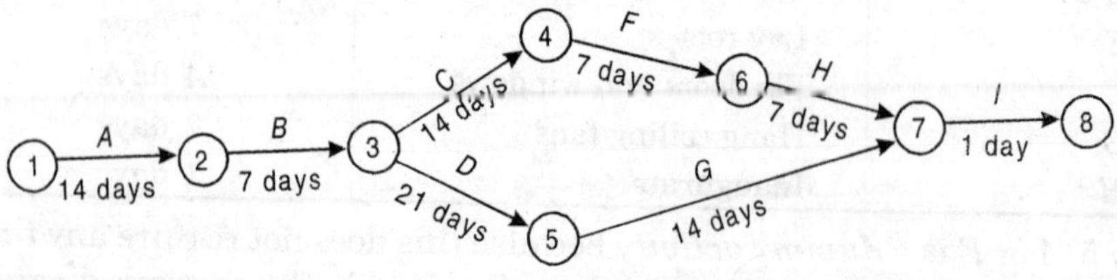

Fig. 3.6 *Network diagram of house construction with dummy activity omitted.*

This network indicates that activity *F* can be taken up as soon as activity *C* ends, which is not correct because of the fact that activity *F* is also dependent on activity *D*. As such in order to show that activity *F* depends on activity *D* also an arrow with dashed line (called dummy activity) is placed between events 4 and 5. The effect of dummy activity *E* is that it constrains activity *F* from beginning, soon after the completion of activity *C*, until activity *D* has been accomplished.

The network diagrams shown in Fig. 3.7 are also drawn for the same case with dummy activity omitted. However, due to omission of dummy activity the following difficulties are faced.

(i) In Fig. 3.7(a) activity *F* has been restrained from starting until both the activities *C* and *D* have been accomplished. Activity *G* has emanated from event 4 at which activities *C* and *D* have ended. This has resulted in

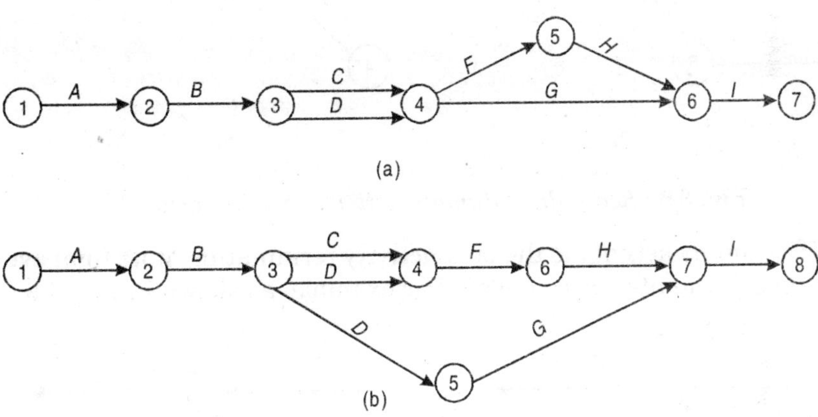

Fig. 3.7 *Net work diagrams of house construction with dummy activities omitted.*

activities *C* and *D* becoming immediate predecessors of activity *G* which is not true. The immediate predecessor of activity *G* is only activity *D* and not activity *C* as has been indicated in Fig. 3.7(a) which is not correct

(ii) In order to eliminate the difficulty faced in (i) above, activity *D* may be drawn twice as shown in Fig. 3.7 (b). However, this would also not be satisfactory because for a single activity only one arrow should be used. If more than one arrow is used for the same activity, it would make the network diagram too confusing and it would become very difficult to find where the project stood at any point of time.

3.4.1 Redundant Dummy Activities

While drawing network diagrams it is always convenient to use initially dummy activities liberally. However, this may clutter the network diagram and confuse its user. Therefore it becomes essential to remove such dummy activities which are redundant. It should, however, be noted that the removal of such dummy activities does not affect the project duration. The redundant or unnecessary dummy activities can be identified as follows.

1. If a dummy activity is the only activity emanating from its initial circle, it can be removed by putting the initial and final circles together into one circle, keeping other connecting activities or jobs in their original positions. For example, as shown in Fig. 3.8 (a) dummy activity *D* is the only activity emanating from event 5 and therefore it has been removed by putting events 5 and 2 together in a single event 2 as shown in Fig. 3.8 (b).

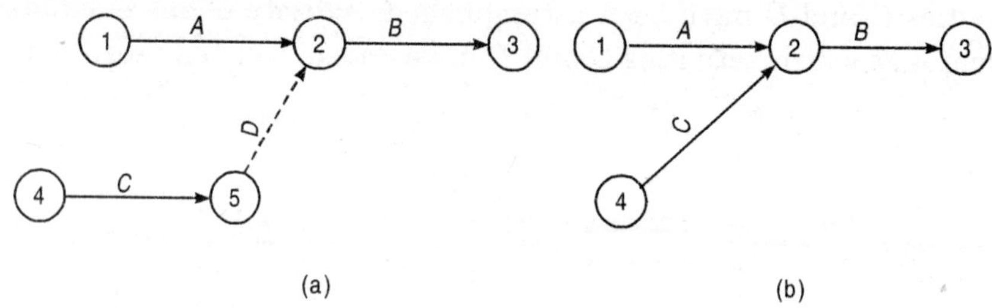

Fig. 3.8 *Redundant dummy activity and its removal.*

2. If a dummy activity is the only activity terminating at its final event or circle then it can also be removed. For example, as shown in Fig. 3.9 (a)

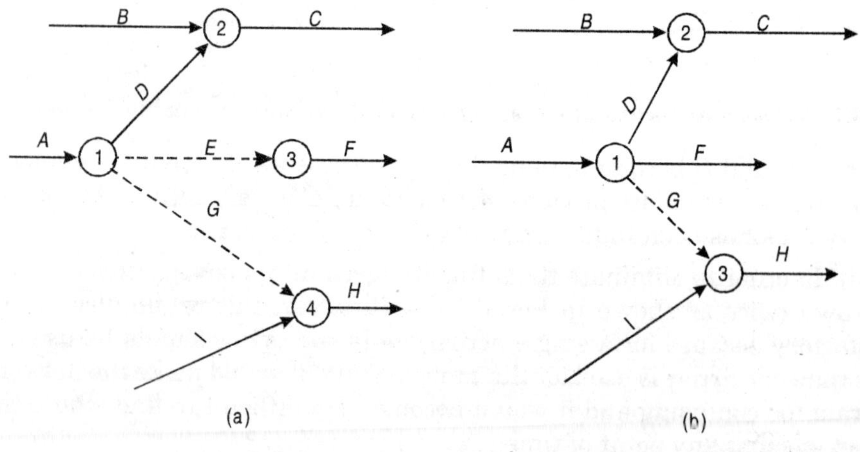

Fig. 3.9 *Redundant dummy activity and its removal.*

dummy activity *E* (which is the only activity ending at event 3) can be removed. The modified network diagram would be as shown in Fig. 3.9 (b) in which the events 1 and 3 have been merged into a single event renumbered as 1.

3. If two or more activities have same sets of predecessors, then these activities can be arranged so as to emanate from a single event or circle. Thus as shown in Fig. 3.10 (a) activities *E*, *F* and *G* have same sets of predecessors viz., *A* and *B* and therefore activities *E*, *F* and *G* have to be rearranged to emanate from single event renumbered as 4 in Fig. 3.10 (b). Also the redundant dummy activities as shown in Fig. 3.10 (a) falling between activities *A*, *B* and *E*, *F*, *G* have been eliminated in Fig. 3.10 (b).

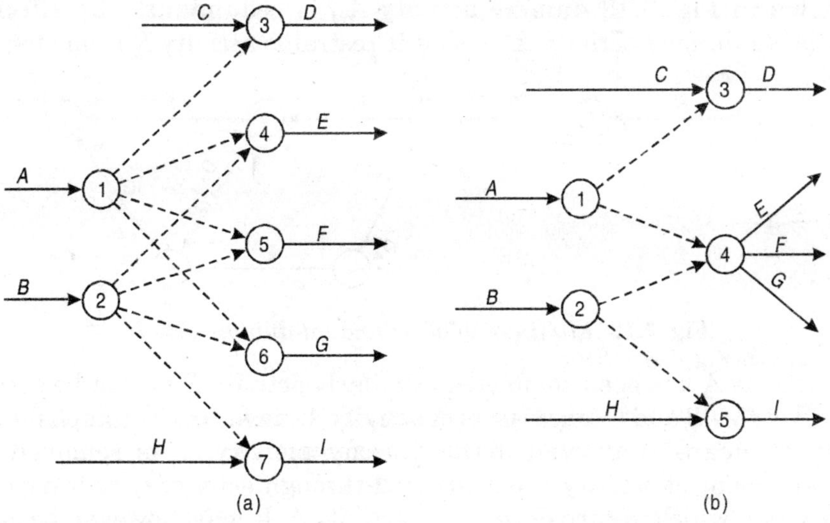

Fig. 3.10 *Redundant dummy activities and their elimination.*

4. If two or more activities have same sets of successors, latter having other predecessors as well, then these two or more activities may be

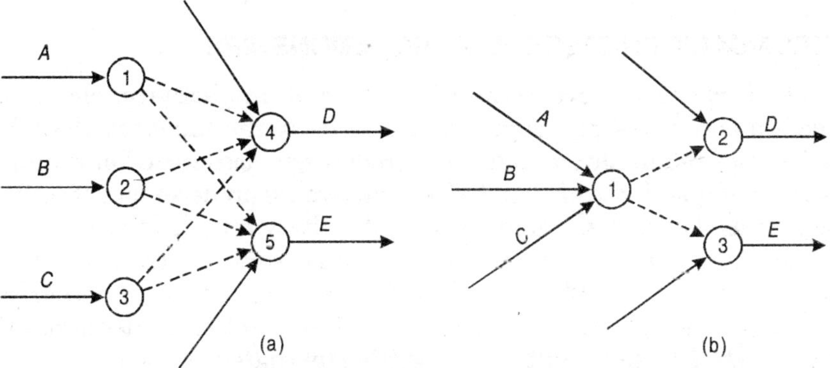

Fig. 3.11 *Reduction of dummy activities by eliminating the redundant dummy activities.*

rearranged so as to end at a single event or circle and thereupon connected by dummy activities to their successors. For example, as shown in Fig. 3.11 (a) activities A, B and C have identical successors viz., D and E. The network diagram has been modified as shown in Fig. 3.11 (b) in which activities A, B and C have been rearranged to be terminated at a single event or circle and then connected by dummy activities to their successors. As a result of this rearrangement the number of dummy activities between activities A, B and C, and D and E has been reduced from 6 to only 2.

5. Dummy activities which show predecessor relations already implied by other activities whether dummy or regular can be eliminated. For example, as shown in Fig. 3.12 dummy activity A_1, is redundant. The effect of introducing dummy activity A_1 is that it restrains activity E from starting

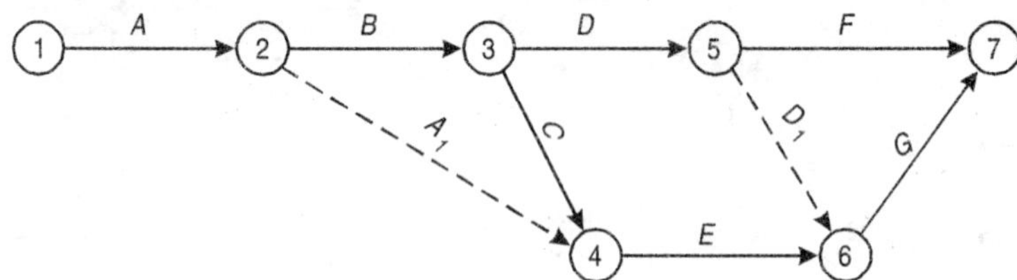

Fig. 3.12 *Elimination of redundant dummy activity.*

until activity A has been completed. Similarly activity E cannot be started until activities B and C (successors of activity A) have been accomplished. It therefore means that even if the dummy activity A_1 is removed the commencement of activity E is restricted through activity C as it depends on activity B which in turn depends on activity A. It may, however, be noted that dummy activity D_1 is not redundant because it restrains activity G from commencing until activity D has been accomplished. The dummy activity D_1 is introduced between activities D and G to show that activity G is also a successor to activity D and this relationship is not implied otherwise.

3.5 REDUNDANT PREDECESSOR RELATIONSHIPS

If in a set of *immediate predecessor activities* of any activity, one of the activities is a predecessor for some other activity in the same set, then that activity becomes redundant in that set of predecessor activities. For example, it is assumed that activities I, J and M are immediate predecessors of activity P and activities J and M are predecessors of activity I, then activities J and M are redundant in the set of immediate predecessors of activity P. This is so because activity I precedes activity P and hence activities J and M will automatically do so as they precede activity I. In a set of predecessors the activities which are redundant can be safely eliminated.

Generally the redundant activities can be spotted easily, but if the trail of predecessor activities is long it may not be that easy to locate the redundant activities. Thus in the above example if activities *J* and *M* were not immediate predecessors of activity *I* but were predecessors of activity *K* which preceded activity *L*, which in turn was a predecessor of activity *I*, then redundancy of activities *J* and *M* in the set of immediate predecessors of activity *P* would not be so apparent.

When a list of predecessors for each activity in a network is prepared it is convenient to put down more immediate predecessor than are necessary, but in doing so some of the immediate predecessors may in fact be more distant predecessors (that is, predecessors of predecessors) rather than really immediate predecessors. This, however, does not affect the network logic but inclusion of unnecessary activities in a set of predecessors would make the drawing of network difficult as number of dummy activities would be needed resulting in more computer time and expenses. As such as far as possible the set of predecessor activities should contain only those immediate predecessor activities which are of the same set or which are not redundant. For removing the redundancies the following method may be adopted.

3.5.1 Method of Removing Redundancies

Prepare a table having as many rows and columns as there are activities in the project. Activities are then listed in both the rows and the columns in *topological order*. A list of activities is said to be in topological order if no activity appears in the list until all its predecessors have been listed and all the successors of an activity would come after that activity has been listed. The general procedure is to look at each row and mark the activity's immediate predecessors with cross (×) and its more distant predecessors with a circle. Now start from the row for the first activity that has predecessors and mark cross (×) in the column corresponding to each immediate predecessor. The starting activities will, however, have blank rows. Next check the rows of each of these predecessors for their predecessors. If the predecessors of an activity has a mark either a cross (×) or a circle in its row then place a circle in the same column position of the row of the original activity. Do this for each immediate predecessor, and then move on to the next activity, first marking its predecessors with cross (×) marks and then more distant predecessors with circles. When the table is completed, if any cross (×) is circled, it is a redundant predecessor for the activity in its row and the same can be eliminated from the list of predecessors of that activity.

The procedure discussed above is illustrated by the following example.

Activity	*Immediate Predecessors*
A	–
B	*A*
C	*A*

Contd.

Contd.

Activity	*Immediate Predecessors*
D	*B,C*
E	*B, D*
F	*C, D*
G	*B, C, D, E, F*

The activities are already in topological order, so the following table is prepared with activities appearing on both rows and columns. The activities which have immediate predecessors are marked with cross (×) in their rows against the corresponding columns of the immediate predecessors.

Predecessors

	A	*B*	*C*	*D*	*E*	*F*	*G*
A							
B	×						
C	×						
D		×	×				
E		×		×			
F			×	×			
G		×	×	×	×	×	

Now in each row, all the immediate predecessors are checked for their predecessors (immediate or otherwise) and these are noted with circles in the corresponding rows against the corresponding column positions of the predecessors, For example, in the row of activity *D*, activities *B* and *C* are shown as predecessors. Both these activities *B* and *C* have activity *A* as a predecessor, so a circle is placed in the row of activity *D* under the column of predecessor *A*. In the row of activity *E*, activities *B* and *D* are shown as immediate predecessors which in turn have activity *A* and activities *B* and *C* respectively as their predecessors. Thus circles are placed in the row of activity *E* under the columns of predecessors *A*, *B* and *C* which causes the cross (×) under the column of predecessor *B* to be circled. By continuing in similar fashion through the row of activity *G*, the table would appear as follows.

	A	*B*	*C*	*D*	*E*	*F*	*G*
A							
B	×						
C	×						
D	○	×	×				
E	○	⊗	○	×			
F	○	○	⊗	×			
G	○	⊗	⊗	⊗	×	×	

Note the cross (×) marks which are circled because as stated earlier they represent the redundant predecessor activities. Thus predecessor activity *B* is redundant for activity *E* ; predecessor activity C is redundant for activity *F*; and predecessor activities *B, C* and *D* are redundant for activity *G*. All these redundant predecessors may be eliminated without changing the logic of the network and hence the above table showing activities and immediate predecessors may be modified as follows.

Activity	*Immediate Predecessors*
A	—
B	*A*
C	*A*
D	*B, C*
E	*D*
F	*D*
G	*E, F*

The above procedure can be performed by hand for small projects, but for larger projects it would be tedious without the help of a computer.

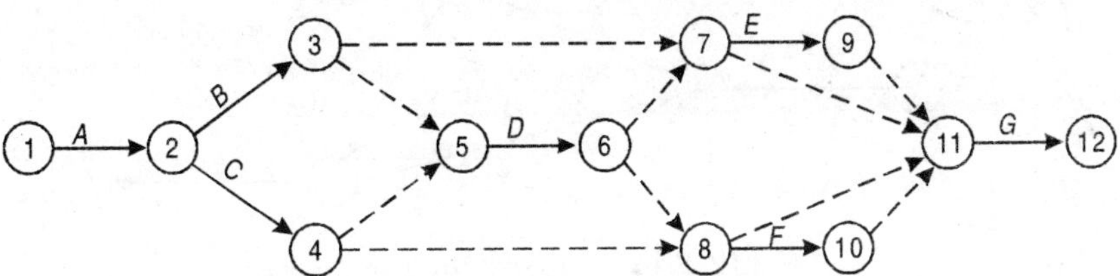

(a) On the basis of original table including redundant predecessors.

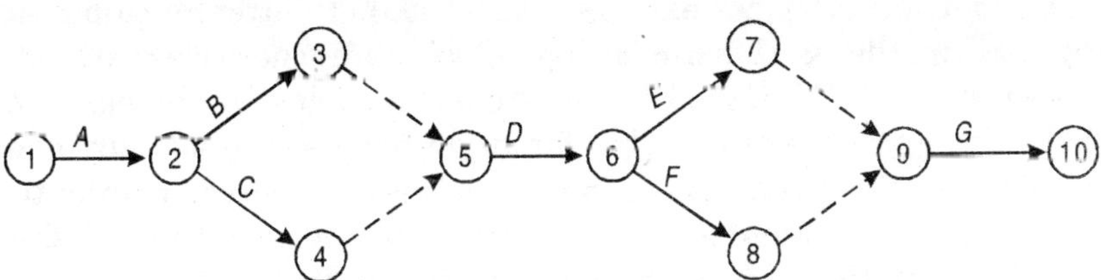

(b) On the basis of modified table eliminating redundant predecessors.

Fig, 3.13 *Network diagram.*

In respect of the original as well as the modified tables, network diagrams are drawn as shown in Fig. 3.13. It may be noted that the network diagram shown in Fig. 3.13 (a) has large number of dummy activities because it includes various redundant predecessors. On the other hand the network diagram shown in Fig. 3.13 (b) is quite compact because it has been drawn on the basis of table as modified by eliminating the redundant predecessors. It may, however, be noted that modification of table by eliminating the redundant predecessors does not affect the logic of the network.

3.6 CYCLES

A *cycle* (or *loop*) in a network is any path of activities that leads back into itself. Figure 3.14 shows a network diagram having a cycle. It may be noted that in general the arrows in a network point from left to right, but in the cycle some of the arrows point from right to left. The existence of a cycle in a network will be indicated if an activity shows up as a distant predecessor of itself. Cycles are more serious than simple redundancies, as cycles represent logical errors in the network and they must be removed before network calculations can be performed. However, as regards redundancies it is desirable but not absolutely necessary to remove them.

In the cycle shown in Fig. 3.14 activity *C* follows activity *B* ; activity *D* follows activity *C* ; and activity *B* follows activity *D*. However, none of these three activities could ever be listed in topological order because its predecessor would not have been listed and successors would come before that activity is listed. For example, activity *B* cannot be listed until its predecessor activity *D* has been listed and activity *D* cannot be listed until

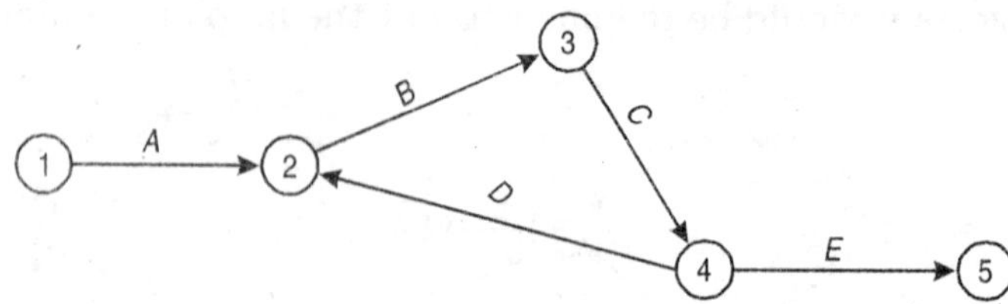

Fig. 3.14 *Network having a cycle.*

its predecessor activity *C* has been listed. Thus one simple method to determine whether cycles exist in a network is to attempt to put activities in topological order. If this can be done successfully, no cycles exist, otherwise cycles exist. By this method the existence of cycles can be easily detected manually in smaller networks, but for larger networks assistance of computer may be needed for this purpose. Once a cycle is discovered, in order to remove it, the project data must be rechecked for the accuracy of the stated predecessor relationships of activities in the cycle.

3.7 EVENTS

An event is a specific accomplishment of an activity or activities at a recognizable point of time. It denotes certain stages of a project. For example, in a project of building a space rocket, *'design of rocket engine started'*, *'design of rocket engine completed'*, *'manufacturing of rocket engine commenced, 'rocket engine manufactured'*, *'control equipments fixed*, etc., are events. Thus, an event is start and completion of an activity but not the actual performance of the activity. Moreover, whereas the activities consume time and resources, the events do not consume time or resources.

As indicated earlier in network diagram events are generally represented by circles which are referred to as nodes. The events are numbered for their identification. Figure 3.15 illustrates two events. Each of these two events represent a significant point in a project at a specific point of time.

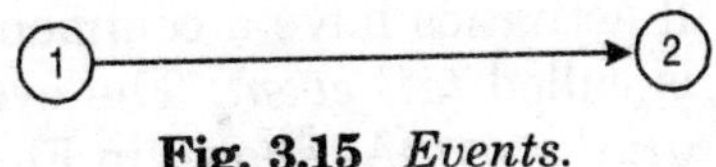

Fig. 3.15 *Events.*

Thus event 1 could represent *'rocket engine manufactured'* and event 2 could represent *'rocket engine mounted'*.

Thus an event must conform to the following three criteria:

(1) An event must represent a significant point in a project at a specific point of time.

(2) An event is the start or completion of an activity.

(3) An event does not require time or other resources.

3.7.1 Successor and Predecessor Events

Events are connected by activities to form a network. Events that come before another event are called *predecessor events* to that event. Events which come immediately before another event without any intervening events are called *immediate predecessor events* to that event.

Similarly events which follow another event are called *successor events* to that event and those events which follow another event without any intervening events are called *immediate successor events* to that event.

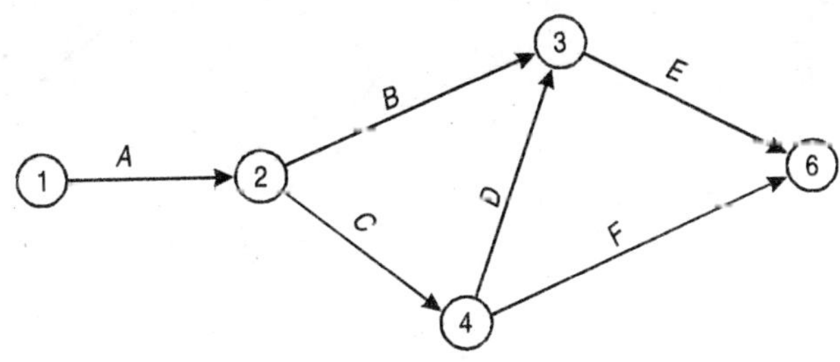

Fig. 3.16 *Successor and predecessor events.*

For example, in the network shown in Fig. 3.16 event 2 is *predecessor event* to events 3,4 and 6 and event 2 is *immediate predessor event* to events 3 and 4. On the other hand in the same figure event 3 is *successor event* to events 1, 2 and 4 and event 3 is *immediate successor event* to events 2 and 4.

3.7.2 Head and Tail Events

On the basis of the position of events in a network they may be classified as

(1) Head event (2) Tail event

1. Head Event. All activities have a termination point. This point is marked by an event which is called *head event.* If a particular event marks completion of the project then it is called *final event.* As shown in Fig. 3.17 (a) and (b) events 3 and 7 are *head events.*

2. Tail Events. All activities have a commencement point marked by an event. This event is called *tail event.* The event with which a project commences is called *initial event.* As shown in Figs. 3.17 (c) and (d), events 4 and 5 are *tail events.*

It may be noted that the expression head event or tail event is always in relation to the activity with which it is connected. For example, as shown in Fig. 3.17 (e) event 12 is *head event* for activity *X* and *tail event* for activity *Y*. Similarly as shown in Fig. 3.17 (f) event 9 is *head event* for activities *L* and *M* and *tail event* for activities *N* and *O*. It may, however, be noted that except initial and final events all events serve dual function i.e., they are head events for some activities and tail events for other activities. Hence all events except initial and final events are generally classified as *dual role events.*

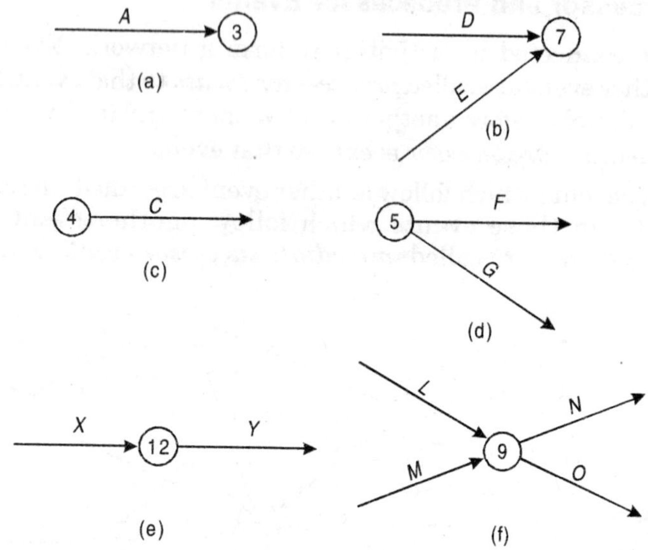

Fig. 3.17 *Head and Tail events.*

3.7.3 Numbering the Events

It is essential to number all the events or node points in a network. This would facilitate the identification of the activities joining the events or node points in the network in terms of the event numbers or node numbers at the tail and head of the activity. The event numbering should, however, be done in such a manner that they reflect their logical sequence. For sequential numbering of the events a rule devised by D.R. Fulkerson may be adopted which involves the following steps.

(i) In any network there is a single initial event which has arrows coming out of it and none entering it. Number this initial event as '1'.

(ii) Neglect all arrows emerging from the initial event numbered 1. This will create one or more new initial events.

(iii) Number these new initial events as 2, 3, 4, etc.

(iv) Again neglect all emerging arrows from these newly numbered events which will create a few more new initial events.

(v) Follow step (iii).

(vi) Continue this operation until the last event, which has no emerging arrows from it, is numbered.

The above noted procedure is illustrated by the following example.

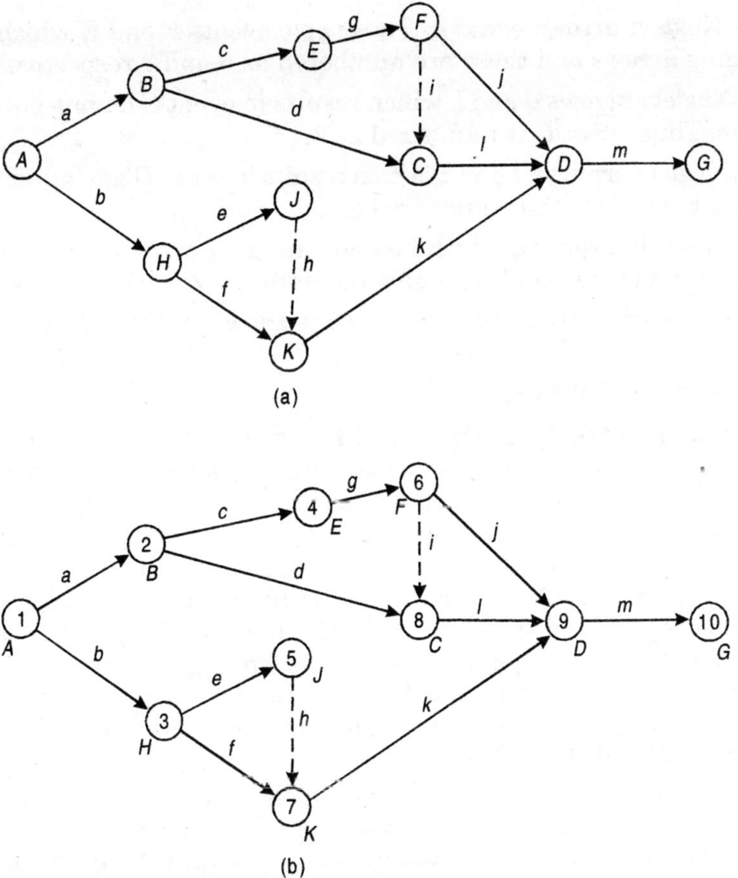

Fig. 3.18 *Network with (a) events not numbered (b) events numbered.*

Consider a network shown in Fig. 3.18 (a) in which the events are to be numbered. By applying Fulkerson's rule the numbering of the events may be done as follows.

(i) Event *A* is the initial event and hence it is numbered as 1.

(ii) There are two arrows *a* and *b* emerging from this newly numbered event. Neglecting these arrows yields two events *B* and *H* with no entering arrows, but only emerging arrows. These events are numbered as 2 and 3 respectively.

(iii) From these newly numbered events 2 and 3, arrows *c, d, e* and *f* emerge. Neglecting these arrows, we get events *E* arid *J* which have only emerging arrows. It may, however, be noted that even after neglecting the arrows *e* and *f*, event *K* has an entering arrow *h,* and hence event *K* cannot form initial event. Similarly even after neglecting the arrow *d,* event *C* also cannot form initial event. Thus events *E* and *J* are numbered as 4 and 5 respectively.

(iv) Neglect arrows *g* and *h.* These give events *F* and *K* which have only emerging arrows and these are numbered as 6 and 7 respectively.

(v) Neglect arrows *d* and *i,* which results in event C having only emerging arrows. Thus event *C* is numbered as 8.

(vi) Neglect arrows *j, l* and *k,* which results in event *D* having only emerging arrows. Event *D* is thus numbered as 9.

(vii) Finally event *G,* which has no emerging arrows, will form the final event or end event and it is numbered as 10.

The network with events numbered is shown in Fig. 3.18 (b).

3.7.4 Skip Numbering

In a small network where there are limited events, usually no modifications are required to be made and hence the numbering of the events may be done serially as in the case of foregoing example. However, in large networks, often extensive modifications may have to be made either before the network is finalized or during the progress of the project. In such cases provision must be made to add new events and number them without necessitating renumbering of the various events in the network. This can be achieved by a process of numbering known as *skip numbering.* There are several ways by which skip numbering may be done. In one of the ways the events are numbered in multiples of 10 i.e., numbering the events as 10 (initial), 20, 30, 40, etc. If an event is added later it can be assigned a number which lies between the number of immediately preceding event (predecessor event) and that of the immediately succeeding event (successor event). Another way by which skip numbering can be achieved is by leaving out such numbers as 8, 9 ; 18,19 ; 28, 29 ; etc., in the initial network.These left out numbers can be assigned to the newly added events arising out of the modification of the initial network.

3.8 GUIDELINES FOR CONSTRUCTION OF NETWORK

There are certain conventions for drawing a network. It is important to keep these conventions in view for drawing a correct network and hence the same are discussed below.

1. The initial event (or node) has only emerging (or out going) arrows. In a network there is only one initial event (or node).

2. The final event (or node) has only entering (or incoming) arrows. In a network there is only one final event (or node).

3. The arrows denoting activities should point from left to right. However, if the arrow is vertical it may point in upward or downward direction.

4. Arrows emanating from or converging at an event should have large angles between them for the sake of clear presentability.

5. An event is said to have taken place only when all the activities (arrows) leading to it have been accomplished, and no activity can start until the event from which it is emanating has taken place.

6. All events, wherever they may appear in a network diagram, should be connected by relevant arrows. Further there must not be any dead end left except the final event. If any event other than final event is left as dead end then the network would not show correct picture of the project. For example, as shown in Fig. 3.19 event 4 has been left unconnected with event 5 and hence it cannot be found at which event the project would be accomplished, as it could be either at event 4 or at event 5.

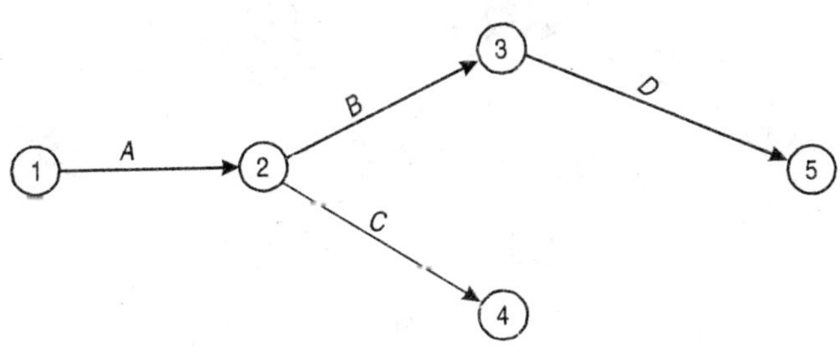

Fig. 3.19 *Event left unconnected.*

7. One arrow should represent only one activity. Two or more arrows should not be used for a single activity, as also two or more activities should not be represented by a single arrow, otherwise it would lead to a lot of confusion for the user of the network. Thus the networks shown in Fig. 3.20 (a) and (b) are incorrect. In the network shown in Fig. 3.20 (a) two arrows have been used for a single activity P. However, out of the two arrows, one arrow can be removed by using a dummy activity as shown in Fig. 3 20 (c). Similarly in the network shown in Fig. 3 20 (b) one arrow has been used for two activities P and Q. The network for this case may, however, be rectified as shown in Fig. 3.20 (d).

8. **The arrows should be straight lines. Curved arrows should be avoided.**

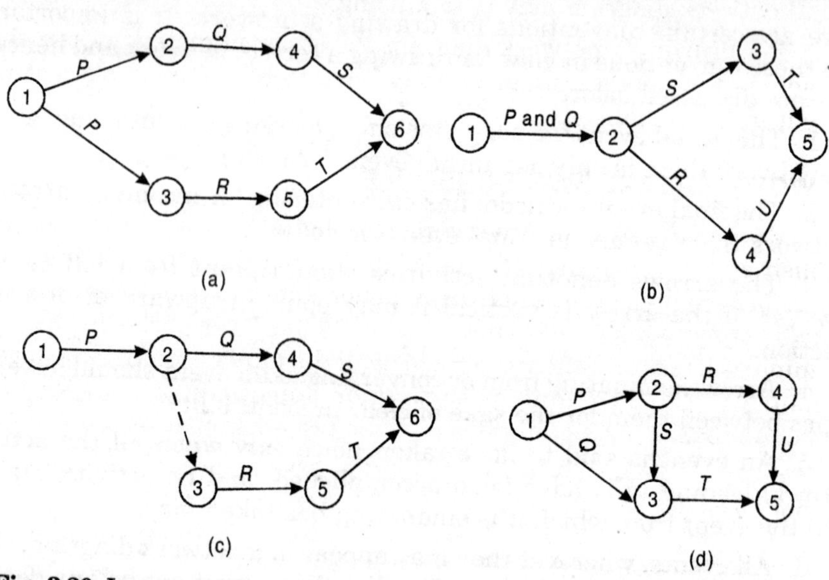

Fig. 3.20 *Incorrect and corrected networks following the rule of single activity–single arrow.*

9. **Arrows should not cross each other [Fig. 3.21 (a)]. However, if crossing is unavoidable then bridging may be done as illustrated in Fig. 3.21 (b).**

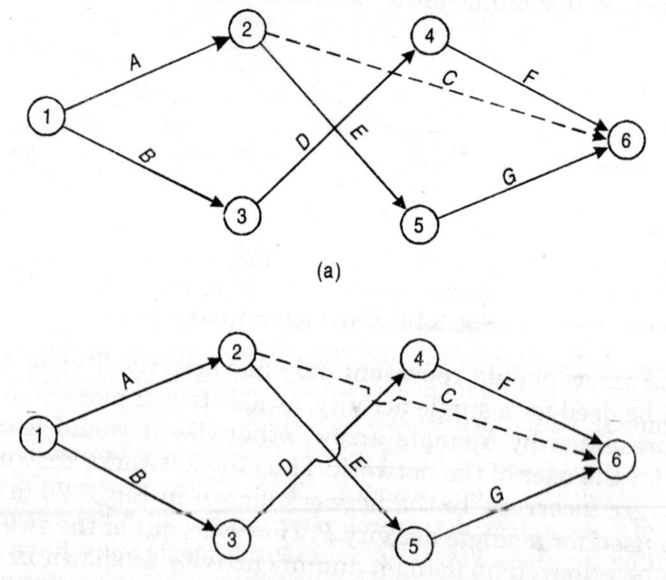

Fig. 3.21 *Incorrect and correct method of drawing the arrows crossing each other.*

10. The size of the network diagram should be reasonably large because a small network diagram may be confusing.

11. For drawing a network diagram use of pencil instead of pen should be made as the network diagram may have to be modified several times before it may be finalised.

3.9 WORK BREAKDOWN SCHEDULE

Before the construction of a network may be taken up, it is necessary to establish and link together the major and minor objectives of the project. The pictorial representation of these major and minor objectives is called '*work breakdown schedule*'. This schedule is not a network. Instead it is a preliminary diagram of the way in which all the minor objectives go together to ensure the attainment of the major objective. It represents the interrelationships among all phases of the project in a systematic way.

A complex project may have thousands of events and activities which may not be easily recognised individually. A *work breakdown schedule* not only gives an overview of the project but it also helps to identify the events and activities individually.

The development of the work breakdown schedule begins with the establishment of the major objective at the top level. The major objective is then divided into minor (or supporting) objectives which come in second level. These minor (or supporting) objectives are again broken down into sub-component parts at the third level. The sub-division of the objectives continues to successively lower levels until the entire project is reduced to such a degree of detail where end-items finally become manageable.

Figure 3.22 shows step by step procedure for preparing work breakdown schedule. The major objective is established first which in this case is building of a house and is shown at level 1. The supporting objectives are (i) survey and site preparation, (ii) masonry, (iii) carpentry, (iv) electric fittings, (v) water and sanitary fittings, (vi) finishing, which are shown at level 2. Each of these supporting objectives are further subdivided. For example, 'masonry' has been shown with a further subdivision into (i) footings, (ii) pillars, (iii) walls, (IV) partitions, (v) chimney, which are shown at level 3. The 'footings' a supporting objective of masonry has been further subdivided into (i) concrete mixing, (ii) laying form, (iii) mixing and placing concrete, (iv) curing, (v) form removal, which are shown at level 4.

It is thus seen that work breakdown schedule is essentially a top-down approach towards the preparation of PERT/CPM network. The type and complexity of the project determine the number of levels into which the project is to be divided. The large complex projects may have even 10 or more levels and it would be almost impossible to determine the interconnections among all the events and activities without first making the work breakdown schedule.

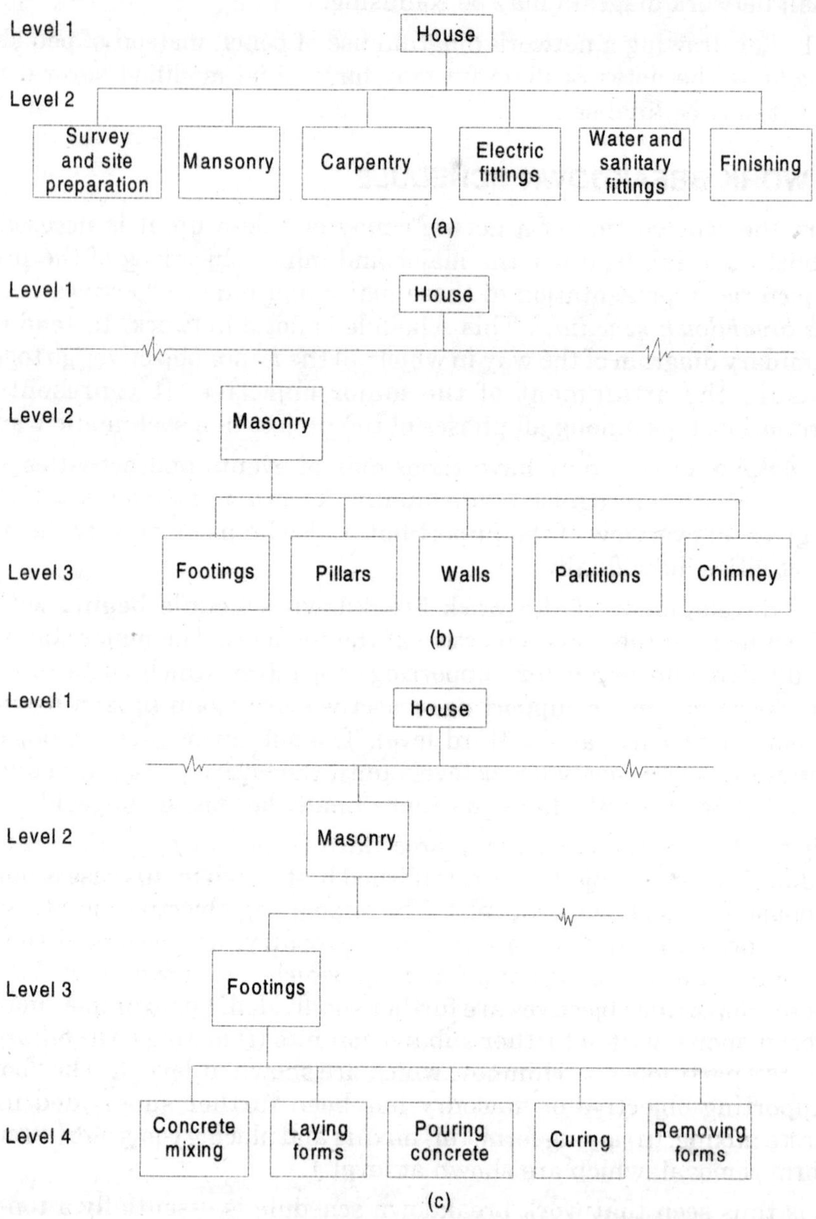

Fig. 3.22 *Work breakdown schedule for house construction project.*

3.10 FORWARD AND BACKWARD PLANNING

The PERT network may be drawn by adopting one of the two approaches. One approach is to start from the initial event (or starting event) and consider the other events and activities until the end event (or final event) is reached. This process of drawing network is known *as forward planning,* (or *forward planning process).* It is evident that in this process one would think "which event comes next?" and "which events can take place concurrently?" The other approach is to start from the end event (or final event) and proceed backward until the initial event (or starting event) is reached. This process of drawing network is known as *backward planning* (or *backward planning process).* In this process keeping the final goal or final event in view one works backward thinking that for achieving the final goal or final event which events should take place. In certain complex situations it may not be convenient to adopt forward planning because the activities in this process are not end-event oriented. In such situations the backward planning may be more conveniently adopted. For example in the case of a project of launching of a satellite one may work backward starting from the final goal or final event to several earlier events. However, in actual practice one cannot strictly adhere to either the forward planning or the backward planning procedures for drawing a network. A combination of both the procedures is usually adopted in which case the network is traversed back and forth several times until a satisfactory network is obtained.

3.11 COMBINING NETWORKS

In large projects there may be certain operations which may be carried out independently. For each of such operations smaller subnetworks may be prepared. These subnetworks may then be combined to form a composite or master network for the entire project. In combining the various subnetworks the events which are common to two or more subnetworks are superimposed on each other. These events are called *interface events* and are noted with a special designation such as a circle circumscribed by a hexagon (Fig. 3.23) or by a completely filled circle. Moreover the interface events are also represented by a special size. The procedure followed for combining the networks is explained by the following example.

Consider a project involving the design and production of an airplane. This project involves two independent operations viz., procurement of engine and manufacturing of airframe. However, both these operations must be taken up simultaneously so that a completed airframe will be ready for engine installation. A detailed description of the activities and events involved for the procurement of the engine is given in Table 3.4 and the corresponding network is shown in Fig. 3.23 (a).

TABLE 3.4 *Description of activities and events involved for the procurement of engine*

Activity No.	*Activity description*	*Event description*
100–102	Prepare plans and specification for engine	102–Bids and specifications completed; source located
101–102	Locate sources for engine procurement	102–Bids and specifications completed ; source located
102–103	Forward plans and specifications to eligible bidders	103–Plans and specifications received by bidders
103–104	Analyze bids received and award contract	104–Contract signed
104–105	Maintain procurement follow-up action with successful bidder	105–Completed engine received
105–106	Test engine	106–Test completed
106–107	Instal engine in airframe	107–Engine mated to airframe

Table 3.5 gives a detailed description of the activities and events involved in the manufacture of airframe and the corresponding network is shown in Fig. 3.23 (b).

TABLE 3.5 *Description of the activities and events involved in manufacturing of airframe*

Activity No.	*Activity description*	*Event description*
10–11	Perform initial design work	11–Airframe design completed
11–12	Procure required materials for airframe	12–Material received
11–13	Prepare necessary jigs and fixtures for assembly of airframe	13–Jigs and fixtures completed
13–12	A dummy activity showing that jigs and fixtures must be available before assembly can begin	
12–14	Assemble airframe	14–Airframe completed
14–15	Instal engine in airframe	15–Engine mated to airframe

From Figs. 3.23 (a) and (b) and the descriptions of the activities and events in Tables 3.4 and 3.5 it is obvious that events 15 and 107 are the same event-engine mated to airframe. Thus when the two networks of Figs. 3.23 (a) and (b) arc combined the events 15 and 107 are superimposed on each other. This is accomplished in Fig. 3.23 (c). However, the network shown in Fig. 3.23 (c) has no network-beginning event and hence it looks a bit disconnected. As such a network-beginning event (number 1) may be introduced which would result in creating three activities 1–10,1–100 and 1–101, all of which may be described as 'project go-ahead notice given to airframe and engine sections'. The resulting network would appear as shown in Fig. 3.24 in

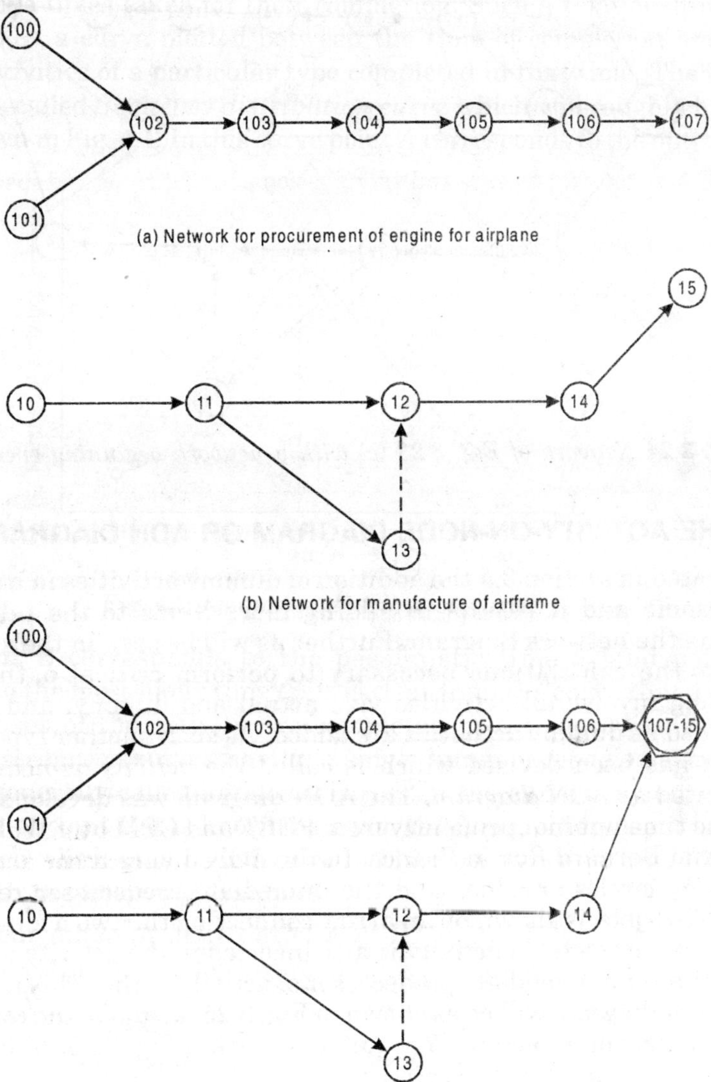

(a) Network for procurement of engine for airplane

(b) Network for manufacture of airframe

(c) Master network formed by combining networks (a) and (b).

Fig. 3.23

which event 1 has been shown as interface event since it is common to both the networks.

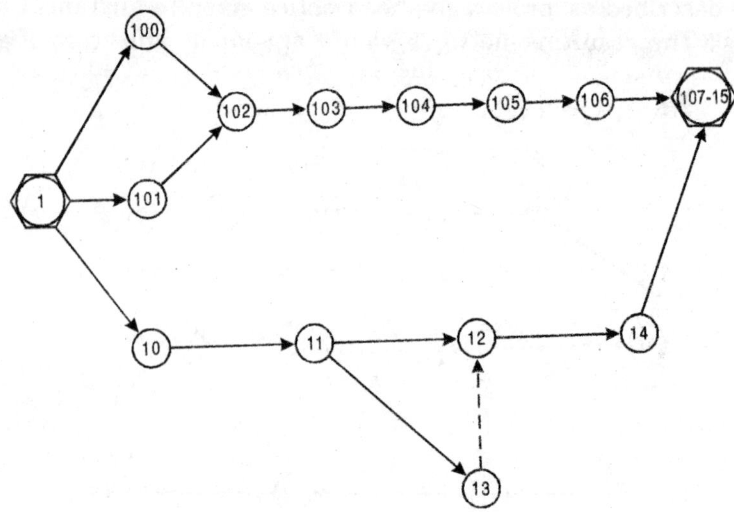

Fig. 3 24 *Network of Fig. 3.23 (c) with a network beginning event added.*

3.12 THE ACTIVITY-ON-NODE DIAGRAM OR AON DIAGRAM

As indicated in section 3.4 the addition of dummy activities in a network is cumbersome and it results in adding more items to the table and in enlarging the network diagram. Further as will be seen in the subsequent chapters the calculations necessary to perform critical path or PERT scheduling involve all activities viz., actual and dummy, and hence are lengthened as dummy activities are added. As such another type of project network has been devised which is called the *activity-on-node diagram* abbreviated as AON *diagram.* The AON diagram was developed at about the same time but independently from PERT and CPM by J.W. Fondahl in U.S.A. and Bernard Roy in France. In the AON diagram the activities are denoted by circles or nodes and the immediate predecessor relationship between two jobs is shown by an arrow connecting the two nodes. The time required to complete an activity is also inserted in the activity node. Thus, if activity a is an immediate predecessor of activity *b,* then this relationship on the AON diagram will be as shown in Fig. 3.25 (a) and in the conventional network diagram (or arrow diagram) as shown in Fig. 3.25(b). In the AON

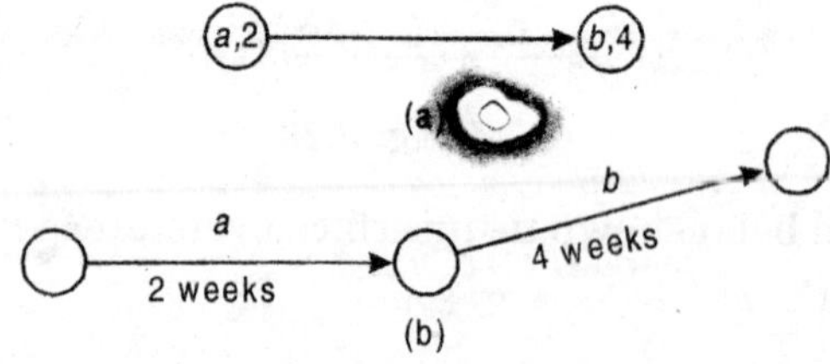

Fig. 3.25 *Immediate predecessor activities shown in (a) AON diagram and (b) Conventional network diagram (or arrow diagram).*

diagram arrow's point is at the node of the successor activity. The main advantage of the AON diagram is that no dummy activities are required to be added in this diagram. This fact is indicated by the following example.

List of activities and their immediate predecessors are given below.

Activities	*Immediate predecessors*
a	–
b	–
c	–
d	*a, b*
e	*b*
f	*b, c*

For this case the conventional network diagram (or arrow diagram) is shown in Fig. 3.26 (a). It may be observed that in this diagram two dummy activities b_1 and b_2 have to be included because activities *d* and *f* have, in addition to activities *a* and *c* respectively, activity *b* as a common immediate

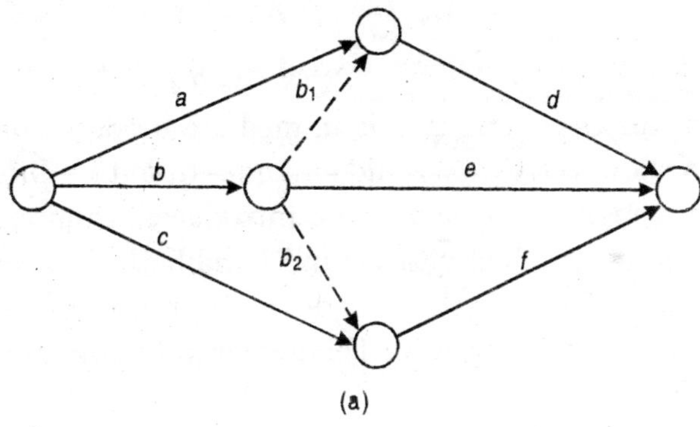

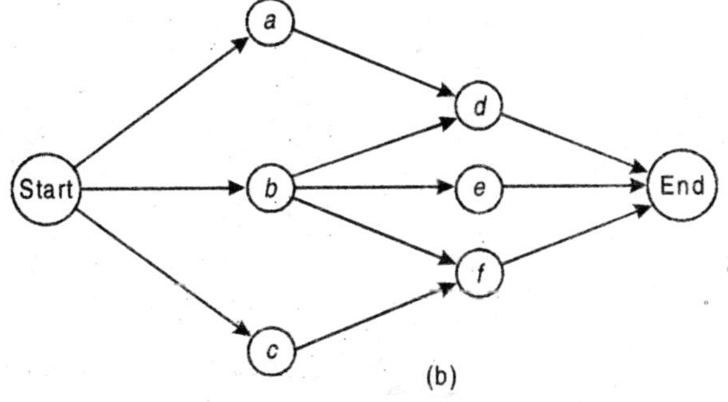

Fig. 3.26 *Comparison between the conventional network diagram (or arrow diagram) and the AON diagram.*

predecessor. The AON diagram for this case is shown in Fig. 3.26 (b) in which a circle is drawn for each activity and it is joined with its immediate successor by an arrow. Thus no dummy activities are required in the AON diagram.

Although the AON diagrams are simpler to explain, more readily understood by nontechnical users and easier to amend but still the conventional network diagrams are more prevalent because these were developed first and became firmly established. However, the AON diagrams are more popular in Europe and especially used in the construction industry.

ILLUSTRATIVE EXAMPLES

Example 3.1 *Draw a network diagram with the following activities.*

Job identification	*Immediate predecessors*
a	—
c	—
d	*a*
e	*c*
f	*a, b, c*

Solution In this case activity *a* is immediate predecessor of activities *d* and *f* and both these activities would emanate from two different circles or nodes, dummy activity will have to be introduced. Similarly activity *c* is immediate predecessor of activities *e* and *f* and both these activities would emanate from two different circles or nodes and hence in this case also dummy activity will have to be introduced. The network diagram for this case is as shown in Fig. Ex. 3.1.

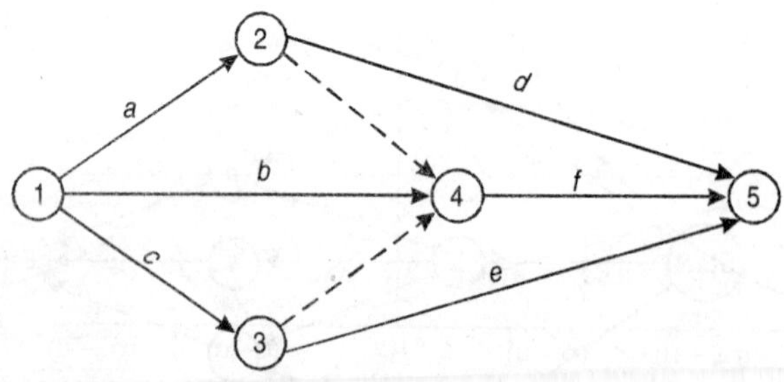

Fig. Ex. 3.1

Example 3.2 *Draw a network diagram with the following data.*

Job identification	*Immediate predecessors*
a	—
b	—
c	—
d	*a*
e	*c*
f	*a, b, c, d*
g	*a, b, c, e*
h	*a, b, c*

Solution The network diagram for this case is shown in Fig. Ex. 3.2.

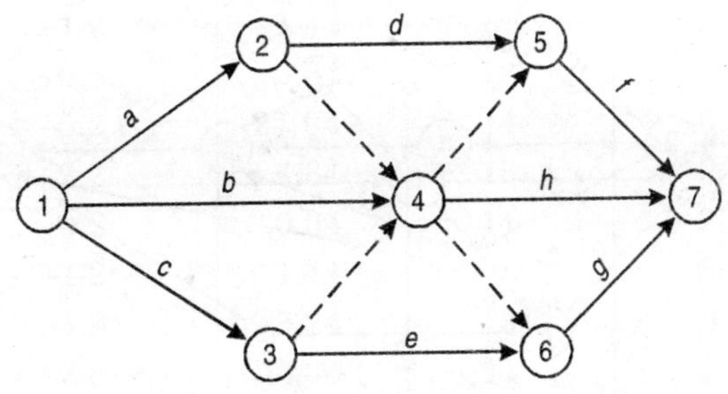

Fig. Ex. 3.2

Example 3.3 *A project consists of 10 activities as detailed below. Draw an arrow-diagram representation of the project.*

Job or Activity	*Immediate predecessors*
A	–
B	*A*
C	*A*
D	*A*
E	*B*
F	*C*
G	*D*
H	*D*
I	*E, F, G*
J	*H, I*

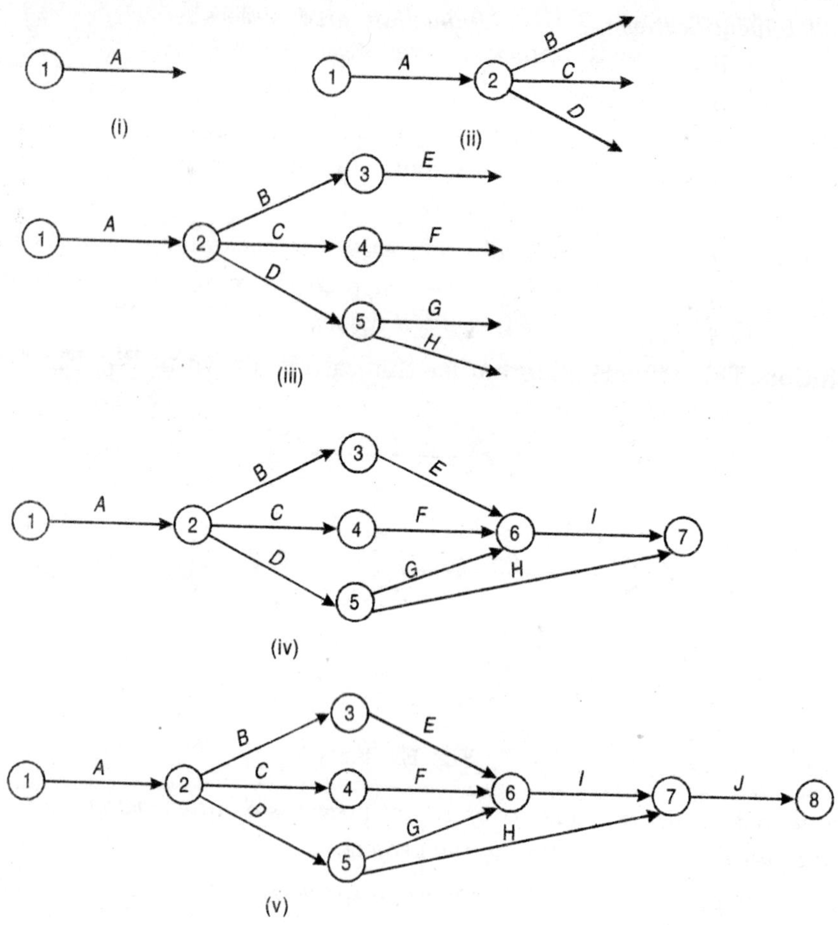

Fig. Ex. 3.3

Solution The arrow-diagram (or network diagram) has been drawn step by step for proper understanding.

(i) Activity *A* is preceded by no activity and therefore it is shown as starting from initial event 1.

(ii) Activities *B, C, D* succeed activity *A* and therefore these have been shown as emanating from event 2 at which activity *A* terminates.

(iii) Activities *E, F* and *G* depend on activities *B, C* and D respectively. Similarly activity *H* depends on activity *D*. Thus activities *E, F, G* and *H* can be initiated only after accomplishment of activities *B, C* and *D*. Thus events 3, 4 and 5 are head events for activities *B, C* and *D,* and tail events for activities *E, F, G* and *H.*

(iv) Since activities *E*, *F* and *G* precede activity *I*, these have been terminated at a single node 6 at which activity *I* emanates. Thus all the three activities *E*, *F* and *G* have been shown as immediate predecessors of activity *I*.

(v) Activity *J* succeeds activities *I* and *H* and therefore both these activities have been joined at node 7 so that they can be shown as immediate predecessors of activity *J*. The last activity *J* is also terminated at node 8 which marks the completion of the project.

Example 3.4 *A project manager was interested in developing a network for a project involving 20 jobs labeled from A to J. He listed all its predecessors as best as he could determine as indicated below.*

Job	*Immediate predecessor*	*Job*	*Immediate predecessor*
A	–	K	G
B	–	L	F, G, K
C	–	M	H, I
D	A, B	N	H, I, J, L
E	A, B, C	O	J, K, L
F	A, B, C	P	M, N
G	C	Q	O, P
H	D, E	R	J, K, L,O
I	D, E, F	S	N, Q, R
J	F, G	T	O, S

Determine which predecessors shown in the table are redundant. Draw the network using as few dummy jobs as possible.

Solution The redundant predecessors may be determined as indicated in the following table.

From this table it is observed that predecessor job *G* is redundant for job *L*; predecessor job *K* is redundant for job *O*; predecessor jobs *J*, *K* and *L* are redundant for job *R*. Besides these it may be observed from the table that job *N* will be completed much before job *S* will commence. Similarly job *O* will also be completed much before job *T* will commence. Hence even though these facts are not depicted in the table, from logical consideration predecessor job *N* may be considered to be redundant for job *S*, and predecessor job *O* may be considered to be redundant for job *T*.

Thus in this case that various redundant predecessors are as listed below.

Jobs	*Redundant predecessors*
L	*G*
O	*K*
R	*J, K, L*
S	*N*
T	*O*

Predecessors

Jobs	*A*	*B*	*C*	*D*	*E*	*F*	*G*	*H*	*I*	*J*	*K*	*L*	*M*	*N*	*O*	*P*	*Q*	*R*	*S*	*T*
A																				
B																				
C																				
D	×	×																		
E	×	×	×																	
F	×	×	×																	
G			×																	
H	○	○	○	×	×															
I	○	○	○	×	×	×														
J	○	○	○			×	×													
K			○				×													
L	○	○	○			×	⊗				×									
M				○	○	○		×	×											
N				○	○	○	○	×	×	×	○	×								
O						○	○			×	⊗	×								
P								○	○	○		○	×	×						
Q										○	○	○	○	○	×	×				
R						○	○			⊗	⊗	⊗			×					
S								○	○	○	○	○		×	○	○	×	×		
T										○	○	○		○	×		○	○	×	

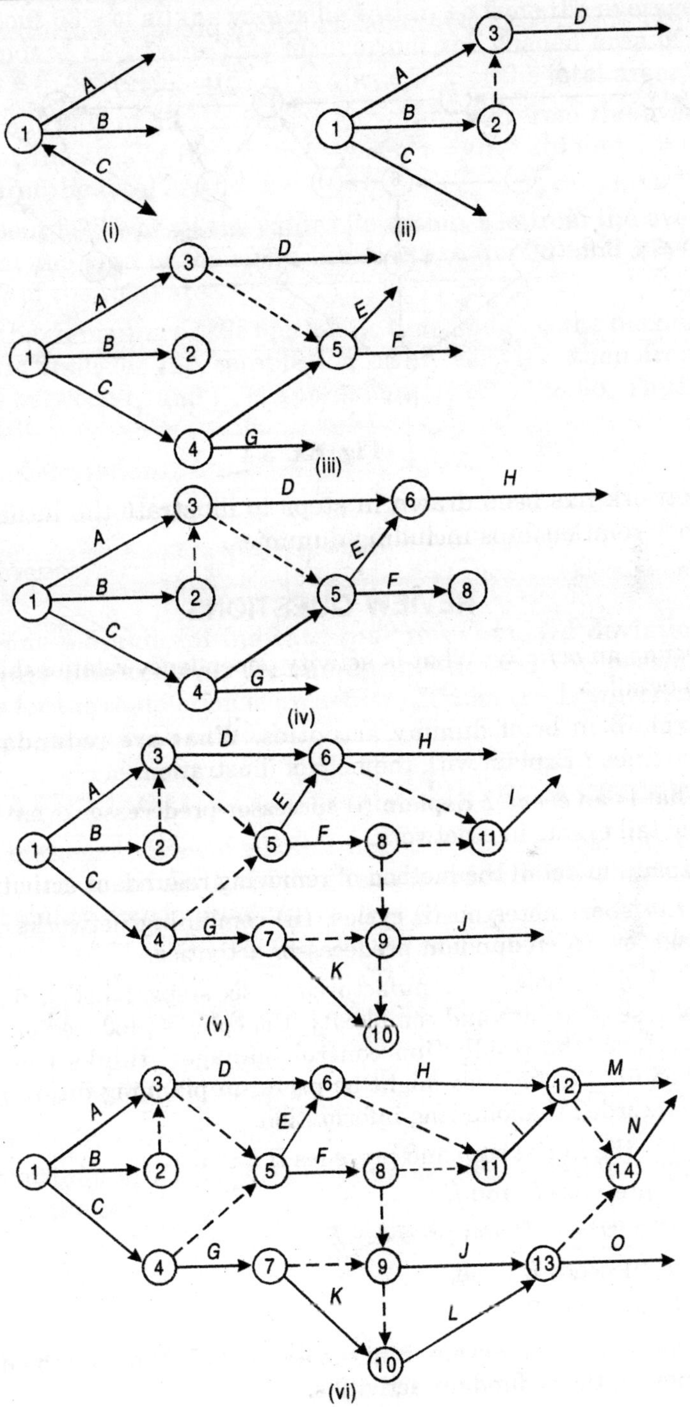

Fig. Ex. 3.4

Contd.

Contd.

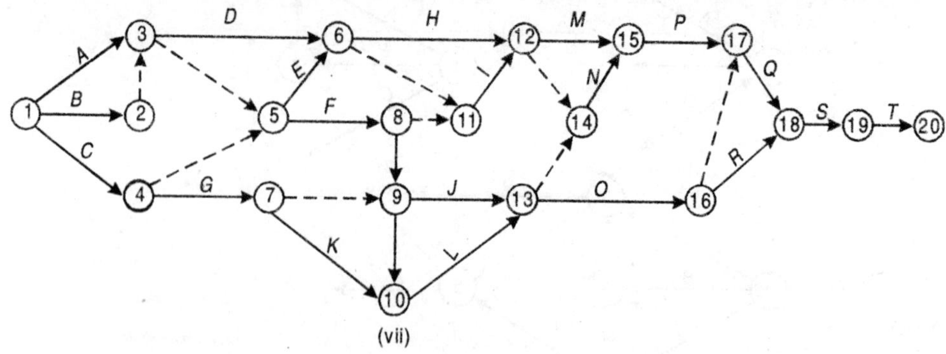

(vii)

Fig. Ex. 3.4

The network has been drawn in steps to illustrate the incorporation of dependency relationships including dummies.

REVIEW QUESTIONS

3.1 Define an *activity*. What is activity dependency relationship ? Discuss in detail.

3.2 Explain in brief dummy activities. What are redundant dummy activities ? Explain with the help of illustrations.

3.3 What is an *event* ? Explain (i) successor-predecessor events ; (ii) head and tail events in a network.

3.4 Explain in detail the method of removing redundant activities.

3.5 Write short notes on (i) cycles, (ii) combining networks ; (iii) AON diagram ; (iv) redundant predecessor activities.

3.6 The Rubik's cube is manufactured in six steps, labelled *A* through *F*. Because of its size and complexity, the cube is produced one at a time. Mr. Zero, the production control manager, thinks that networks scheduling techniques might be useful in planning future production. He recorded the following information:

(i) *A* is the initial step and precedes *B* and *C* ;

(ii) *C* precedes *D* and *E* ;

(iii) *B* succeeds *D* and precedes *E* ;

(iv) *F* succeeds *E* ; and

(v) *D* precedes *F*.

(a) Draw an arrow diagram from the above data. Simplify the diagram by removing the redundant activities.

(b) Draw an activity-on-node diagram. After rechecking the network it was concluded that *B* was really a predecessor of *D* rather than *vice versa*.

3.7 From the following data draw the arrow diagram.

This must be completed	*Activity duration*	*Before this can start*	*Activity duration*
A	30	*C*	–
B	7	*D*	–
B	–	*G*	–
B	–	*K*	–
C	10	*D*	–
C	–	*G*	–
D	14	*E*	–
F	10	*F*	–
F	7	*H*	–
F	–	*I*	–
F	–	*L*	–
G	21	*I*	–
G	–	*L*	–
H	7	*J*	15
I	12	*J*	–
K	30	*L*	15

3.8 A project consists of 12 activities from *A* to *L*. The order in which the activities fall is as follows : Activity *A* comes first and precedes *B*, *C* and *D*. Both *B* and *C* must be completed before *E* starts and *C* and *D* must come before *F*, but *G* and *H* can start as soon as *D* is completed. Activity *I* succeeds *D*, *E*, *F* and *G*. Activities *J* and *K* succeed *G*, *H* and *I* but precede activity *L*.

(a) Eliminate redundant predecessor activities with the help of precedence matrix and list the immediate predecessors for each activity.

(b) With the list in (a) above draw

(i) arrow diagram (ii) AON diagram.

3.9 Following jobs along with their immediate predecessors have been listed by a project manager. Remove the redundant predecessor activities from the list of immediate predecessors and draw (a) arrow diagram ; and (b) Activity-on-node diagram.

Activity	*Immediate predecessors*	*Activity*	*Immediate predecessors*
A	—	*K*	*G*
B	—	*L*	*F, G, K*
C	—	*M*	*H, I*

Contd.

Contd.

D	*A, B*	*N*	*H, I, J, L*
E	*A,B, C*	*O*	*J, K, L*
F	*A, B,C*	*P*	*M, N*
G	*C*	*Q*	*O, P*
H	*D, E*	*R*	*J, K, L, O*
I	*D, E, F*	*S*	*N, Q, R*
J	*F, G*	*T*	*O, S*

3.10 Draw a PERT network for the following project:

(i) *A* is the first of start event and *K* the end event

(ii) *J* is a successor event to *F*.

(iii) *C* and *D* are successor events to *B*.

(iv) *D* is a preceding event to *G*.

(v) *E* and *F* occur after event *C*.

(vi) *E* precedes *F*.

(vii) *C* restrains the occurrence of *G* and *G* precedes *H*.

(viii) *H* precedes *J*

(ix) *F* restrains the occurrence of *H*.

(x) *K* succeeds event *J*.

4

Chapter

PERT : Time Considerations — Estimation and Computation

4.1 INTRODUCTION

PERT, which in its abbreviated form stands for *Programme Evaluation and Review Technique,* is used for planning, scheduling and monitoring the project. PERT was developed in 1957–58 by U.S. Navy in collaboration with a consulting firm of engineers Booz, Allen and Hamilton, to evolve a procedure for monitoring the Polaris Missile Programme. Since then this technique has been used most frequently in the aerospace industries in particular and in various research and development types of projects in general. These projects are known as *once through type* or *nonrepetitive type* projects because in such projects there is little or no past history on which the network construction and time estimates may be based. Moreover in such projects there is large amount of uncertainty in the development of new system, and also uncertainty about the time required for developmental research, engineering design and ultimate construction, about the specific activities and sometimes about the configuration of the end product itself. PERT takes specific account of some of these uncertainties and hence it is usually preferred for these projects. Further a PERT network is event oriented i.e., in this network interest is focussed upon the start or completion of events rather than on the activities themselves. The activities that take place between the events are not specified. It, however, assumes that the activities and their network relationships have been well defined but it allows for uncertainties in activity times. In other words in PERT the duration of an activity, is not fixed or is not deterministic. Thus for each activity in the project network, not only is an estimate made of the *most probable time* required to complete the activity, but some measure of uncertainty is also noted in this estimate as indicated in the next section.

4.2 TIME ESTIMATES

In order to take into account the uncertainties involved in the activity times three kinds of time estimates are generally made for each activity in PERT which are as mentioned below:

1. The optimistic time estimate
2. The pessimistic time estimate
3. The most likely time estimate.

1. The Optimistic Time Estimate. This is the shortest possible time in which an activity can be completed under ideal conditions. Thus this time estimate represents the time in which the activity would be completed if everything went perfectly well without any problems or adverse conditions being developed during the execution of the activity. In arriving at this time estimate no provisions are made for delays or setbacks and better than normal conditions are assumed to prevail during the execution of the activity. This time estimate is denoted by t_O.

2. The Pessimistic Time Estimate. This is the maximum possible time that would be required to complete the activity. Thus this time estimate represents the time required to complete the activity if everything went wrong and abnormal situations prevailed. However, this estimate does not include the possible effects of major catastrophes such as floods, fires, earthquakes, etc., or that of labour strikes or unrest etc. This time estimate is denoted by t_P.

3. The Most Likely Time Estimate. This is the time required to complete the activity if normal conditions prevail. This time estimate lies between the optimistic and the pessimistic time estimates. Thus this time estimate reflects a situation where normal conditions are prevailing, things are as usual and there is nothing exciting. This time estimate is denoted by t_L.

The three time estimates are based on the previous experience of carrying out similar activities. These time estimates are expressed in days, weeks or months and represent calendar dates and not actual working days. However, these time estimates are not always easy to prepare, but together they give useful information about the expected uncertainties of an activity.

4.3 FREQUENCY DISTRIBUTION

As stated earlier the three time estimates are based on the previous experience in regard to the time taken for the completion of activities of a particular type under diverse conditions. Further some sort of a relationship may be established between the number of activities of a particular type and the various times taken for their completion. Such a relationship may be expressed by a curve plotted between the time of completion and the number of activities of a particular type completed in that time. The curve so obtained is called *frequency distribution curve* which will roughly have a shape as shown in Fig. 4.1. In this curve point A corresponds to the optimistic

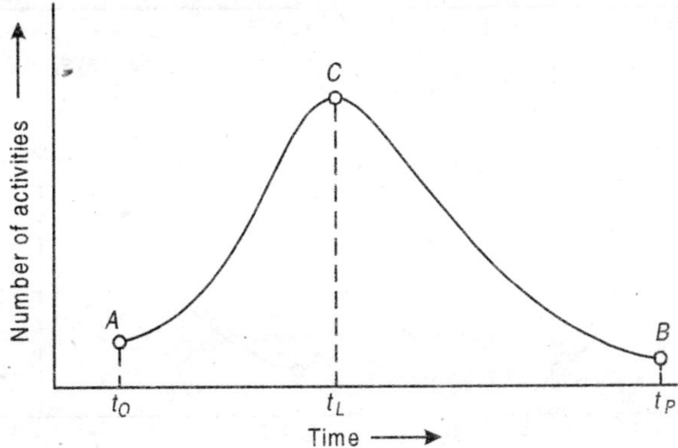

Fig. 4.1 *Frequency distribution curve.*

time t_O, point B corresponds to the pessimistic time t_P and point C corresponds to the most likely time t_L. It is clear from the curve that a large number of cases of the activity are completed in the most likely time. Frequency distribution curves having a single hump or *mode* as shown in Fig. 4.1 are generally called *unimodal curves.* If the curve is symmetrical on either side of point C it is known as a *normal curve,* otherwise it is said to have a *skew* which may be left or right sided as shown in Fig. 4.2 and explained with the following example.

Consider four different activities of a PERT network for each of which the three time estimates in days were obtained as follows.

Activity No.	t_O	t_L	t_P
1	4	7	10
2	6	7	10
3	4	7	8
4	6	7	8

The frequency distribution curves for the above noted activities are as shown in Fig. 4.2. The curve in Fig. 4.2 (a) has left sided skew and it corresponds to activity No. 2.

The curves in Figs. 4.2 (b) and (c) are symmetrical about the peak C and hence these are normal (or unskewed) curves which correspond to activities No. 1 and 4 respectively. The difference in these two curves being that the

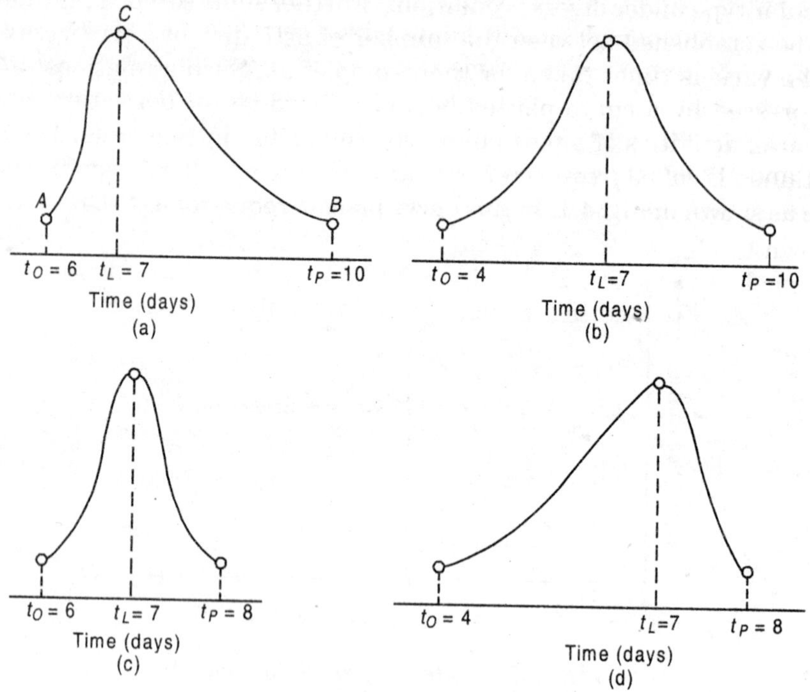

Fig. 4.2 *Frequency distribution curves.*

curve of Fig. 4.2 (b) has a wider base as compared to that of Fig. 4.2 (c). This is so because for activity No. 1 there is wider range of variation between t_O and t_P as compared to that for activity No. 4. The curve in Fig. 4.2 (d) has right sided skew and it corresponds to activity No. 3.

The method of preparing a frequency distribution curve is explained with the help of the following example.

Consider a large multi-storey building construction project in which the times in days required for driving 66 piles of the same dimensions are given in Table 4.1.

TABLE 4.1 *Times in days for driving piles*

10	11	16	13	14	17
12	10	14	11	9	19
14	12	9	12	12	18
8	16	11	14	13	15
11	18	15	13	16	14
13	14	12	11	14	12
12	15	10	8	15	13
15	10	17	13	13	18
17	13	19	11	10	12
16	9	15	13	16	14
13	12	11	10	11	17

From Table 4.1 it is observed that the minimum time taken for the completion of the pile driving is 8 days which corresponds to the optimistic time t_O, while the maximum time taken is 19 days which corresponds to the pessimistic time t_P. The time for pile driving varies from 8 to 19 days. Table 4.2 gives the number of piles driven in 8, 9, 10, 11, 12, 13, 14, 15, 16, 17, 18 and 19 days respectively.

The data of Table 4.2 is plotted to obtain the frequency distribution curve as shown in Fig. 4.3. From the curve the most likely time t_L corresponding to the peak of the curve is found to be 13 days. The frequency distribution curve obtained in this case is not symmetrical about its peak but it has a left sided skew.

TABLE 4.2 *Number of Piles driven in 8 to 19 days*

Days of completion	*No. of piles driven in these days*	*Days of completion*	No. *of piles driven in these days*
8	2	14	8
9	3	15	6
10	6	16	5
11	8	17	4
12	9	18	3
13	10	19	2

If the time of completion of activities has a large range (i.e., the difference between the longest and the shortest time taken by the activity for its

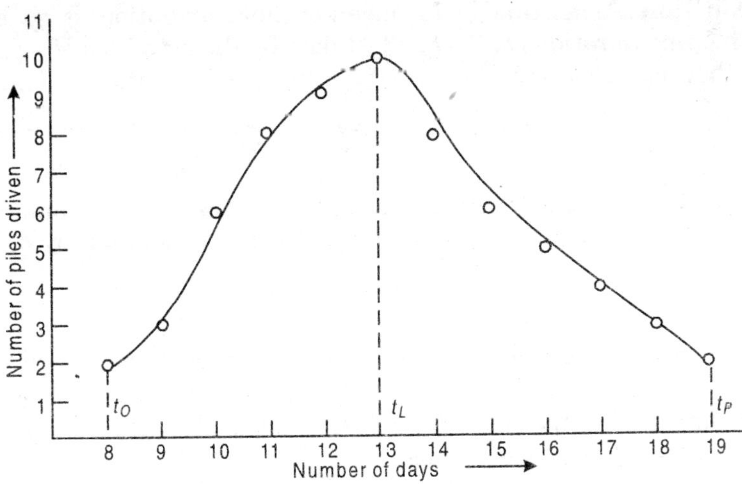

Fig. 4.3 *Frequency distribution curve in respect of data of Table 4.2.*

completion) then this range is divided into some number of equal or unequal smaller ranges and the number of activities falling in each smaller range is counted. A plot of number of activities versus the corresponding smaller range of completion time is prepared which is obtained as a bar chart. Such a bar chart is also called a *histogram.* In drawing the histogram the adjacent ranges are made to touch each other i.e., no gap is left between them. If the mid-points of the top sides of the rectangles of the histogram are joined by straight lines then and *frequency polygon* is obtained. If the interval of the smaller ranges is reduced the frequency polygon will consist of short but a large number of straight lines. In the limit the frequency polygon will assume the shape of a frequency distribution curve.

4.4 MEAN, VARIANCE AND STANDARD DEVIATION OF THE DISTRIBUTION

From the frequency distribution curve prepared by using the data for the varying durations of time taken by the activities of a particular type the only aspect of the characteristics of the distribution that is noticeable is the range i.e., the difference between the longest and the shortest time taken by the activity. However, a more complete description of the distribution would be obtained if the various other aspects of the characteristics of the distribution as indicated below are computed.

1. Mean time or average time (called the mean of the distribution)
2. Deviation
3. Variance
4. Standard deviation.

1. **Mean Time.** Mean time t_m (or mean of the distribution) is given by the sum of the time durations $t_1, t_2, t_3, ... t_n$, taken by the activities of a particular type for their completion divided by the number of activities n. Thus

$$t_m = \frac{t_1 + t_2 + t_3 + ... + t_n}{n} = \frac{\Sigma t}{n} \quad ...(4.1)$$

2. **Deviation.** The difference between the time under consideration and the mean time is known as deviation, which is denoted by δ. Thus

$$\delta = t - t_m \quad ...(4.2)$$

where δ = deviation of any time t from the mean time t_m ; and

t = time under consideration for which deviation is being found.

3. **Variance.** The mean of the square of the deviations is known as variance. It is denoted by σ^2. Thus

$$\sigma^2 = \frac{\Sigma \delta^2}{n} = \frac{\Sigma (t - t_m)^2}{n} \quad ... (4.3)$$

Variance is a measure of the dispersion or spread of data.

For computing the variance the following steps are involved:

(i) Obtain the mean of the distribution by Eq. 4.1.

(ii) Determine the deviation of each time from the mean by Eq. 4.2.

(iii) Find the square of these individual deviations.

(iv) Find the mean of the square of the deviations which is equal to variance.

TABLE 4.3 *Computation of deviation and variance*

Time taken t	*Deviation* $\delta = t - t_m$	δ^2	*Time taken t*	*Deviation* $\delta = t - t_m$	δ^2
10	–3.2	10.24	13	–0.2	0.04
12	–1.2	1.44	11	–2.2	4.84
14	+0.8	0.64	12	–1.2	1.44
8	–5.2	27.04	14	+0.8	0.64
11	–2.2	4.84	13	–0.2	0.04
13	–0.2	0.04	11	–2.2	4.84
12	–1.2	1.44	8	–5.2	27.04
15	+1.8	3.24	13	–0.2	0.04
17	+ 3.8	14.44	11	–2.2	4.84
16	+ 2.8	7.84	13	–0.2	0.04
13	–0.2	0.04	10	–3.2	10.24
11	–2.2	4.84	14	+ 0.8	0.64
10	–3.2	10.24	9	–4.2	17.64
12	–1.2	1.44	12	–1.2	1.44
16	+2.8	7.84	13	–0.2	0.04
18	+4.8	23.04	16	+2.8	7.84
14	+0.8	0.64	14	+0.8	0.64
15	+1.8	3.24	15	+1.8	3.24
10	–3.2	10.24	13	–0.2	0.04
13	–0.2	0.04	10	–3.2	10.24
9	–4.2	17.64	16	+2.8	7.84
12	–1.2	1.44	11	–2.2	4.84
16	+ 2.8	7.84	17	+3.8	14.44
14	+ 0.8	0.64	19	+5.8	33.64
9	–4.2	17.64	18	+4.8	23.04
11	–2.2	4.84	15	+1.8	3.24
15	+ 1.8	3.24	14	+0.8	0.64

Contd

Table 4.3 Contd

12	−1.2	1.44	12	−1.2	1.44
10	−3.2	10.24	13	−0.2	0.04
17	+ 3.8	14.44	18	+ 4.8	23.04
19	+ 5.8	33.64	12	−1.2	1.44
15	+ 1.8	3.24	14	+ 0.8	0.64
11	−2.2	4.84	17	+ 3.8	14.44

It may be noted that though some of the deviations may be negative, their squares will always be positive and hence variance will always be positive. Further variance cannot have zero value unless each individual deviation is equal to zero.

4. **Standard Deviation.** The square root of the variance is known as standard deviation which is denoted by σ. Thus

$$\sigma = \sqrt{\frac{(t-t_m)^2}{n}} \qquad \text{...(4.4)}$$

All the above noted quantities are computed for the data given in Table 4.1. The computations are shown in Table 4.3. For the 66 time observations, we have

$$\Sigma t = 871$$

$$\therefore \qquad t_m = \frac{\Sigma t}{n} = \frac{871}{66} = 13.20$$

Also $\qquad \Sigma\delta^2 = 478.44$

∴ Variance, $\qquad \sigma^2 = \frac{\Sigma\delta^2}{n} = \frac{478.44}{66} = 7.25$

∴ Standard deviation

$$\sigma = \sqrt{7.25} = 2.69$$

4.5 PROBABILITY DISTRIBUTION

In general probability means chance or likelihood of something happening and hence it is connected with chance and uncertainty. As indicated earlier the three time estimates made for each activity of a PERT network have inherent uncertainties. As such the time duration of each activity of a PERT network may be considered to follow a probability distribution rather than frequency distribution. A probability distribution is a distribution of probability values for all possible outcomes. Mathematically probability is defined as the ratio of the number of times a particular event can occur to the total number of likely events involved. The value of probability therefore always ranges from 0 to 1. If an event has a probability of 1, then it is certain to occur, and if its probability is zero it can never occur. Any value of probability between 1 and 0 for an event represents a possible occurrence of the event. Further for any event closer is the value of probability to 1, more certain is the occurrence of that event. The method for the computation of probability for any event is explained by the following example.

Consider an example of sinking of wells for the well foundation of a long bridge. It is assumed that in all 25 wells are to be sunk under varying circumstances and the durations of time taken are as follows:

4 wells are sunk in 40 days each
6 wells are sunk in 60 days each
8 wells are sunk in 90 days each
5 wells are sunk in 100 days each
2 wells are sunk in 110 days each.

From the given data the probability of sinking a well within 40 days is equal to the ratio of the number of wells sunk in 40 days to the total number of wells sunk i.e., (4/25) = 0.16 or 16% probability. Similarly, the probability of sinking a well within 90 days will be

$$\frac{4+6+8}{25} = 0.72 \text{ or } 72\%$$

and that of sinking a well within 100 days will be

$$\frac{4+6+8+5}{25} = 0.92 \text{ or } 92\%$$

A probability distribution curve is a plot of a function $f(x)$ called *probability density function (pdf)* or *probability function,* with the height of the curve standardized so that the area under the curve is equal to unity, i.e.,

$$\int_{-\infty}^{+\infty} f(x) = 1$$

Since the probability distribution curve is represented by an equation of the type $y = f(x)$, the height or the ordinate of the curve at any point x is equal to $f(x)$. Figure 4.4 shows a typical probability distribution curve. It may,

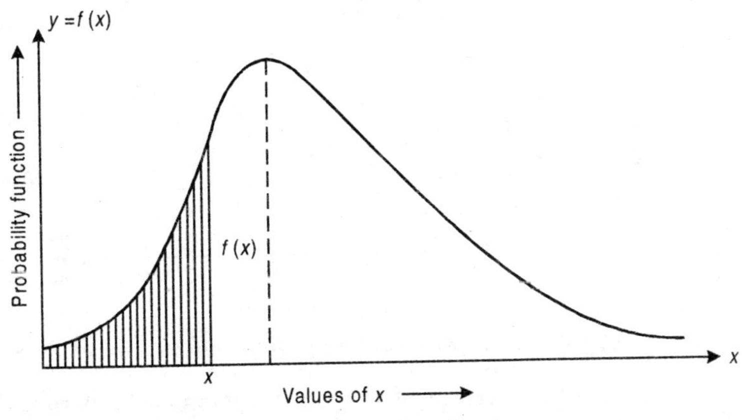

Fig. 4.4 *Probability distribution curve.*

however, be noted that the ordinate $f(x)$ of the curve at any point x does not give the probability. The probability value at any point x is given by the ratio of the shaded area (i.e., area to the left of the point x) to the total area of the curve. Since the total area of the curve is equal to unity, the probability value at any point x is equal to the shaded area only. If x represents the activity duration time t and $y = f(x) = f(t)$, then probability distribution curve for activity duration time may be obtained from which the three time estimates for each activity of a PERT network may be readily made.

The probability distribution curve may be either symmetrical about its apex or it may be unsymmetrical about its apex (or it may be skewed). If the curve is symmetrical about its apex then it is said to have *normal* or *Gaussian distribution.* The normal or the Gaussian distribution is one of the very important probability distributions since it has a wide range of practical applications. It is sometimes referred to as the bell-shaped distribution because the curve resembles a bell. However, the time durations of individual activities of a PERT network usually do not follow the normal distribution but they follow another distribution called Beta-distribution (or β-distribution) which unlike normal distribution is unsymmetrical about its apex (or is skewed). Both the types of probability distributions viz., normal probability distribution and Beta probability distribution are described in the subsequent sections.

4.6 NORMAL PROBABILITY DISTRIBUTION OR NORMAL DISTRIBUTION

Figure 4.5 shows a typical normal probability distribution curve. It may be seen that the curve is symmetrical about the point $x = \mu$, where μ is the

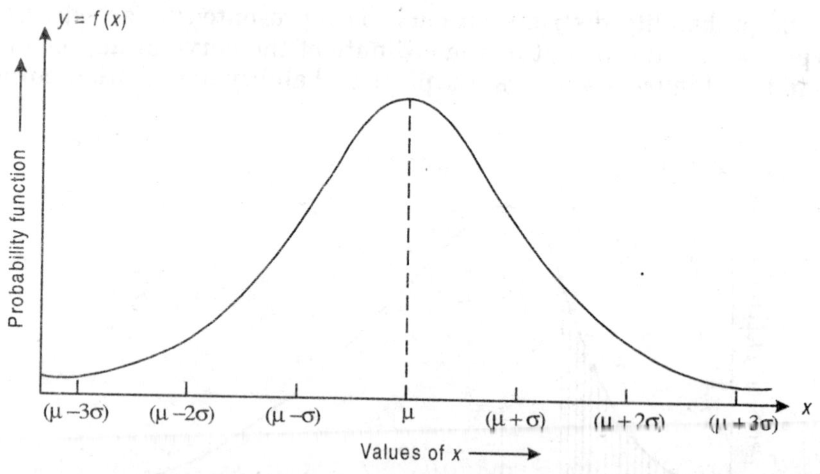

Fig. 4.5 *Normal probability distribution curve.*

mean of the distribution. Some of the observations which may be made from this curve (Fig. 4.5) are as follows.

(i) About 68% of all the values lie within $\pm\sigma$ from the average, where σ is the standard deviation. This means that the shaded area of the curve between $x = (\mu - \sigma)$ and $x = (\mu + \sigma)$ is about 68% of the total area.

(ii) About 95% of all the values lie within $\pm 2\sigma$ from the average. This means that the area of the curve between $x = (\mu - 2\sigma)$ and $x = (\mu + 2\sigma)$ is about 95% of the total area.

(iii) About 99.7% of all the values lie within $\pm 3\sigma$ from the average. This means that the area of the curve between $x = (\mu - 3\sigma)$ and $x = (\mu + 3\sigma)$ is about 99.7 of the total area.

If t_O is the minimum or the optimistic time and t_P is the maximum or the pessimistic time for the completion of an activity, then from (iii) the difference between t_P and t_O is approximately equal to 6σ. Thus

Standard deviation $$\sigma = \frac{t_P - t_O}{6} \qquad \text{... (4.5)}$$

and variance $$\sigma^2 = \left(\frac{t_P - t_O}{6}\right)^2 \qquad \text{... (46)}$$

Equations 4.5 and 4.6 indicate that the standard deviation and the variance are affected only by the optimistic and the pessimistic time estimates for the completion of an activity. These are, however, not affected by the most likely time estimate.

4.7 BETA PROBABILITY DISTRIBUTION OR BETA DISTRIBUTION

For most of the activities of a PERT network, Beta probability distribution curve is found to give satisfactory results. Figure 4.6 shows two typical Beta probability distribution curves. The curve of Fig. 4.6 (a) has skew to the left and hence it represents the beta distribution for an optimistic estimator, while the curve of Fig. 4.6 (b) has skew to the right and hence it represents beta distribution for a pessimistic estimator. As shown in Fig. 4.6 points A and B are made to coincide with the optimistic time t_O and the pessimistic time t_P respectively, i.e., the range is equal to $(t_P - t_O)$ in both cases. Further the mode of the curve is made to coincide with the most likely time t_L.

For a distribution of this type also the standard deviation is approximately one sixth of the range, i.e.,

$$\sigma = \frac{(t_P - t_O)}{6}$$

The variance is therefore equal to

$$\sigma^2 = \left(\frac{t_P - t_O}{6}\right)^2$$

Both the above noted expressions for standard deviation and variance are same as those given by Eqs. 4.5 and 4.6. Further as mentioned earlier variance is a measure of the dispersion and since it depends on the range

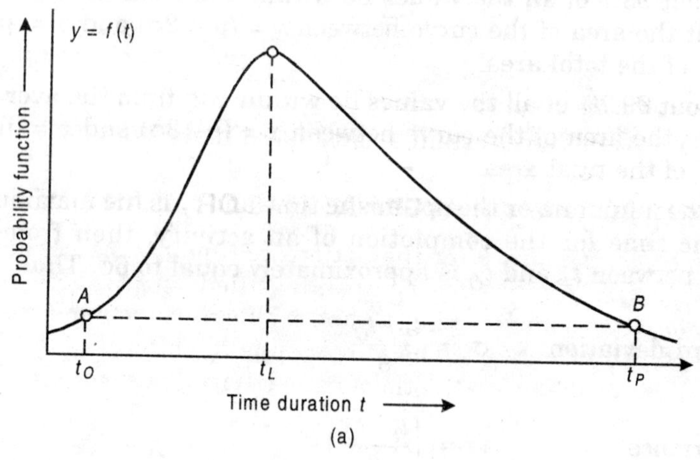

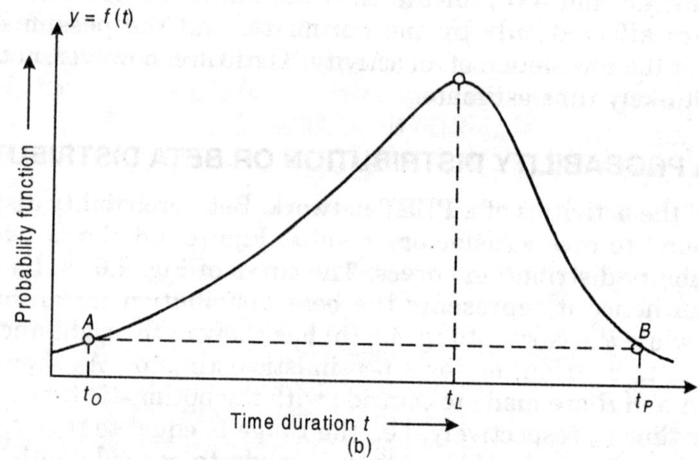

Fig. 4.6 *Beta probability distribution curves.*

$(t_P - t_O)$ larger the variance greater will be the uncertainty. This fact is explained by the following example.

For the completion of a particular activity the three time estimates obtained from two persons, *X* and *Y*, are as noted below :

	t_O	t_L	t_P
Estimate by *X* :	7	9	11
Estimate by *Y* :	6	8	12

The variance

$$\text{for } X : \sigma^2 = \left(\frac{11-7}{6}\right)^2 = 0.44$$

$$\text{for } Y : \sigma^2 = \left(\frac{12-6}{6}\right)^2 = 1.00$$

Hence, Y was more uncertain about his estimate than X.

4.8 EXPECTED TIME OR AVERAGE TIME OR MEAN TIME

The three time estimates viz., the optimistic time t_O, the pessimistic time t_P, and the most likely time t_L are identified on the beta probability distribution curve and by using t_O and t_P the variance and the standard deviation can be calculated. The next step is to obtain the average or the mean time taken for the completion of an activity. The average or the mean time taken for the completion of an activity is commonly called the *expected time* and is denoted by t_E. If the exact shape of the probability distribution curve is known, the expected time t_E could be accurately calculated. However, since the precise curves are generally not available, the use of an approximation is made. It has been indicated by the statisticians that in beta distribution the average or the expected time is obtained by adding together one-sixth of the optimistic time, two-thirds of the most likely time and one-sixth of the pessimistic time. Thus

$$t_E = \frac{1}{6}t_O + \frac{2}{3}t_L + \frac{1}{6}t_P$$

or

$$t_E = \frac{t_O + 4t_L + t_P}{6} \qquad \text{...(47)}$$

The above expression for t_E is based on the weighted average method in which it may be considered that a weightage of 1 is given to the optimistic time t_O, a weightage of 4 is given to the most likely time t_L, and a weightage of 1 is given to the pessimistic time t_P. A larger weightage given to the most likely time t_L is justified because the chance of completion of the activity in the most likely time t_L is much more than in the optimistic time t_O or in the pessimistic time t_P.

Equation 4.7 is one of the most important equations in PERT analysis as it facilitates the computation of the average or the expected time t_E from the three time estimates. The average or the expected time indicates that there is a fifty-fifty chance of the activity being completed within that time. As such a vertical ordinate through the average or the expected time t_E will divide the area under the probability distribution curve into two equal halves. Further if the estimated times t_O, t_L and t_P are such that the average or the estimated time t_E computed with these times comes out to be equal to t_L, then in view of the above fact it is evident that in all such cases the probability distribution curve will be symmetrical about the mode or apex of the curve. This would happen in all the cases in which $(t_L - t_O) = (t_P - t_L)$ i.e., when the most likely time t_L is equal to the mean of the optimistic time t_O and the pessimistic time t_P.

4.8.1 EXPECTED TIME FOR ACTIVITIES IN SERIES

When there are number of activities in series, the expected time for the entire path along the activities can be found by first finding the expected time t_E for each activity and then taking their sum. Alternatively by adding t_O, t_L and t_P for each of the activities the optimistic time t_O, the most likely time t_L and the pessimistic time t_P for the entire path are obtained from which the expected time t_E can be computed. Illustrative Example 4.1 shows the computations of expected time for individual activity and for activities in series.

The expected time or the average time calculated from the three time estimates for an activity enables to find the critical path in simple networks. A *critical path* is defined as the longest or the most time-consuming path of activities from the beginning to the end of a network. As indicated in Illustrative Example 4.2 by summing up the expected times for the various activities along the different paths the critical path may be found. There can be more than one critical path through a network. However, in large networks, for determining the critical path or paths in a systematic manner it is essential to calculate for each event two time estimates viz., the earliest expected time and the latest allowable time. The critical path is then obtained by connecting those events for each of which the earliest expected time is equal to the latest allowable time. Both the earliest expected time and the latest allowable time which refer to events are discussed in the subsequent sections.

4.9 EARLIEST EXPECTED TIME

The *earliest expected time* is the time in which an event can be expected to be completed. It is denoted by T_E and is written either above or below the node or event circle in the network diagram. The earliest expected time T_E is computed by adding the expected times (t_E's) of all the activities of the activity path leading to that event. If more than one activity paths lead to that activity then the maximum of the sum of the expected times (t_E's) along the various paths will give the earliest expected time.

1 —(3–4–6, t_E = 4.17)→ 2 —(7–9–19, t_E = 9.33)→ 3 —(10–13–17, t_E = 13.17)→ 4

T_E = 0 | T_E = 4.17 | T_E = 13.50 | T_E = 26.67

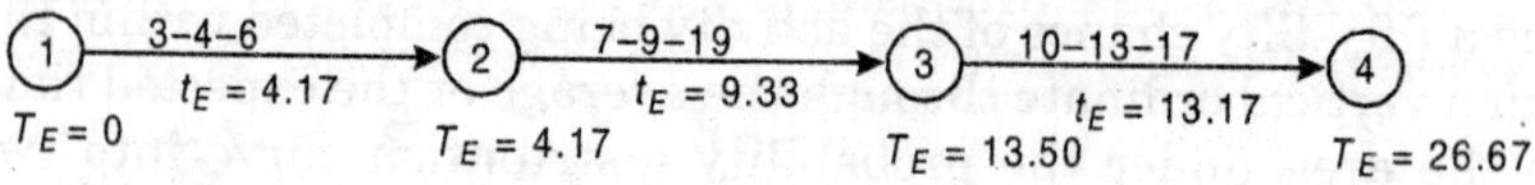

Fig. 4.7 *Simple network having single activity path.*

For example consider a simple network shown in Fig. 4.7 in which there is only one activity path. The three time estimates (t_O, t_L and t_P) of each activity are shown on each activity arrow. From the three time estimates for the activities, the expected times have been calculated and the same are written below each activity arrow. Assuming event 1 as the initial event, for this event $T_E = 0$. The expected time for the completion of activity 1–2 is 4.17 and hence the earliest expected time T_E for event 2 is 4.17. Since event 3 occurs after the completion of activities 1–2 and 2–3, the earliest expected time T_E for event 3 is (4.17 + 9.33) = 13.50. Similarly the earliest expected time T_E for event 4 is (4.17 + 9.33 + 13.17) = 26.67.

Next consider a network shown in Fig. 4.8 in which the expected time T_E for each activity is shown along the activity arrows. In this network event 7 is connected by two activity paths, these being 1–2, 2–4,4–7 and 1–3, 3–5, 5–7. In the first path 1–2–4–7, T_E for the event 7 is (7 + 10 + 15) = 32. In the second path 1–3–5–7, T_E for the same event 7 is (9 + 11 + 14) = 34. Since no event can be considered to have reached or occurred until all activities leading to that event are completed, it may be concluded that event 7 cannot be considered reached or occurred until activities 1–3, 3–5, 5–7 have all been completed. Hence the earliest expected time for event 7 is 34.

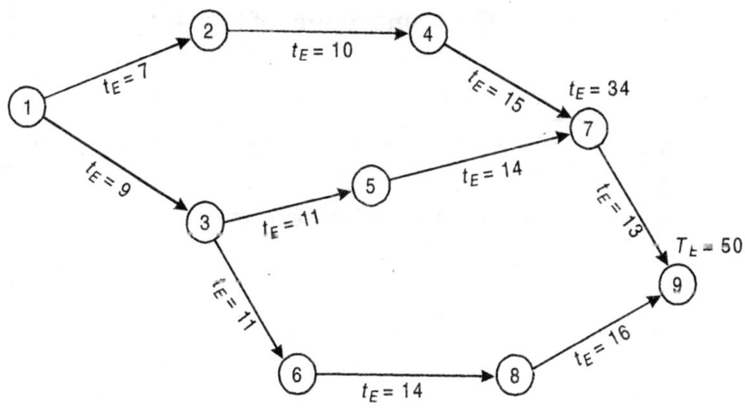

Fig. 4.8 *Network having number of paths leading to a single event.*

In the same network now event 9 is considered. There are three paths leading to event 9, these being 1–2, 2–4, 4–7, 7–9 ‘; 1–3, 3–5, 5–7, 7–9 ; and 1–3, 3–6, 6–8, 8–9. In the first path 1–2–4–7–9, T_E for event 9 is (7 +10 +15 +13) = 45. In the second path 1–3–5–7–9, T_E for the same event 9 is (9 + 11 + 14 + 13) = 47. In the third path 1–3–6–8–9, T_E for the same event 9 is (9 + 11 + 14 + 16) = 50. Hence the earliest expected time for event 9 is 50, the largest of the three values obtained.

4.10 RULE FOR EVALUATING T_E FOR ANY EVENT

A rule has been established to evaluate T_E for any event so that when dealing with large networks the computational work can proceed without making frequent references to the network diagram and also to help in making the entries in a tabular form. The rule to evaluate T_E for any event may be expressed as follows:

T_E (successor event) = T_E (predecessor event) + t_E (activity)

In this rule, the T_E for any successor event is obtained by adding the value of T_E for the predecessor event to the value of t_E for the activity connecting the predecessor and the successor events. Symbolically, if i and j refer to the predecessor and successor events respectively and if $i–j$ refers to the activity connecting events i and j (Fig. 4.9 a), then the rule can be written as

$$T_E^j = T_E^i + t_E^{ij} \quad \text{...(4.8)}$$

where the superscripts refer to the events (i and j) or the activity $(i - j)$. When there are more than one predecessor event for a successor event j, this rule needs modification because an event j cannot occur until all activities leading to that event are completed as described in section 4.9. Therefore T_E^j for the event j will be equal to the maximum of $(T_E^{\,i} + t_E^{ij})$ along various activity paths leading to the event), i.e.,

$$T_E^i = \text{maximum of } (T_E^i + t_E^{ij}) \quad \text{... (4.9)}$$

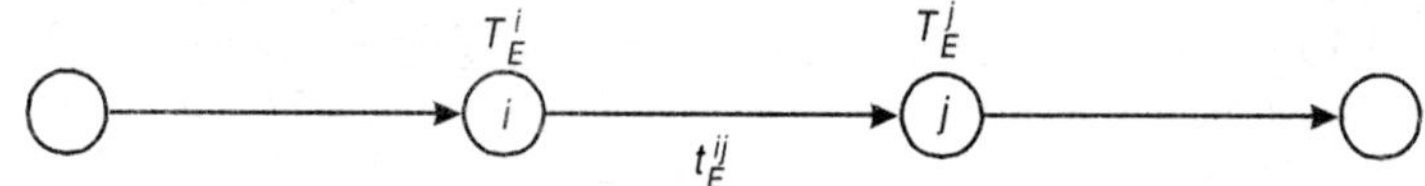

An event having (a) single predecessor event

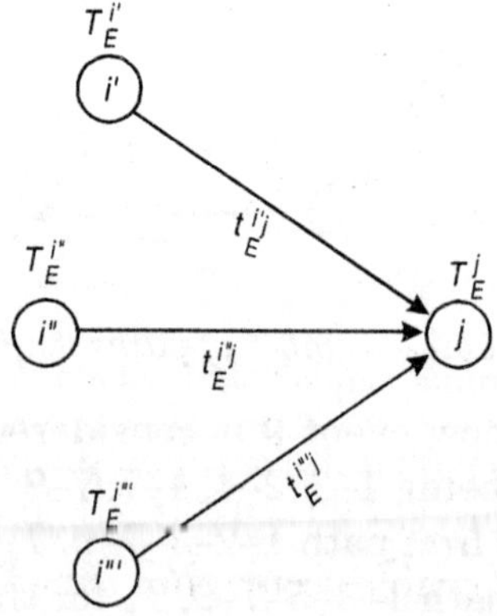

(b) Three predecessor events.

Fig 4.9

For example as shown in Fig. 4.9 (b) event j has three predecessor events i', i'' *and* i''', with the three activities $(i'-j)$, $(i''-j)$ and $(i'''-j)$ leading to it. The earliest expected time T_E^j for the event j will be the maximum of

$(T_E^{i'} + t_E^{i'j})$, $(T_E^{i''} + t_E^{i''j})$ and $(T_E^{i'''} + t_E^{i'''j})$

The application of this rule for evaluating T_E for any event is indicated in Illustrative Example 4.3.

4.11 LATEST ALLOWABLE OCCURRENCE TIME OR LATEST ALLOWABLE TIME

The latest time by which an event must occur to keep the project on schedule is known as the *latest allowable occurrence time* or the *latest allowable time*. It is denoted by T_L and is written either above or below the node or event circle in the network diagram. For every project it is usual to decide the completion time of the project which is known as *contractual obligation time* or *scheduled completion time* and is denoted by T_s. This time evidently refers to the latest allowable occurrence time of the end event i.e., $T_s = T_L$ of the end event. The computation of the latest allowable occurrence time T_L of the events may be done as mentioned in the following example.

Consider a simple network as shown in Fig. 4.10. It is assumed that the contractual obligation time T_s for the project is 31 units. This means that the end event 4 must occur 31 units of time after the project is initiated.

Thus for the end event $T_L^4 = T_s = 31$.

The activity 3–4 takes 13.17 units of time for its completion. Hence event 3 cannot occur later than (31—13.17) = 17.83 units of time after the initiation of the project.

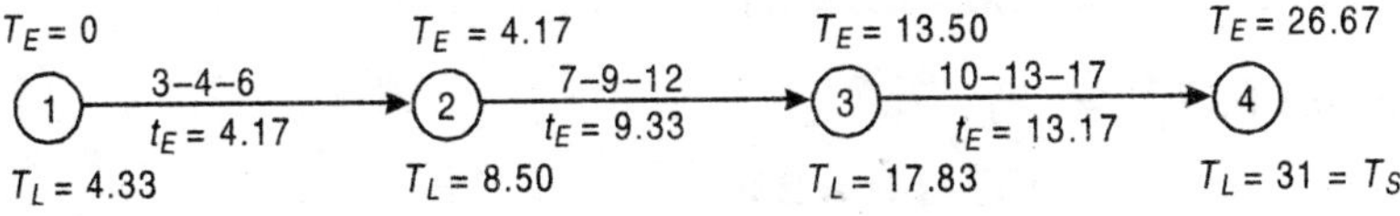

Fig. 4.10 *Simple network having single activity path.*

Since activity 2–3 takes 9.33 units of time, the latest allowable occurrence time for event 2 is therefore (17.83 – 9.33) = 8.50.

Similarly, the latest allowable occurrence time for event 1 is (8.50 – 4.17) = 4.33.

These values of the latest allowable occurrence time T_L for each event are indicated below the corresponding event circle in Fig. 4.10.

The significance of T_L for the events in the network may be indicated by the following analysis.

It is assumed that the project is started as per schedule, i.e., event 1 occurs at time zero. Activity 1–2 is carried out as planned with $T_E^2 = 4.17$. Since $t_E^{2-3} = 9.33$, the earliest expected time T_E^3 is 13.50. If, due to any reason such as labour problem or non-availability of materials, activity 2–3 is delayed, the maximum delay that can be tolerated is (17.83 – 13.50) = 4.33 units of time after the occurrence of event 2 since, for event 3, the latest allowable occurrence time is $T_L^3 = 17.83$. The same type of analysis can be applied to other activities also.

Next consider a network shown in Fig. 4.11 in which the expected time t_E for each activity and the earliest expected time for each event are shown. It is assumed that the contractual obligation time for the project is 50 units, i.e., $T_s = 50$. The latest allowable occurrence time for the end event is therefore $T_L^9 = 50$.

The latest allowable occurrence time for the other events may be obtained as follows.

For event 8, $T_L^8 = T_L^9 - t_E^{8-9}$
$= (50 - 16) = 34$

For event 6, $T_L^6 = T_L^8 - t_E^{6-8}$
$= (34 - 14) = 20$

For event 7, $T_L^7 = T_L^9 - t_E^{7-9}$
$= (50 - 13) = 37$

For event 5, $T_L^5 = T_L^7 - t_E^{5-7}$
$= (37 - 14) = 23$

Event 3 has two successor events viz., event 5 and event 6. Hence the two values of T_L^3 are obtained as under.

$$T_L^3 = T_L^5 - t_E^{3-5}$$
$$= (23 - 11) = 12$$

and
$$T_L^3 = T_L^6 - t_E^{3-6}$$
$$= (20 - 11) = 9$$

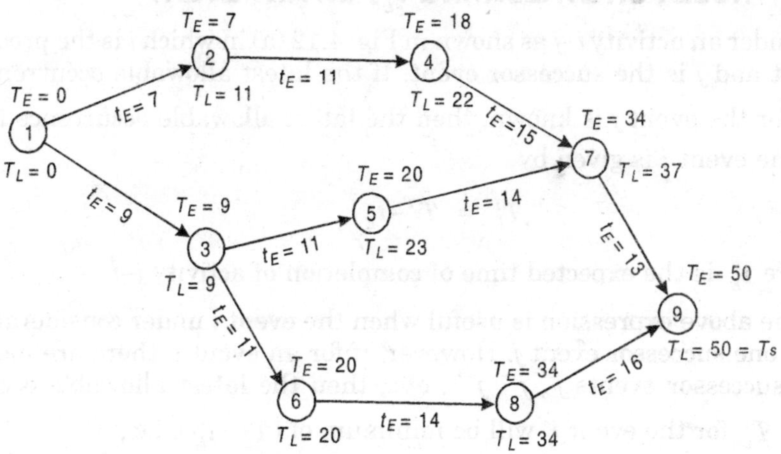

Fig. 4.11 *Network having number of paths leading to a single event.*

Out of these two values of the latest allowable occurrence time for the event 3, the one which is minimum will be the appropriate value and hence $T_L^3 = 9$. This is so because if event 6 cannot occur later than 20 units of time after the beginning of the project, then since activity 3–6 takes 11 units of time for its completion, event 3 cannot occur later than (20–11) = 9 units of time after the beginning of the project. However, if a higher value of $T_E^3 = 12$ is permitted then since T_L^6 will be equal to (12+11) = 23, the event 6 will be late by 3 units of time which is not desirable. Hence in all such cases out of the various values of T_L a minimum value is to be selected.

For event 4, $T_L^4 = T_L^7 - t_E^{4-7}$
$= (37 - 15) = 22$

For event 2, $T_L^2 = T_L^4 - t_E^{2-4}$
$= (22 - 11) = 11$

Again event 1 has two successor events viz., event 2 and event 3. Hence the two values of T_L^1 are obtained as under.

$$T_L^1 = T_L^2 - t_E^{1-2} = (11 - 7) = 4$$

and

$$T_L^1 = T_L^3 - t_E^{1-3} = (9 - 9) = 0$$

Thus as explained earlier out of these two values of the latest allowable occurrence time for the event 1, the minimum value viz., $T_L^1 = 0$ will be the appropriate value.

4.12 RULE FOR EVALUATING T_L FOR ANY EVENT

Consider an activity *i–j* as shown in Fig. 4.12 (a) in which *i* is the predecessor event and *j* is the successor event. If the latest allowable occurrence time T_L^j for the event *j* is known, then the latest allowable occurrence time T_L^i for the event *i* is given by

$$T_L^i = T_L^j - t_E^{ij} \qquad ...(4.10)$$

where t_E^{ij} is the expected time of completion of activity *i–j*.

The above expression is useful when the event *i* under consideration has only one successor event *j*. However, if for an event *i*, there are more than one successor events j', j'', j''', etc., then the latest allowable occurrence time T_L^i for the event j' will be minimum of $(T_L^j - t_E^{ij})$, i.e.,

$$T_L^i = \text{minimum of } (T_L^j - t_E^{ij}) \qquad ...(4.11)$$

This is because if the higher of the various values is taken, the latest allowable occurrence time for the successor events will also be increased, thus suggesting a delay in the project completion.

Thus as shown in Fig. 4.12 (b) there are three successor events j', j'' and j''' to event *i*. The latest allowable occurrence time T_L^i for the event *i* will be the minimum of $\left(T_L^{j'} - t_E^{ij'}\right), \left(T_L^{j''} - t_E^{ij''}\right)$ and $\left(T_L^{j'''} - t_E^{ij'''}\right)$

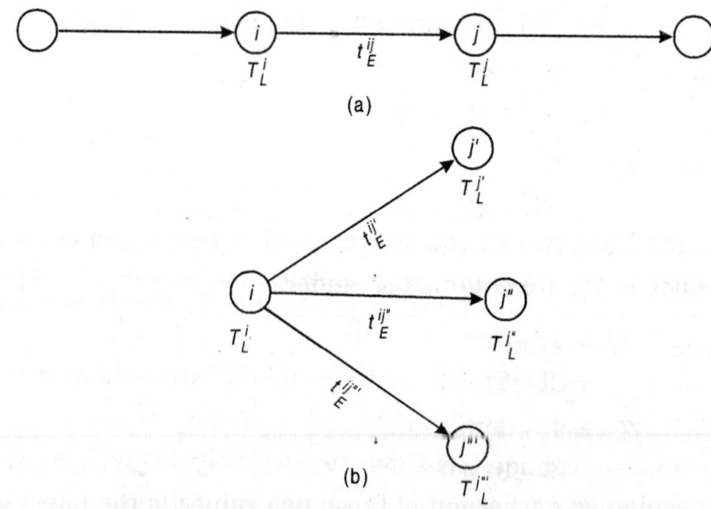

Fig. 4.12 *An event having (a) single successor event; (b) three successor events.*

4.13 FORWARD PASS AND BACKWARD PASS

For calculating the earliest expected time T_E for the occurrence of an event the computations are started from the initial event and ended with the end event or the last event. This is called the *forward pass.* For calculating the latest allowable time T_L for the occurrence of an event the computations are started from the end event and ended with the initial event. This is known as the *backward pass.* Also, when the calculations are done in the tabular form, the computations of the earliest expected time are started from the bottom and that of the latest allowable time are started from the top of the table. Generally the computations for T_E and T_L may be done in a *combined tabular form* as indicated in Table (c) of Illustrative Example 4.3. The enteries in various columns of Table (c) are done as mentioned below.

In column 1 the event numbers are entered starting with the initial event and proceeding in the direction of increasing numbers of the events.

In column 2 the predecessor events and in column 6 the successor events to the events of column 1 are entered. An event under consideration (column 1) may have one or more than one predecessor events (column 2), and one or more than successor events (column 6). A horizontal line is drawn after entering all the predecessor and successor events to every event of column 1.

In columns 3, 4 and 5 the computations for the earliest expected times of the events are done. In column 3 activity times t_E^{ij} are entered where j is the event under consideration (column 1) and i is the predecessor event (column 2). T_E^j is computed by using Eq. 4.8 as

$$T_E^j = T_E^i + t_E^{ij}$$

Where there are more than one predecessor events, several values of T_E^j are obtained, which are entered in column 4. The maximum value of T_E^j is underscored. This underscored value is the appropriate value of the earliest expected time for the event under consideration (column 1) and it is entered as T_E in column 5. Thus for the computation of T_E the forward pass is used starting with the initial event and proceeding in the downward direction(↓) in the table. It may be observed that in this case T_E for the last event comes out to be 48 units of time.

In columns 7, 8 and 9 the computations for the latest allowable occurrence time of the events are done. In column 7 activity times t_E^{ij} are entered where i is the event under consideration (column 1) and j is the successor event (column 6). T_L^i is computed by using Eq. 4.10 as

$$T_L^i = T_L^j - t_E^{ij}$$

Computations are done by backward pass, starting with the end event and proceeding upwards (↑) in the table. For the end event T_L is always taken equal to the contractual obligation time T_s, which in turn is usually taken equal to T_E for the end event. Thus for the end event $T_L = T_S = T_E$ which in this case is equal to 48 units of time.

Where there are more than one successor events, several values of T_L^i are obtained, which are entered in column 8. The minimum value of T_L^i is underscored. This underscored value is the appropriate value of the latest allowable occurrence time for the event under consideration (column 1) and is entered as T_L in column 9.

Thus for each of the events of column 1, T_E is given in column 5 and T_L is given in column 9.

ILLUSTRATIVE EXAMPLES

Example 4.1. *Three activities 10—20, 20–30 and 30–40 of a network are shown in Fig. Ex. 4.1 with their individual time estimates t_O, t_L and t_P marked on them. Compute the expected time for each activity and for the series of activities.*

(10) —5-7-9→ (20) —6-8-12→ (30) —5-11-13→ (40)

Fig. Ex. 4.1

Solution Computations are shown in the following table.

Activity	t_O	t_L	t_P	$t_E = \frac{t_O + 4t_L + t_P}{6}$
10–20	5	7	9	7.00
20–30	6	8	12	8.33
30–40	5	11	13	10.33
				$\Sigma t_E = 25.66$

Alternatively

$$\Sigma t_O = 5 + 6 + 5 = 16$$

$$\Sigma t_L = 7 + 8 + 11 = 26$$

$$\Sigma t_P = 9 + 12 + 13 = 34$$

$$\Sigma t_E = \frac{\Sigma t_O + 4\Sigma t_L + \Sigma t_P}{6}$$

$$= \frac{16 + 4 \times 26 + 34}{6} = 25.66$$

Example 4.2. In *a network shown in Fig. Ex. 4.2 for each activity the optimistic, the most likely and the pessimistic time estimates are given. If10 and 100 are the start and the end events respectively, find the critical path through the network.*

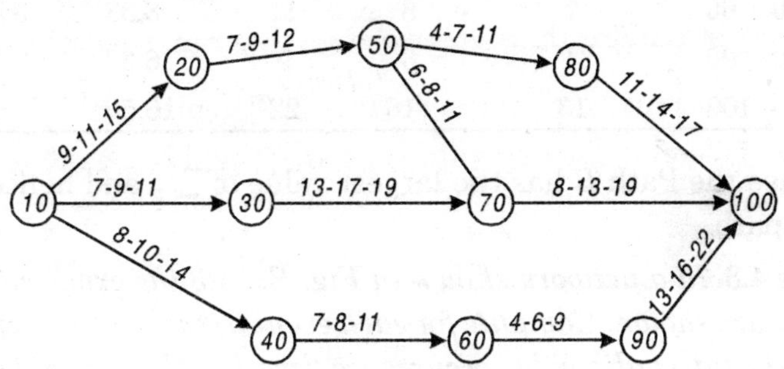

Fig. Ex. 4.2

Solution There are four paths from the start event to the end event as given below.

A : 10–20–50–80–100

B : 10–20–50–70–100

C : 10–30–70–100

D : 10–40–60–90–100

The values of t_E for each activity as well as for the entire path are calculated and tabulated in the following table.

TABLE for Example 4.2

	Activity	t_O	t_L	t_P	t_E	Σt_E
	10 – 20	9	11	15	11.33	
Path *A*	20 – 50	7	9	12	9.17	41.67
	50 – 80	4	7	11	7.17	
	80 – 100	11	14	17	14.00	
	10 – 20	9	11	15	11.33	
	20 – 50	7	9	12	9.17	
Path *B*	50 – 70	6	8	11	8.17	41.84
	70 –100	8	13	19	13.17	
	10 – 30	7	9	11	9.00	
Path *C*	30 – 70	13	17	19	16.67	
	70 – 100	8	13	19	13.17	38.84

Contd.

Table Ex. 4.2 Contd.

Activity		t_o	t_L	t_P	t_E	Σt_E
	10 – 40	8	10	14	10.33	
Path *D*	40 – 60	7	8	11	8.33	37.34
	60 – 90	4	6	9	6.33	
	90 – 100	13	16	22	16.50	

In this case the Path *B* has the largest value of Σt_E and hence Path *B* is the critical path.

Example 4.3. *In a network shown in Fig. Ex. 4.3 the expected time t_E for each activity are shown. Compute for each event (i) the earliest expected time T_E, and (ii) the latest allowable occurrence time T_L. Also compute the values of T_E and T_L in a combined tabular form. Events 10 and 100 are the start and the end events respectively. The contractual obligation time for the project may be assumed to be equal to T_E^{100}.*

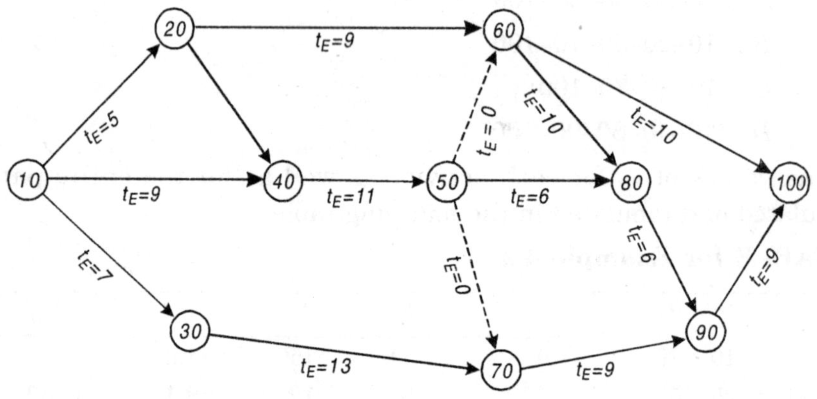

Fig. Ex. 4.3

Solution The computations for T_E and T_L are done in tabular form and the same are shown in Tables 4.3 (a) and (b). For convenience in computations the entries in the tables are made by starting with the end event. Table Ex. 4.3(c) shows the computations for T_E and T_L, in a combined tabular form. The values of T_E and T_L for each event are shown in Fig. Ex. Sol. 4.3.

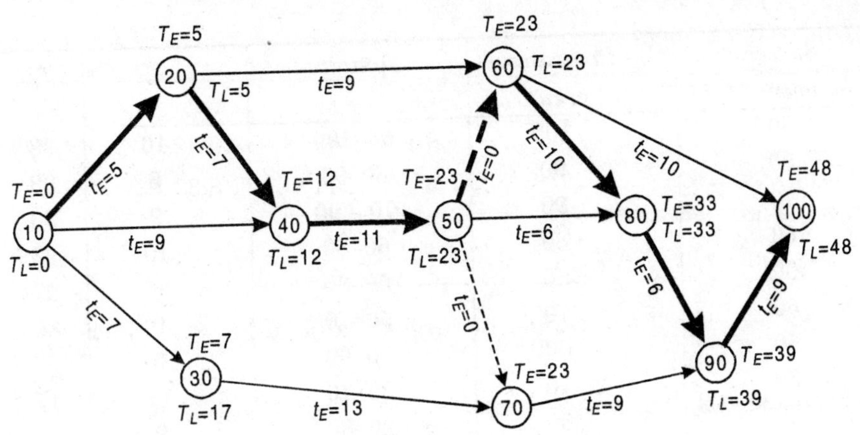

Fig. Sol. Ex. 4.3

TABLE Ex. 4.3 (a) *Computation of Earliest expected time T_E*

Successor event j	*Predecessor event i*	*Activity i – j*	t_E^{ij}	T_E^j
100	90	90–100	9	48
100	60	60–100	10	33
90	80	80–90	6	39
90	70	70–90	9	32
80	60	60–80	10	33
80	50	50–80	6	29
70	50	50–70	0	23
70	30	30–70	13	20
60	20	20–60	9	14
60	50	50–60	0	23
50	40	40–50	11	23
40	20	20–40	7	12
40	10	10–40	9	9
30	10	10–30	7	7
20	10	10–20	5	5

TABLE Ex. 4.3 (b) *Computation of latestallowable occurrence time T_L*

Successor event j	*Predecessor event i*	*Activity i – j*	t_E^{ij}	T_L^i
90	100	90–100	9	39

Contd.

Table Ex. 4.3 Contd.

Successor event j	*Predecessor event i*	*Activity i – j*	t_E^{ij}	T_L^i
60	100	60–100	10	38
80	90	80–90	6	33
70	90	70 – 90	9	30
60	80	60–80	10	23
50	80	50–80	6	27
50	70	50–70	0	30
50	60	50–60	0	23
30	70	30–70	13	17
20	60	20–60	9	14
40	50	40–50	11	12
20	40	20–40	7	5
10	40	10–40	9	3
10	30	10–30	7	10
10	20	10–20	5	0

TABLE Ex. 4.3 (c) *Computation for T_E and T_L*

Event No.	*Earliest expected time (↓)*				*Latest occurrence time (↑)*			
	Predecessor event (i)	t_E^{ij}	T_E^J	T_E	*Successor Event j*	t_E^{ij}	T_L^i	T_L
(1)	(2)	(3)	(4)	(5)	(6)	(7)	(8)	(9)
10	—	—	0	0	20	5	0	0
					30	7	10	
					40	9	3	
20	10	5	5	5	40	7	5	5
					60	9	14	
30	10	7	7	7	70	13	17	17
40	10	9	9	12	50	11	12	12
	20	7	12					
50	40	11	23	23	60	0	23	23
					70	0	30	
					80	0	27	
60	20	9	14	23	80	10	23	23
	50	0	23		100	10	38	

Contd.

Table Ex. 4.3 (c) Contd.

(1)	(2)	(3)	(4)	(5)	(6)	(7)	(8)	(9)
70	30	13	20	23	90	9	30	30
	50	0	23					
80	50	6	29	33	90	6	33	33
	60	10	33					
90	70	9	32	39	100	9	39	39
	80	6	39					
100	60	10	33	48	—	—	48	48
	90	9	48					

REVIEW QUESTIONS

4.1 Write a brief note on the three estimates made for each activity in PERT.

4.2 What do you understand by frequency distribution curve? Indicate with the help of neat sketches the different types of frequency distribution curves.

4·3 Define mean, variance and standard deviation of a distribution.

4.4 Discuss briefly the beta probability distribution. How does it differ from a normal probability distribution?

4.5 How can you determine (i) most likely time, (ii) variance, (iii) standard deviation from the frequency distribution?

4.6 Explain how beta distribution is more suitable for PERT analysis. Indicate how can you determine the expected time and standard deviation in this case.

4.7 The time estimates for three activities *A*, *B* and *C* are as follows :

	Optimistic time	*Most likely time*	*Pessimistic time*
A	11	13	15
B	7	9	13
C	6	11	13

Determine the expected time and variance for each activity. Which activity has more reliable time estimates ?

4.8 Explain the term 'earliest expected time'. Formulate an expression for determining the same.

4.9 What do you understand by 'latest allowable occurrence time'? How do you determine it ?

4.10 In a network shown in the Fig. Rev. Q. 4.10, the three time estimates for each of the activities are indicated. Calculate the variance and the expected time for each activity. Enter the values in a tabular form.

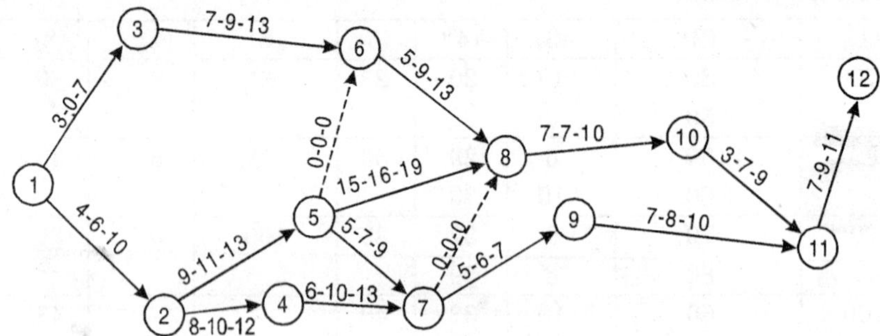

Fig. Rev. Q. 4.10

4.11 If 1 is the start event and 12 is the end event in the network of Rev. Q. 4.10, determine the critical path based on (a) the most likely time estimate for each activity, and (b) the expected time obtained in Rev. Q. 4.10.

4.12 For the network of Rev. Q. 4.10 calculate (a) the earliest expected time, and (b) the latest allowable occurrence time for each event. Make the entries in a combined tabular form. Also enter these values against the respective event circles.

4.13 A father notes that when his teenage daughter uses the telephone, she takes no less than 5 minutes for a call and sometimes as much as 1 hour. Fifteen minutes calls are more frequent than calls, of any other duration. If daughter's phone call were an activity in PERT project:

(a) What would be the phone call's expected duration?

(b) What estimate would you give for its variance?

(c) In scheduling the project, how much time would you allocate for the phone call? [*Ans.* (a) 20.83 minutes; (b) 84.03; (c) 20.83 minutes]

4.14 (a) What is the basic concept of PERT?

(b) The three time estimates activity of a project are given below:

Activity	t_O*(days)*	t_L*(days)*	t_P *(days)*
1–2	2	5	14
1–3	3	12	21
2–4	5	14	17
3–4	2	5	8
4–5	1	4	7
3–5	6	15	30

(i) Draw the network diagram.

(ii) Find the expected duration and variance of each activity.

(iii) Determine the expected project duration.

(iv) Find the variance and standard deviation of the entire project

5

Chapter

PERT : Network Analysis

5.1 SLACK OR SLACK TIME

In chapter 4 two time estimates for any event have been discussed. These being the earliest expected time T_E and the latest allowable occurrence time T_L. The difference between the latest allowable occurrence time and the earliest expected time of an event is known as *slack* (or *slack time*). It is denoted by S. Thus,

$$S = T_L - T_E \quad ...(5.1)$$

Since both T_L and T_E refer to events the term slack refers to an event. Hence the above expression may be written as

$$S_j = T_L^j - T_E^j \quad ...(5.2)$$

where S_j is slack for event j.

Consider a network shown in Fig. 5.1 in which the values of t_E^{ij}, T_L^j and T_E^j are indicated along the arrows and the events. The values of S^j obtained for each event are shown in Table 5.1.

TABLE 5.1 *Computation of slack*

Event No.	T_E	T_L	$S = T_L - T_E$
10	0	0	0
20	5	5	0
30	7	17	10
40	12	12	0
50	23	23	0
60	23	23	0
70	23	30	7
80	33	33	0
90	39	39	0
100	48	48	0

In this case it may be observed that the slack for all events, except for events 30 and 70 is zero. The slack for event 30 is 10 units of time. This means that even if the event 30 occurs 10 units of time late the scheduled

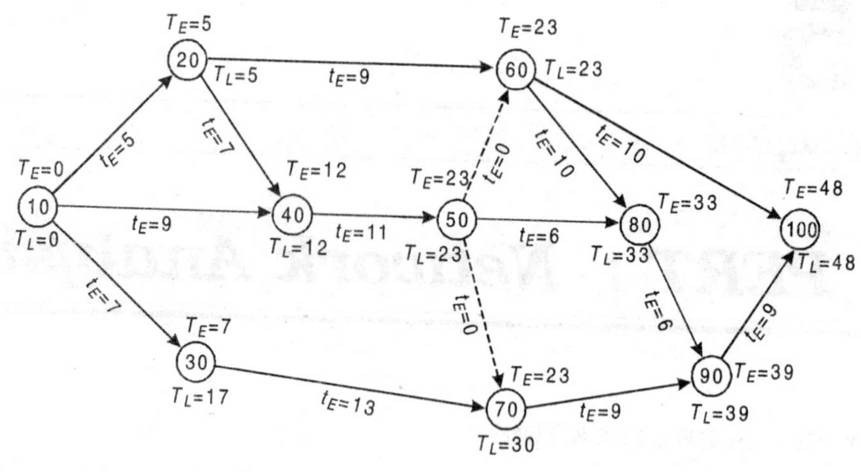

Fig. 5.1 *Network for computing slack.*

completion date of the project will not be affected. In other words, after the commencement of the project or the start event 10, event 30 can occur at 7+(0 to 10) units of time later. Similarly the slack for event 70 is 7 units of time. This means that even if the event 70 occurs 7 units of time late the scheduled completion date of the project will not be affected. Again in other words, after the completion of event 50, event 70 can occur at 0 + (0 to 7) units of time later. The other events 10, 20, 40, 50, 60, 80, 90 and 100 do not have any slack time and these events are termed as critical events because their occurrence is critical.

In the network of Fig. 5.1 if it is assumed that the scheduled completion time T_S for the project is equal to 52 units of time (i.e., $T_S \neq T_E^{100}$) then $T_L = T_S = 52$. Consequently the values of T_L for all other events will also change. Since the values of T_E for all the events remain unchanged the values of S will change as given in Table 5.2. It may be noted that in this case none of the events have slack time equal to zero. However, each of the events 10, 20, 40, 50, 60, 80, 90 and 100 has a minimum slack time equal to 4 and hence these may be termed as critical events.

The slack thus gives an idea of the extra time that is available for the completion of some of the activities. Further it reveals those areas which have an excess of resources so that these may be rearranged. The slack also spots those areas, which are potential trouble areas, i.e., the areas of zero or minimum slack.

TABLE 5.2 *Comutation of Slack*

Event No.	T_E	T_L	$S = T_L - T_E$
10	0	4	4
20	5	9	4
30	7	21	14
40	12	16	4
50	23	27	4
60	23	27	4
70	23	34	11
80	33	37	4
90	39	43	4
180	48	52	4

Depending upon the relative magnitudes of T_L and T_E, slack can be positive, zero and negative.

Positive slack. Positive slack is obtained when T_L is more than T_E, for an event. It is an indication of an ahead of schedule condition and also a condition of excess resources.

Zero slack. Zero slack is obtained when T_L is equal to T_E, for an event. It is an indication of an on schedule condition and also a condition of adequate resources.

Negative slack. Negative slack is obtained when T_L is less than T_E for an event. This will happen when the scheduled time of completion T_S (and hence T_L) of a project is less than T_E of the end event. It is an indication of a behind of schedule condition and also a condition of lack of resources.

5.2 CRITICAL PATH

A *critical path* is the path in a project network which, commencing from the initial event, connects the events having zero or minimum slack times and terminates at the end event. As explained in section 5.1 the events having zero or minimum slack times are termed as critical events because any delay in their occurrence will result in the delay of the scheduled completion of the project. Hence a critical path is the one which connects the critical events in a project network. Further the activities along a critical path are also referred to as critical activities because these activities are critical in determining the duration of the project. It may further be noted that a critical path is the longest path in terms of time connecting the initial and the end events in a project network. In other words a critical path is the most time-consuming path from the beginning to the end of the network. For example, in the network shown in Fig. 5.2, by summing up the earliest expected times for the various events along the different paths it is found that the path 10–20–40–50–60–80–90–100 is the critical path which would consume 48 units of time. It may, however, be noted that in the same network there are certain other paths connecting the events with zero slack times such as 10–20–40–50–60–100, but the total time consumed by these paths being less none of these paths are the critical paths. The critical path is distinctly marked in the network, usually by a thick line as shown in Fig. 5.2.

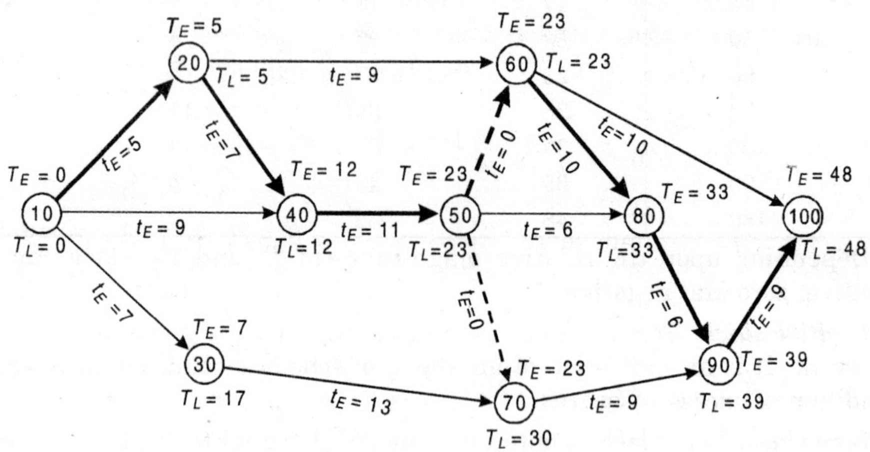

Fig. 5.2 *Network with a critical path*

5.2.1 Multiple Critical Paths

Generally there is only one critical path in a project network. However, there may be more than one critical path in a project network, which is then said to have *multiple critical paths.* If the critical paths are such that no activities are common in them, then these are termed as *independent critical paths.* For example in the network shown in Fig. 5.3 there are only two paths both of which are critical paths as shown in Fig. 5.3.

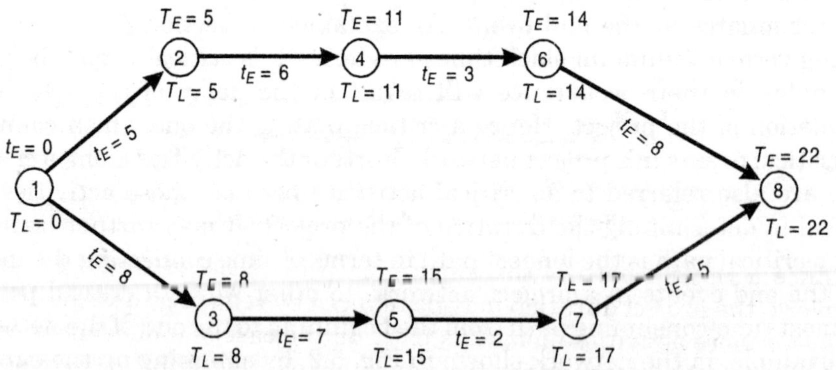

Fig. 5.3 *Network with two independent critical paths.*

Path	Time units consumed
1–2–4–6–8	22
1–3–5–7–8	22

Since none of the activities are common in these two critical paths these are termed as independent critical paths.

In the network shown in Fig. 5.4 there are in all six paths out of which there are three critical paths as given below:

Path	Time units consumed
1–2–4–7–8	10
1–2–5–6–8	10
1–3–4–7–8	10

none of which is an independent critical path. The remaining three paths which are not critical are as follows:

Path	Time units consumed
1–3–5–7–8	7
1–2–5–7–8	8
1–3–5–6–8	9

It may be noted that although this network contains only eight events it has three critical paths. Thus for a network having large number of events the problem would be rendered fairly complicated and it would not be possible to solve it by hand calculation but would necessitate, the use of computers.

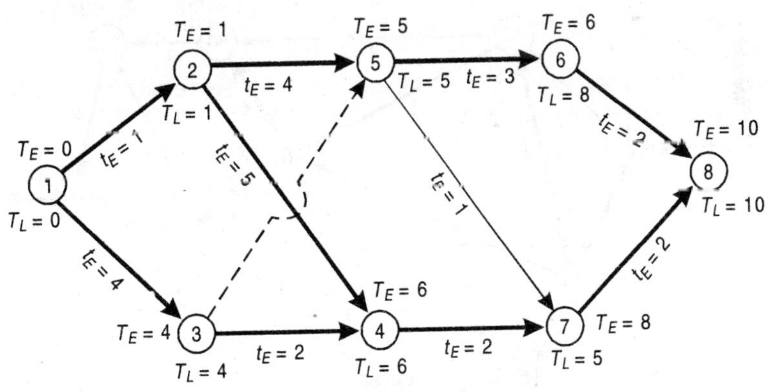

Fig. 5.4 *Network with three critical paths*

Since a critical path is the longest path in terms of time in a project network, the project duration may be reduced by reducing the time duration of one or more activities along this path. In the case of independent critical paths in a project network the time duration of atleast one activity on each path will have to be reduced to reduce the project duration. However, if the critical paths have one or more activities in common then the project duration may be reduced by reducing the time duration of one or more common activities.

5.2.2 Semi-critical Path or Sub-critical Path

A *semi-critical path* or *sub-critical path* is the path in a project network which connects those events which have the slack next lower than that for the critical events. For example in the network shown in Fig. 5.5 the values of t_E, T_E and T_L are given. The slack for each of the events are calculated as given in Table 5.3.

TABLE 5.3 *Computation of slack*

Event	*Slack*	*Event*	*Slack*
10	0	70	0
20	0	80	0
30	0	90	1
40	0	100	0
50	1	110	0
60	1	120	0

The events 10, 20, 30,40, 70, 80, 100,110 and 120 have slack time equal to zero and hence the critical path is 10–20–30–40–70–80–100–110–120

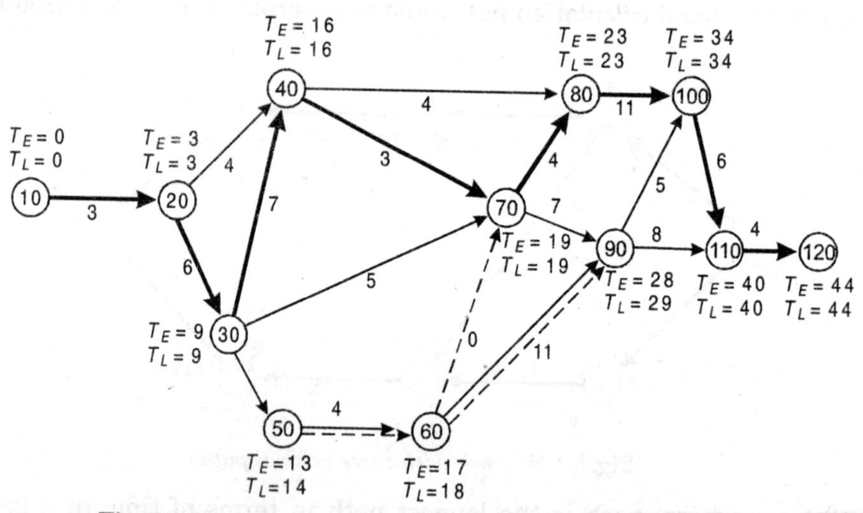

Fig 5.5 *Network showing critical and semi-critical paths*

which is shown by thick lines. The events 50, 60 and 90 have the next lower slack time equal to 1 and hence the path 50–60–90 is the semi-critical or sub-critical path which is shown by dotted lines drawn adjacent to the corresponding activity arrows in Fig. 5.5. Selection of a semi-critical or sub-critical path is a matter of individual judgement. As such instead of the path 50–60–90, the path 30–50–60–90–110 may be considered as the semi-critical or sub-critical path.

5.3 PROBABILITY CONCEPTS AND THEIR APPLICATION TO NETWORK ANALYSIS

From the assumed or given scheduled completion time of the project the latest allowable occurrence time of each event may be calculated from which the critical path may be determined. However, it is also necessary to determine the probability of completion of the project within the scheduled completion time for which the probability theory is applied to the network analysis as explained below.

Each activity *i–j* is given three estimates t_O, t_L and t_P and by assuming β-distribution for each activity the expected time or mean time t_E for the completion of the activity is given by

$$t_E = \frac{t_O + 4t_L + t_P}{6}$$

The meaning of the expected time is that there is a fifty-fifty chance that the activity *i–j* will be completed within the expected time t_E. Thus if the distribution curve for activity *i–j* is as shown in Fig. 5.6, a vertical line

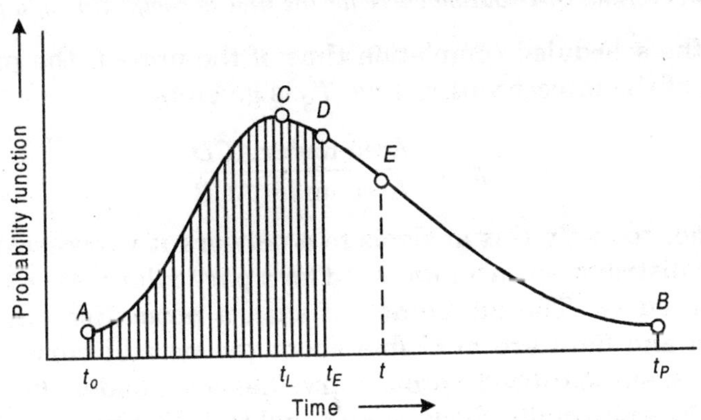

Fig. 5.6 *β-distribution curve for an activity of a project*

corresponding to t_E would divide the area under the curve into two equal parts and hence the probability of completion of the activity in time t_E would be 1/2. The probability of completion of the activity within some other time t would be given by the ratio of the area under the curve upto the vertical line at t and the total area under the curve, i.e., the probability of completion of the activity within time t is given by

$$p = \frac{\text{Area under } ACE}{\text{Area under } ACB}$$

Although the distribution curve for the time taken to complete each activity of a project resembles a β-distribution curve, the distribution curve for the time taken to complete the entire project (consisting of several activities) in general resembles a normal distribution curve as shown in Fig. 5.7. Since sum of the values of t_E for all the activities along the critical path is equal to T_E of the last event, the probability of completion of the project in time T_E is 1/2 (see Fig. 5.7).

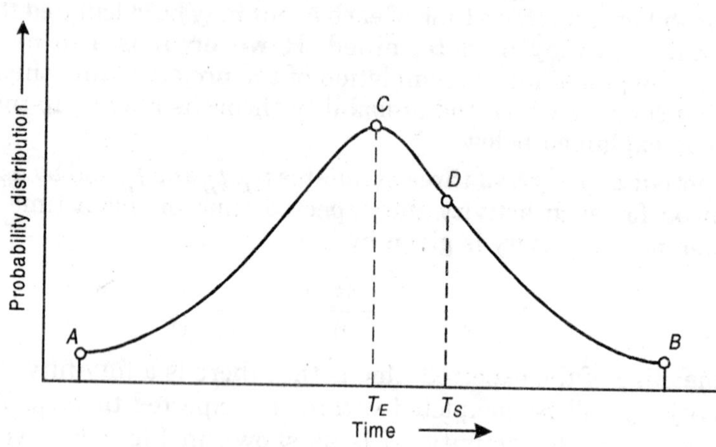

Fig. 5.7 *Normal distribution curve for the time of completion of a project.*

If T_S is the scheduled completion time of the project, the probability of completion of the project within time T_S is given by

$$p = \frac{\text{Area under } ACD}{\text{Area under } ACB}$$

Thus in order to apply this analysis to a network it is necessary to reduce the random distribution curve obtained for a particular network to a normal distribution curve. The advantage of such a normalisation is that the information and data are available about the normal curve in books on probability. A standardized normal curve has area under the entire curve equal to unity and standard deviation equal to 1. Further it is symmetrical about the mean value T_E. Hence the area under the curve AC is 50% of the total area under the entire curve ACB. The area under the curve ACD depends on the location of T_S along the time axis. The point T_E can be taken as reference point and the distance $T_E\,T_S$ can be expressed in terms of standard deviation. For example, if T_S is to the right of T_E at a distance of 1 standard deviation, then the area enclosed by ACD is 84.1%. If T_S is to the left of T_E at a distance of 1 standard deviation, then the area enclosed is 15.9%. These statements can be made in a slightly different way. A distance of $+\,1.0\sigma$ from the mean corresponds to 84.1% probability, and a distance of $-\,1.0\sigma$ corresponds to 15.9% probability as shown in Fig. 5.8.

Table 5.4 gives the values of probability corresponding to the normal deviate i.e., the distance from the mean expressed in terms of σ.

TABLE 5.4 *Normal Distribution Function*

Normal Deviate (–)	*Probability* (%)	*Normal Deviate* (+)	*Probability* (%)
0	50.0	0	50.0
– 0.1	46.0	+ 0.1	54.0
– 0.2	42.1	+ 0.2	57.9
– 0.3	38.2	+ 0.3	61.8
– 0.4	34.5	+ 0.4	65.5
– 0.5	30.8	+ 0.5	69.2
– 0.6	27.4	+ 0.6	72.6
– 0.7	24.2	+ 0.7	75.8
– 0.8	21.2	+ 0.8	78.8
– 0.9	18.4	+ 0.9	81.6
– 1.0	15.9	+ 1.0	84.1
– 1.1	13.6	+ 1.1	86.4
– 1.2	11.5	+ 1.2	88.5
– 1.3	9.7	+ 1.3	90.3
– 1.4	8.1	+ 1.4	91.9
– 1.5	6.7	+ 1.5	93.3
– 1.6	5.5	+ 1.6	94.5
– 1.7	4.5	+ 1.7	95.5
– 1.8	3.6	+ 1.8	96.4
– 1.9	2.9	+ 1.9	97.1
– 2.0	2.3	+ 2.0	97.7
– 2.1	1.8	+ 2.1	98.2
– 2.2	1.4	+ 2.2	98.6
– 2.3	1.1	+ 2.3	98.9
– 2.4	0.8	+ 2.4	99.2
– 2.5	0.6	+ 2.5	99.4
– 2.6	0.5	+ 2.6	99.5
– 2.7	0.4	+ 2.7	99.6
– 2.8	0.3	+ 2.8	99.7
– 2.9	0.2	+ 2.9	99.8
– 3.0	0.1	+ 3.0	99.9

In order to make use of the probability values given in Table 5.4 the random distribution curve obtained for a particular network needs to be reduced to

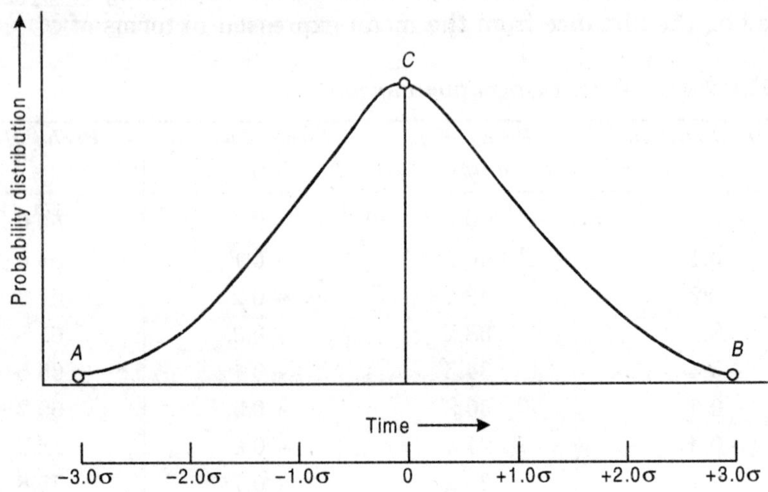

Fig. 5.8 *Normal distribution curve in respect of values given in Table 5.4.*

a normal distribution curve. This may be done on the basis of the Central Limit Theorem discussed below.

5.4 CENTRAL LIMIT THEOREM

This theorem states that in any project if there are n activities involved each having for its time of completion its own β–distribution with mean values $\mu_1, \mu_2, \mu_3, \ldots. \mu_4$ and standard deviations $\sigma_1, \sigma_2, \sigma_3 \ldots.. \sigma_4$ respectively, then (if n is fairly large) the distribution of time for the completion of the project as a whole will approximately be a normal distribution with mean μ and variance σ^2 given by

$$\mu = \mu_1 + \mu_2 + \mu_3 + \ldots.+ \mu_n \qquad \text{...(5·3)}$$

and

$$\sigma^2 = \sigma_1^2 + \sigma_2^2 + \sigma_3^2 + \ldots..+ \sigma_n^2 \qquad \text{... (5.4)}$$

The average or the earliest expected time for completion of the project is equal to the earliest expected time T_E for the end event which in turn is equal to the sum of the expected or average times t_E for the activities along the critical path, i.e., $T_E = \Sigma t_E$. Since there is 50% probability of completion of any activity within its expected time t_E, there will be 50% probability of completion of the entire project within its earliest expected time T_E. Thus in order to reduce the random distribution curve derived for a particular network to a normal distribution curve the value of T_E calculated for the end event of the network is made to coincide with the modal value of the normal distribution curve. Next the standard deviation σ for the project network is required to be determined. Again σ for the project network may be taken equal to the standard deviation for the critical path of the network which is determined from Eq. 5.4 by summing the variances of the activities along the critical path and taking the square root of the sum. Thus for the project network

$$\sigma = \sqrt{\text{sum of the variances along critical path}}$$

or

$$\sigma = \sqrt{\Sigma\sigma_{ij}^2} \qquad \text{...(5.5)}$$

where σ_{ij}^2 is the variance of activity i–j along the critical path.

Further if T_S is the scheduled completion time of the project then the *normal deviate* or probability factor Z is given by

$$Z = \frac{T_S - T_E}{\sigma} \qquad \text{...(5.6)}$$

For the normal deviate Z obtained from Eq. 5.6 the probability of completion of the project within the scheduled completion time T_S is obtained from Table 5.4.

If may, however, be noted that depending on the magnitudes of T_S and T_E the normal deviate Z may be positive, zero or negative. If $T_S > T_E$, Z is positive and T_S is on the right of T_E, the probability of completion of the project within the time T_S is *more* than 50%. If $T_S = T_E$, Z is zero and T_S coincides with T_E, the probability of completion of the project within the time T_S is just 50%. If $T_S < T_E$, Z is negative and T_S is on the left of T_E, the probability of completion of the project within the time T_S is *less* than 50%.

ILLUSTRATIVE EXAMPLES

Example 5.1 *For the network shown in Fig. Ex. 5.1 determine the critical path, sub-critical path and probability of finishing the project within the scheduled time (a) $T_S = 35$, (b) $T_S = 40$. Also determine the time of completion of the project with a probability of 95%.*

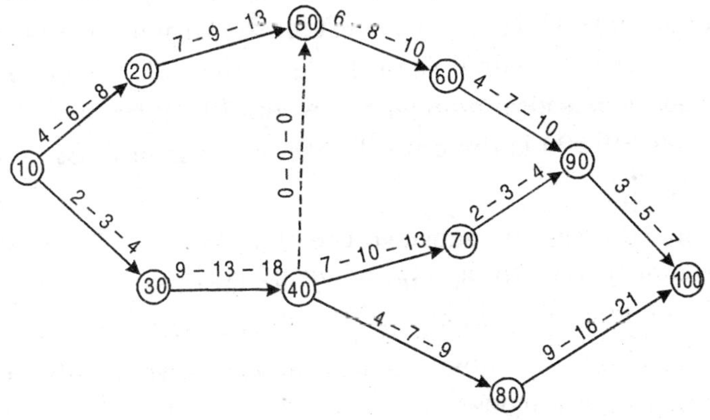

Fig. Ex. 5.1

Solution

The expected time of completion t_E and variance σ^2 are computed for each activity using the following relations:

$$t_E = \frac{t_O + 4t_L + t_P}{6}$$

and
$$\sigma^2 = \left(\frac{t_P - t_O}{6}\right)^2$$

The computed values of t_E and σ^2 are given in Table (A).

TABLE (A) *Computed values of t_E and σ^2*

Activity	t_O	t_L	t_P	t_E	σ^2
10–20	4	6	8	6.00	0.44
10–30	2	3	4	3.00	0.11
20–50	7	9	13	9.33	1.00
30–40	9	13	18	13.17	2.25
40–50	0	0	0	0.00	0.00
40–70	7	10	13	10.00	1.00
40–80	4	7	9	6.83	0.69
50–60	6	8	10	8.00	0.44
60–90	4	7	10	7.00	1.00
70–90	2	3	4	3.00	0.11
80–100	9	16	21	15.67	4.00
90–100	3	5	7	5.00	0.44

The computations for T_E, T_L and slack for the various events are given in Table (B). For the end event T_L is taken equal to its T_E. From Table (B) it is found that the slack is minimum for the events 10, 30,40, 80 and 100. Hence path 10–30–40–80–100 is the critical path which is marked by thick lines on the Fig. Ex. 5.1.

From Table (B) it is further observed that the next lower slack is 2.5 which occurs for events 50, 60 and 90. Therefore the path connecting the events 50, 60 and 90 i.e., path 40–50–60–90–100 is the sub-critical or semi-critical path which is shown by dotted line drawn adjacent to the corresponding activity arrows.

TABLE (B) *Comutation for T_B, T_L and slack*

Earliest expected time ↓					Latest occurrence time ↑				
Event No.	*Predecessor envent (i)*	t_E^{ij}	t_E^j	T_E	*Successor event (j)*	t_E^{ij}	T_E^L	T_L	*Slack S*
10	—	—	0	0	20	6.00	334	0.00	0
					30	3.00	0.00		
20	10	6.00	6.00	6.00	50	9.33	9.34	9.34	3.34
30	10	3.00	3.00	3.00	40	13.17	3.00	3.00	0
40	30	13.17	16.17	16.17	50	0.00	18.67	16.17	0
					70	10.00	20.67		
					80	6.83	16.17		
50	20	9.33	15.33	16.17	60	8.00	18.67	18.67	2.5
	40	0.00	16.17						
60	50	8.00	24.17	24.17	90	7.00	26.67	26.67	2.5
70	40	10.00	26.17	26.17	90	3.00	30.67	30.67	4.5
80	40	6.83	23.00	23.00	100	15.67	23.00	23.00	0
90	60	7.00	31.17	31.17	100	5.00	33.67	33.67	2.5
	70	3.00	29.17						
100	80	15.67	38.67	38.67	–	–	38.67	38.67	0
	90	5.00	36.17						

Standard deviation along the critical path is given by Eq. 5.5 as

$$\sigma = \sqrt{\Sigma\sigma_{ij}^2}$$

where $\Sigma\sigma_{ij}^2$ = sum of variances of the activities along the critical path.

Thus

$$\Sigma\sigma_{ij}^2 = \sigma_{10-30}^2 + \sigma_{30-40}^2 + \sigma_{40-80}^2 + \sigma_{80-100}^2$$

$$= (0.11 + 2.25 + 0.69 + 4.00)$$

$$= 7.05$$

$$\therefore \quad \sigma = \sqrt{7.05} = 2.66$$

The normal deviate Z is given by equation 5.6 as

$$Z = \frac{T_S - T_E}{\sigma}$$

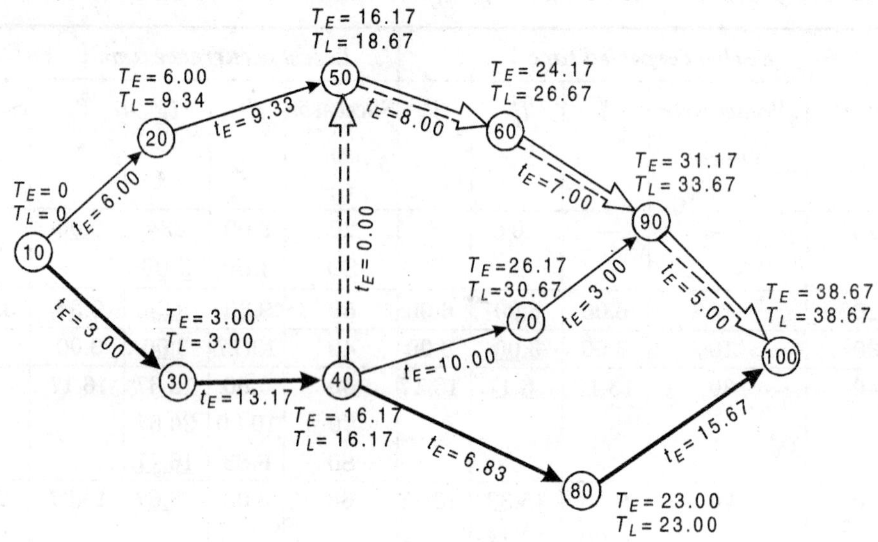

Fig. Ex. 5.1

(a) For $T_S = 35$

$$Z = \frac{35 - 38.67}{2.66}$$

$$= -1.38$$

From Table 5.4, for Z = –1.38, the value of probability = 8.42%.

Hence the probability of completion of the project within the scheduled time T_s = 35 is 8.42%.

(b) For $T_S = 40$

$$Z = \frac{40 - 38.67}{2.66}$$

$$= 0.5$$

From Table 5.4, for Z = 0.5, the value of probability = 69.2%

Hence the probability of completion of the project with in the scheduled time T_S = 40 is 69.2%.

From Table 5.4, for probability of 95%, normal deviate Z = 1.65

The normal deviate Z is given by equation 5.6 as

$$Z = \frac{T_S - T_E}{\sigma}$$

or

$$T_S = \sigma Z + T_E$$

$$= (2.66 \times 1.65) + 38.67$$
$$= 43.06 \approx 43$$

Example 5.2 *A project is expected to take 24 months along the critical path having a standard deviation of 3.6 months. What is the probability of completion of the project within (a) 24 months (b) 18 months and* (c) *30 months ?*

Solution

The normal deviate Z is given by Eq. 5.6 as

$$Z = \frac{T_S - T_E}{\sigma}$$

Given T_E = 24 months and σ = 3.6 months

(a) For T_S = 24 months

$$Z = \frac{24-24}{3.6} = 0$$

From Table 5.4, for $Z = 0$, probability = 50%

(b) For T_S = 18 months

$$Z = \frac{18-24}{3.6} = -1.67$$

From Table 5.4, for $Z = -1.67$, probability = 4.8%

(c) For T_S = 30 months

$$Z = \frac{30-24}{3.6} = 1.67$$

From Table 5.4, for $Z = 1.67$, probability = 95.2%

Example 5.3. *A project is expected to take 60 weeks with a variance of 20.25. Within how many weeks would the project be expected to be completed with the probability of (a) 90%, (b) 70% and* (c) *35%?*

Solution

Standard deviation $\sigma = \sqrt{20.25} = 4.5$

(a) From Table 5.4, for 90% probability normal deviate $Z = 1.28$

From Eq. 5.6, we have

$$Z = \frac{T_S - T_E}{\sigma}$$

$$\therefore \quad T_S = \sigma Z + T_E$$
$$= (4.5 \times 1.28) + 60$$

$= 65.76 \approx 66$ weeks

(b)From Table 5.4, for 70% probability normal deviate $Z = 0.524$

$$T_S = \sigma Z + T_E$$
$$= (4.5 \times .524) + 60$$
$$= 62.358 \approx 62.5 \text{ weeks}$$

(c)From Table 5.4, for 35% probability normal deviate $Z = -0.387$

$$\therefore \quad T_S = aZ + T_E$$
$$= 4.5\,(-0.387) + 60$$
$$= 58.26 \approx 58.5 \text{ weeks.}$$

REVIEW QUESTIONS

5.1 What is the slack time ?

5.2 Does slack time refer to an activity or an event ?

5.3 What do you understand by positive and negative slack ?

5.4 Define critical path and a semi-cricitcal path.

5.5 What is meant by 'the probability of completion of a project within the scheduled time' ?

5.6 Why only critical path is considered in determining the probability of completion of the project within the scheduled time ?

5.7 How do you determine the probability of completion of the project within the scheduled time ?

5.8 How do you standardize or normalize the random curve obtained for a particular network.

5.9 Define normal deviate.

5.10 For the various activities in a project the expected times are as follows :

Activity	*Duration (days)*
0–1	4
1–2	17
1–3	7
2–3	9
1–4	11
3–4	6
4–5	4
4–6	6
5–4	8

If the scheduled completion time of the project is equal to the earliest expected time T_E for the end event, calculate the slack time for each event and identify the critical path.

5.11 For the network shown in the Fig. Rev. Q. 5.11 determine (i) critical path and its standard deviation ; (ii) probability of completion of the project within the scheduled lime $T_S = 40$; (iii) time duration that will provide 80% probability of its completion in time.

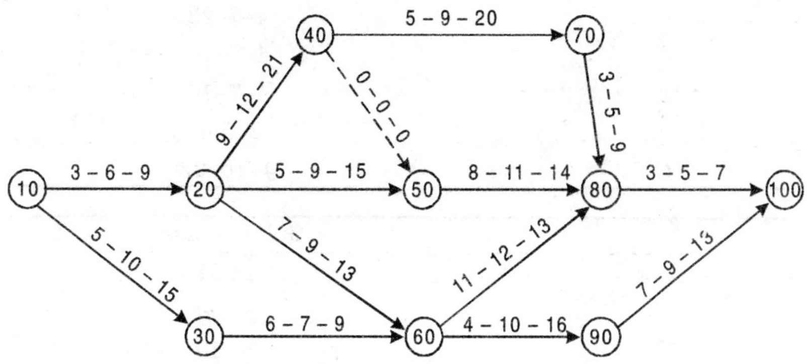

Fig. Rev. Q. 5 .11

5.12 A project consists of 8 activities, code-named based on the type of work as *A, C, E, K, P, R, T* and *Y*. *A* and *E* are initial activities; *T* and *Y* are terminal activities; *T* follows C; *R* follows *P; A* precedes *K; R* precedes *Y; P* follows *E*; and *K* is followed by *C*. The values of t_O, t_L and t_P have been estimated as under. Data on area under the normal probability curve are also given for information. What is the probability of the project being completed in 28 months?

Actiity	*A*	C	*E*	*K*	*P*	*R*	*T*	*Y*
t_o (in months)	5	3	4	6	6	2½	7½	5
t_L (in months)	6	3	8	12	7	3½	9½	7
t_P (in months)	7	3	10	14	8	7½	14½	9

Extracts: Area Under Normal Probablity Curve

	0.00	0.02	0.04	0.06	0.08
0.00	0.5000	0.5080	0.5160	0.5239	0.5319
0.10	0.5398	0.5478	0.5557	0.5636	0.5712
0.20	0.5793	0.5871	0.5948	0.5987	0.6103
0.30	0.6179	0.6255	0.6331	0.6406	0.6480
0.40	0.6554	0.6628	0.6700	0.6772	0.6844
0.50	0.6915	0.6985	0.7054	0.7123	0.7190

5.13 The interdependence of a job consisting of seven activities *A* to *G* is given as

Activity	*A*	*B*	*C*	*D*	*E*	*F*	*G*
Predecessor activity	—	—	*A*	*B*	*A*	*B*	*C, D*
Succeeding activity	*C, E*	*D, F*	*G*	*G*	—	—	—

The time estimates, in days, for each activity are:

Activity	*Time estimates*
A	6–9–18
B	5–8–17
C	4–7–22
D	4–7–16
E	4–7–10
F	2–5–8
G	4–10–22

Z (+)	% *Probability*
0.8	78.81
0.9	81.59
1.0	84.13
1.1	86.43
1.2	88.49

Draw the network and determine the probability of completing the job in 35 days.

5.14 PERT calculations yield a project length of 60 weeks, with variance of 9. Within how many weeks would you expect the project to be completed with probability 0.95? (That is, what is the project length that you would except to be exceeded only 5 percent of the time if the project were repeated many times in an identical manner?) [65 weeks]

5.15 Determine (i) the expected completion time, (ii) Variance, and (iii) the critical path for the following project:

Activity	*A*	*B*	*C*	*D*	*E*	*F*	*G*	*H*
Predecessors	—	—	*A*	*B*	*A*	*C*, *D*	*C*, *D*, *E*	*F*
Optimistic time t_O(days)	1	1	3	1	1	2	2	6
Most likely time t_L (days)	4	5	6	2	2	4	9	6
Pessimistic time t_P (days)	7	9	9	3	9	6	10	6

5.16 The following information applies to a particular project.

Event 0 is the initial event

Event 1 is preceded by event 0

Event 3 is preceded by event 1

Event 4 is preceded by event 1

Event 2 is preceded by event 1

Event 3 is preceded by events 2 and 1

Event 4 is preceded by events 3 and 1

Event 5 is preceded by event 4

For the various activities in the project the expected times are:

Activity	0–1	1–3	1–2	2–3	1–4	3–4	4–5
Duration (days)	3	16	6	8	10	5	3

(i) Draw the arrow diagram for this project

(ii) If the scheduled completion date is equal to the earliest expected time T_E for the end event, calculate the slack time for each event and identify the critical path.

6

Chapter

Network Replanning and Adjustment

6.1 INTRODUCTION

The preparation of a project network is a dynamic process because the project networks once prepared may often be required to be replanned and readjusted and new networks are formulated. The replanning and readjustment or changes in the networks may be necessitated on account of the changes in schedules and also due to revision of plans to achieve better performance in the light of changing conditions. Thus the process of replanning and readjustment of a project network is of prime importance. The various methods adopted for replanning and readjustment of the networks are discussed in the next section.

6.2 METHODS OF NETWORK REPLANING AND READJUSTMENT

The methods commonly adopted for replanning are as noted below:

1. Interchanging resources.
2. Relaxing technical specifications.
3. Changing arrangement of activities.

Each of these methods are described in the following paras.

6.2.1 Interchanging Resources

In this method by readjusting the resources among the various activities of the project the slack times of the various events can be reduced and also the earliest expected time T_E for the end event can be reduced to suit the given conditions. This is explained by means of the following two examples.

In the first case a project network consisting of four activities is considered as shown in Fig. 6.1. It may be noted that in this network the scheduled completion time T_L is less than the earliest expected time T_E for the end event. The activity times noted on the activities of the network indicate that

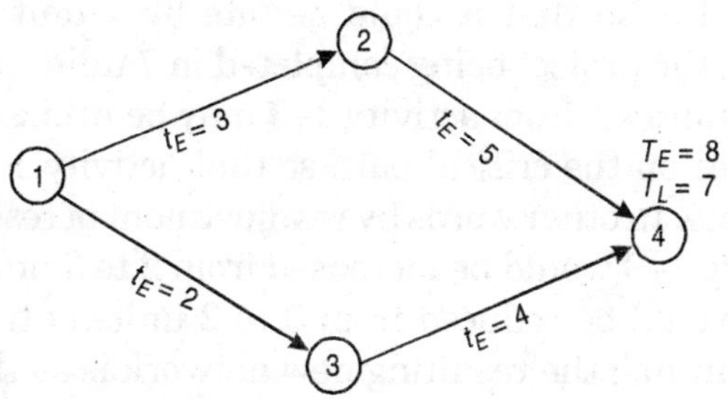

Fig. 6.1 *Network to be used for replanning.*

8 units of time are needed for the completion, but because of some other connecting or coordinating project the scheduled completion time T_L must be 7 units of time, i.e., T_L has to be 1 unit of time sooner than the earliest expected time T_E for the end event 4. Thus in order to shorten the time required to complete the project so that $T_E = T_L = 7$ the following procedure may be adopted.

The values of T_E, T_L and slack for each event in the network are computed as given in Table 6.1 and shown in Fig. 6.2 from which it is observed that in this case only event 3 has positive slack equal to 1 unit of time and rest each of

TABLE 6.1 T_E, T_L *and slack for each event in the network of Fig. 6.2*

Event	T_E	T_L	*Slack*
1	0	–1	–1
2	3	2	–1
3	2	3	1
4	8	7	–1

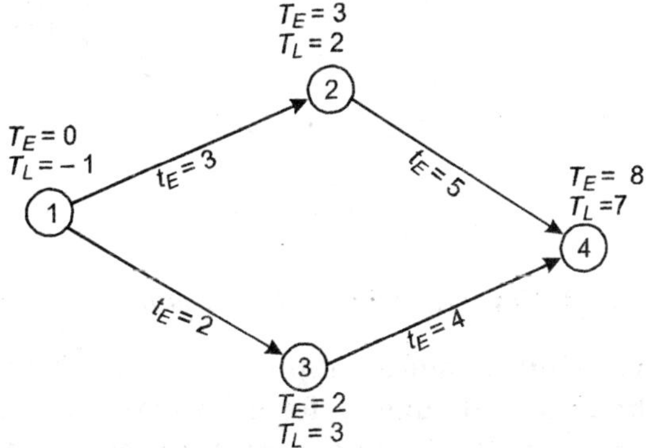

Fig. 6 2 *Network of Fig. 6.1 with the values of* T_E *and* T_L *added for each event.*

the three events has negative slack equal to –1. As indicated in Chapter 5 since the negative slack represents a condition of lack of resources, for readjustment of resources only those events may be considered which have positive slack. Thus in this case some of the resources may be withdrawn from activity 1–3 so that it could be late by 1 unit of time and still not interfere with the project being completed in 7 units of time as desired. The resources withdrawn from activity 1–3 may be utilized on activity 1–2, one of the activities on the critical path so that activity 1–2 could be expedited by 1 unit of time. In other words by readjustment of resources the completion time of activity 1–3 would be increased from 2 to 3 units of time and that of activity 1–2 would be reduced from 3 to 2 units of time. After this simple network replanning the resulting new network is as shown in Fig. 6.3. The values of T_E, T_L and slack for each event in the new network are computed as given in Table 6.2 and the same are also shown in Fig. 6.3. It may be noted that replanning of the network has completely removed the slack time that existed earlier and has reduced the time required to complete the project to the desired value of 7 units of time without adding any new resources.

TABLE 6.2 *T_E, T_L and slack for each event in thenetwork of Fig. 6.3.*

Event	T_E	T_L	*Slack*
1	0	0	0
2	2	2	0
3	3	3	0
4	7	7	0

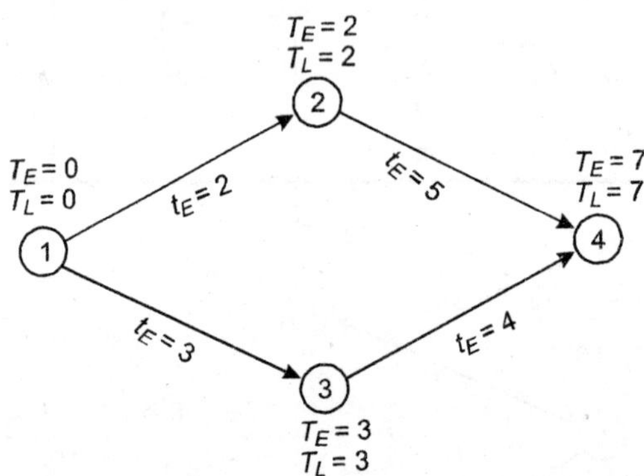

Fig. 6.3 *Network of Fig. 6.1 after simple replanning.*

In another case a slightly more complicated network as shown in Fig. 6.4 is considered. The expected time t_E for each activity is shown in Fig. 6.4 from which the values of T_E, T_L and slack for each event are computed as given in Table 6.3 and shown in Fig. 6.5. The value of the T_L for end event of the network has been arbitrarily set equal to the value of T_E for the end event which is equal to 15 units of time.

TABLE 6.3 *T_E, T_L and slack for each event in the network of Fig. 6.5*

Event	T_E	T_L	*Slack*
1	0	0	0
2	2	5	3
3	5	6	1
4	4	4	0
5	7	9	2
6	12	12	0
7	15	15	0

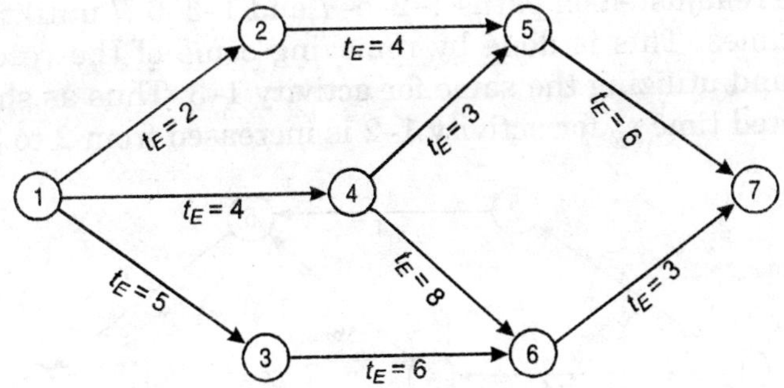

Fig. 6.4 *Network to be used for replanning.*

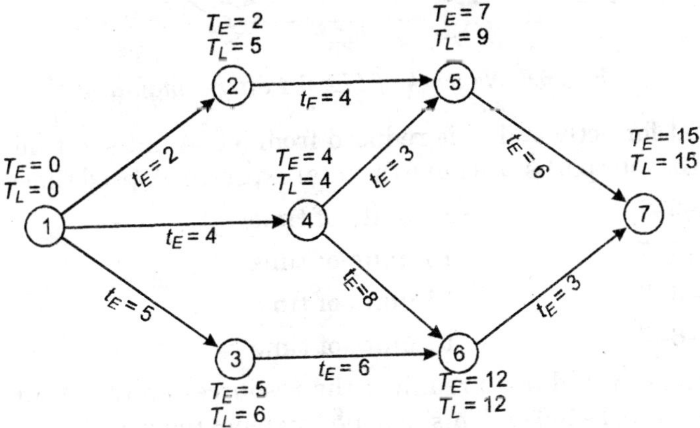

Fig. 6.5 *Network of Fig. 6.4 with the values of T_E and T_L added for each event.*

The purpose of calculating the slack time is to determine whether there is any slack in the system. If there is no slack the chance of reducing the earliest expected time T_E of the end event of the network is slim. In this case the three events viz., 2, 3, and 5 of the network have slack time. Further there are four possible paths through the network as indicated below :

1–2–5–7	12 units of time
1–4–5–7	13 units of time
1–4–6–7	15 units of time (critical path)
1–3–6–7	14 units of time

The sum of the expected elapsed times of all the activities of the network is 41 units of time and hence the readjusted network must also have the sum of the expected elapsed times of all the activities equal to 41.

Now by readjusting the resources among the various activities the network is so replanned that each of the four possible paths through the network requires exactly the same time. Thus to begin with some of the resources are readjusted on paths 1–2–5–7 and 1–3–6–7 until the two path have equal times. This is done by removing some of the resources from activity 1–2 and utilizing the same for activity 1–3. Thus as shown in Fig. 6.6 the expected time t_E for activity 1–2 is increased from 2 to 3 units of

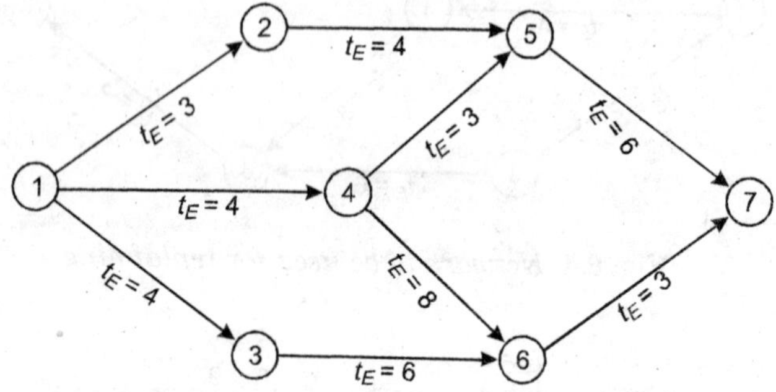

Fig. 6.6 *Network of Fig. 6.4 after repianning.*

time and that for activity 1–3 is reduced from 5 to 4 units of time. With this replanning the four paths will have the total expected elapsed times as follows:

1–2–5–7	13 units of time
1–4–5–7	13 units of time
1–4–6–7	15 units of time
1–3–6–7	13 units of time

The next step would be to readjust the resources on the other two paths viz., 1–4–5–7 and 1–4–6–7. This is done by removing some of the resources from activity 4–5 and utilizing the same for activity 4–6. Thus as shown is Fig. 6.7 the expected time t_E for activity 4–5 is increased from 3 to 4 and that for activity 4–6 is reduced from 8 to 7. With this replanning the four paths will have the total expected elapsed times as follows :

1–2–5–7	13 units of time
1–4–5–7	14 units of time
1–4–6–7	14 units of time
1–3–6–7	13 units of time

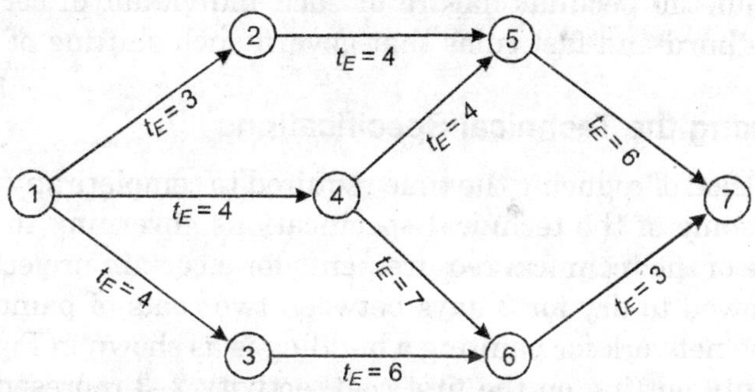

Fig. 6.7 *Network of Fig. 6.6 after replanning.*

The final step would be to readjust the resources among the activities 2–5 and 4–5; and 3–6 and 4–6. Some of the resources are withdrawn from the activities 2–5 and 3–6 and the same are utilized for activities 4–5 and 4–6 respectively. Thus as shown in Fig. 6.8 the expected time t_E for activity 2–5 is increased from 4 to 4.5 and that of activity 4–5 is reduced from 4 to 3.5. Similarly the expected time t_E for activity 3–6 is increased from 6 to 6.5 and that of activity 4–6 is reduced from 7 to 6.5. With this replanning all

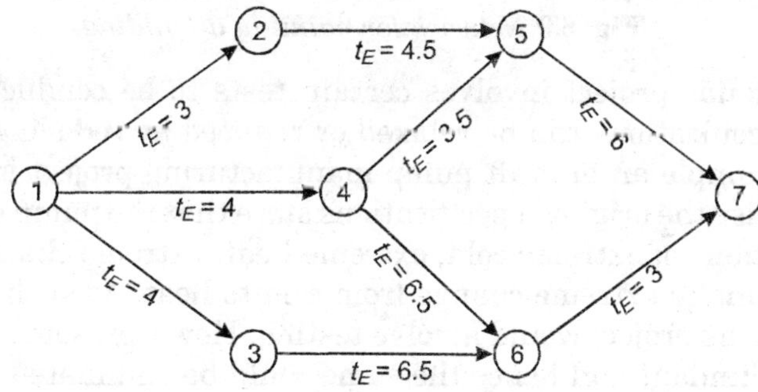

Fig. 6.8 *Network of Fig. 6.7 after replanning.*

the four paths in the network will be balanced with each path having the same total expected elapsed time as indicated below :

1–2–5–7	13.5 units of time
1–4–5–7	13.5 units of time
1–4–6–7	13.5 units of time
1–3–6–7	13.5 units of time

The method of replanning of a project network by readjustment of resources would be possible only if the various activities are of similar type so that the resources withdrawn from one activity may be utilized for the other activity. Further the amount of resources which may be shifted from one activity to another with proportional results in time reduction actually depends upon the peculiar nature of each individual project. There are, however, no hard-and-fast rules that govern such shifting of resources.

6.2.2 Relaxing the Technical Specifications

Another method of reducing the time required to complete any project would be to relax some of the technical specifications governing the project. For example one of the technical requirements for a certain project is that paint must be allowed to dry for 3 days between two coats of paint applied on a building. The network for painting a building is as shown in Fig. 6.9. Activity 1–2 represents putting on the first coat, activity 2–3 represents the drying time and activity 3–4 represents putting on the final coat. The value of the earliest expected time T_E of the end event 4 of the network is 21 days. If the technical specifications are slightly relaxed such that the drying time between the two coats is reduced from 3 days to 2 days, then the value of T_E of the end event of the network would be reduced.

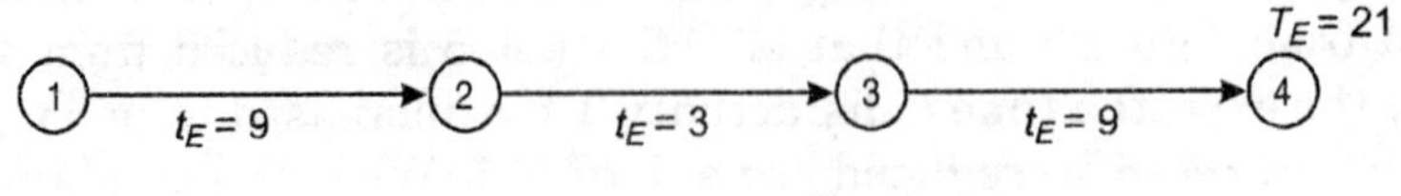

Fig. 6.9 *Network for painting a building.*

If a particular project involves certain tests to be conducted then the technical specifications can be relaxed or reduced by reducing some of the tests. For example an aircraft pump manufacturing project involves lot of testing because the original specifications state that the pump is to be tested under conditions of extreme cold, extreme heat, extreme change from heat to cold and finally extreme change from cold to heat. As such a part of the network for this project would involve testing. However, some of these tests might be redundant and hence the same could be eliminated. Thus in this case by reducing the specifications considerable saving in time can be achieved.

The extent to which the specifications can be relaxed or reduced may be severely restricted in many cases. For example in the process of pouring concrete the specifications require the concrete to cure for at least 5 days before a load is put on it. However, if this specification is arbitrarily reduced to say 2 days, disastrous results would be experienced when the finished concrete is put underload.

6.2.3 Changing the Arrangement of Activities

Often considerable saving of time can be effected by rearranging the structure of the activities in the project network. This may be explained by the following example.

It is considered that a particular finished part must go through three machining operations viz., cut off, grinding and drilling before completion. Assuming that these parts were sent through the machine shop in batches of 100 and all the pieces were to travel along together, the process would be represented in the form of a bar chart as shown in Fig. 6.10. The activities represented in this manner are called *series-connected activities* in PERT terminology, meaning that one activity must be completed before the next activity can be started. As may be seen in Fig. 6.10 this arrangement of activities would involve a relatively longer duration for their completion. However, an alternative arrangement could be that when a few pieces have gone through the cut off operation they may be sent for grinding instead of waiting for the entire batch of 100 pieces to be processed at the cut off section.

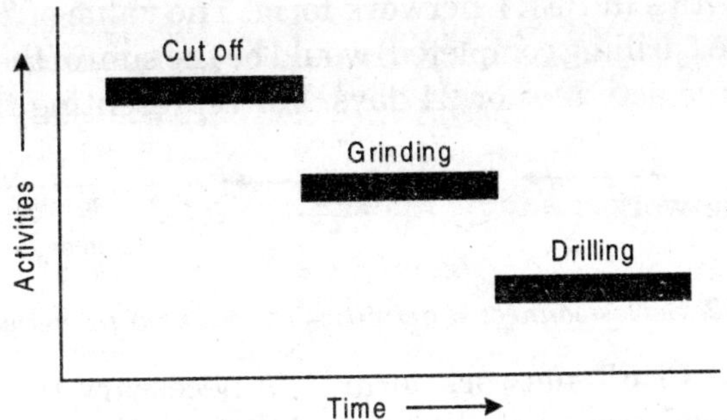

Fig. 6.10 *Series-connected machining activities for batches of 10 pieces.*

Similarly when a few pieces have gone through the grinding process they may be sent to the drilling section instead of waiting until the entire batch of 100 pieces has been processed through cut off and grinding operations. The rearranged activities are as shown in Fig. 6.11 which reflect a considerable

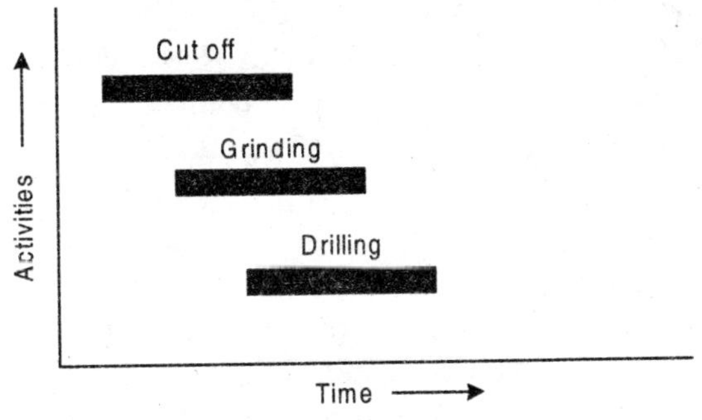

Fig. 6.11 *Activities of Fig. 6.10 rearranged into series-parallel activities.*

saving in time. This rearrangement of activities is commonly termed as change from *series-connected activities to series-parallel activities* in PERT terminology. It means that the activities go on concurrently, i.e., different activities are in operation at the same time. Thus by changing series-connected activities into series-parallel activities the time required to complete a project is considerably reduced.

The bar charts shown in Figs. 6.10 and 6.11 may be replaced by the usual network diagrams used in PERT analysis. For this certain times are assigned to each of these three operations for the batch of 100 pieces as per their requirements. Since each of these three operations may require almost the same time, identical times are assigned as follows :

Cut off	8 days
Grinding	8 days
Drilling	8 days

In Fig. 6.12 these three activities are represented as three series-connected activities in PERT network form. The value of T_E of the network-ending event (i.e., drilling completed) would be the sum of the expected elapsed times of the three activities or 24 days. For representing the series-parallel

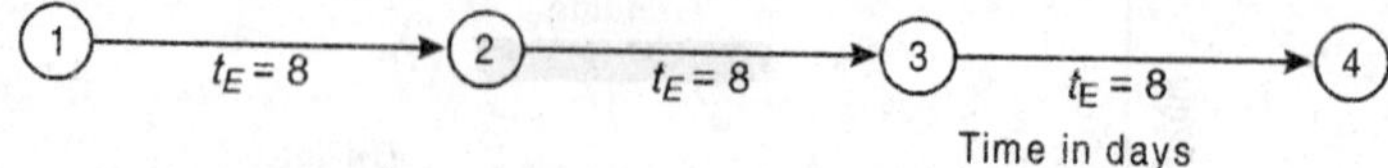

Fig. 6.12 *Series-connected activities represented in network form.*

activities in the PERT network form it is necessary to decide how much time should elapse between the starting of the cut off process and the starting of the grinding operation, and also between the starting of the grinding operation and the starting of the drilling operation. In this case 3 days are assigned for the time that will elapse between the starting of the cut off process and the starting of the grinding operation. Similarly 3 days

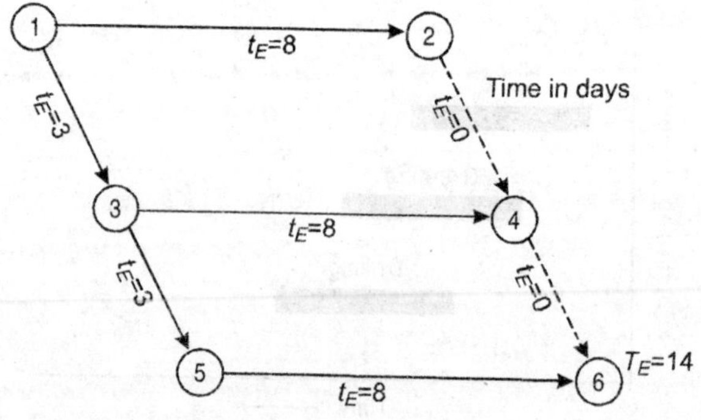

Fig. 6.13 *Series-parallel represented in network form.*

are also assigned for the time that will elapse between the starting of the grinding operation and the starting of the drilling operation. The resulting network is as shown in Fig. 6.13. Table 6.4 explains the various activities of the network shown in Fig. 6.13.

TABLE 6.4 *Explanation of activities in Fig. 6.13*

Activity	*Explanation*
1–2	100 pieces are cut off.
1–3	3 days elapses between start of cut off activity (1–2) and the start of grinding activity (3–4).
2–4	Dummy or zero-time activity to maintain network appearance.
3–4	100 pieces are ground.
3–5	3 days elapses between start of grinding activity (3–4) and start of drilling activity (5–6).
5–6	100 pieces are drilled.
4–6	Dummy or zero-time activity to maintain network appearance.

It may be noted that the rearrangement of the activities from series-connected to series parallel has resulted in reducing the value of T_E of the network-ending event from 24 days to 14 days. The amount of reduction would, however, depend on the time periods assigned to activities 1–3 and 3–5 which represent waiting time between the start of one activity and the accumulation of enough partially processed items to justify the start of the next activity. Thus if larger time values are assigned to these two activities, the T_E of the network-ending event will increase accordingly.

There are various activities which cannot be changed from series-connected to series-parallel. For instance the two related activities of sanding the hull of a boat and then painting it will be series-connected activities only because it will be essential to first finish sanding, clean off the dust and then paint in dirt-free conditions for any acceptable finish. Similarly in another example there may be a case in which a complete item must be produced before any kind of testing can be done. In this case the two activities viz., production of the item and testing of the item cannot go concurrently.

It may, however, be stated that the readjustment and replanning of a project network will become difficult as the number of events contained in the network increases and the network becomes complicated. The analysis of larger and complicated networks would necessitate the use of computers, which is briefly described in Chapter 10.

REVIEW QUESTIONS

6.1 What do you understand by readjustment and replanning of network ?

6.2 What are the different methods of replanning and readjustment of project network ?

6.3 Explain briefly how interchanging of resources can reduce the completion time of a project. Support your answer by examples.

6.4 What is meant by relaxing the technical specifications? How such relaxation can reduce the completion time of a project ?

6.5 Explain by means of an example how by changing the arrangement of the activities the completion time of a project can be reduced.

6.6 Differentiate between series-connected activities and series-parallel activities.

6.7 Narrate some of the examples in which it is not possible to change series-connected activities to series-parallel activities.

7

Chapter

Critical Path Method (CPM)

7.1 INTRODUCTION

Critical Path Method, commonly abbreviated as CPM is identical to PERT in concept and methodology but was developed independently of PERT by Du Pont and Spery Rand Corporation in the year 1957. Both CPM and PERT are the tools used nowadays synonymously for planning, scheduling and control of various projects, though broad differences exist between them. CPM has wide applications in the fields of construction, manufacturing, maintenance, etc. Examples of the applications of CPM in different fields are as follows.

1. Construction of a building or a highway.
2. Scheduling airplane or ship construction and maintenance.
3. Laying railway tracks.
4. Planning and launching of a new product.
5. Closing of accounts books at the year end.
6. Expansion and modernisation of a manufacturing unit
7. Maintenance projects.

7.2 CPM AND PERT—A COMPARISON

1. In CPM emphasis is laid on activities and in PERT on events. Thus CPM network is activity based and PERT network is event based.

2. In CPM, activity times are deterministic i.e., time estimates for completion of activities are fairly accurate, whereas in the case of PERT, activity times are stochastic or probabilistic and are assumed to follow a beta distribution.* Thus CPM is suitable when time estimates can be determined with fair degree of accuracy and costs can be calculated in

* Beta distribution has been discussed in section 4.7 Chapter 4.

advance. For example, for a construction project CPM is suitable because the time estimates for the completion of the project as well as costs of labour, material etc., can be determined in advance with a fair degree of accuracy. On the other hand PERT is suitable when there is extreme degree of uncertainty in the various aspects of the project and control over time outweighs control over costs. For example, for a project of satellite launching PERT is more suitable because in such a project it is extremely difficult even to list all the activities comprehensively.

3. CPM puts emphasis on optimizing resource allocation and minimizing overall cost for a given project execution time and therefore it is cost biased. On the other hand in PERT the emphasis is on shortening and monitoring project execution time without too much concern for cost and therefore it is time biased. Moreover in PERT it is assumed that cost varies directly with time for all activities within the project. Thus when a reduction in time has been effected, it is assumed that a reduction in cost has also been achieved. However, it may not be the case always because in general when the normal time for the completion of an activity is reduced the total cost for the activity may either decrease or increase depending upon the nature of the activity and the manner of achieving the reduction in time.

7.3 CPM-NETWORKS

The networking principles involved in CPM are similar to those considered in the case of PERT. Alike PERT in CPM network also various activities are represented by arrows that are logically connected in order of the sequence of operations. The beginning and the end of each arrow is attached to nodes that symbolise the events. However, the main difference between CPM and PERT networks is that CPM networks are generally activity oriented while the PERT networks are event oriented.

The elements of network have been discussed in detail in Chapter 3. However, as an example consider the network shown in Fig. 7.1. Activities *A*, *B* and *C* can start independently and simultaneously as these are the initial activities preceded by none. Activity *D* can start only when activity A

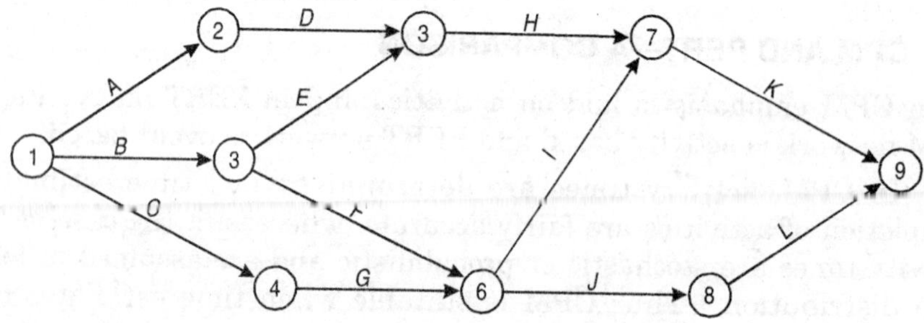

Fig. 7.1 *CPM-setwork*

is completed. Activities E and F can start only when activity B is completed. Similarly activity G cannot occur until activity C is completed. Activity H cannot occur until activities D and E are completed. Activities I and J cannot start until activities F and G are completed. Activities H and I are predecessor activities to activity K and activity L is successor activity to activity J.

7.4 TIME ESTIMATE OF AN ACTIVITY

After the network has been finalized and put on paper, the next step is to estimate the time required for the execution of each activity. As indicated in Chapter 4, PERT makes use of probabilistic approach for obtaining time estimate of an activity because PERT is concerned with uncertainty problems. In probabilistic approach, for each activity, three time estimate viz., optimistic time, most likely time and pessimistic time are obtained and with the help of these three time estimates the expected time t_E for each, activity is calculated. However, CPM is concerned with problems which do not involve significant uncertainties and hence, unlike PERT, CPM does not make use of probabilistic approach for obtaining, time estimate of an activity. In CPM activity times are deterministic because in CPM there exists only one time estimate for each activity. Both the above noted approaches for obtaining time estimate of an activity are presented graphically in Fig. 7.2. In Fig. 7.2 (a) the time estimate of the activity has greater range of variation and hence greater uncertainty, thus probabilistic approach would be required to be used. However, in Fig. 7.2 (b) the time estimate of the activity has a narrow range of variation and hence in this case the activity time estimate is deterministic i.e., it can be determined directly from the plot without necessitating the use of probabilistic approach. Thus as shown in Fig. 7.2 (b) the estimated time t for the activity is 21 weeks. The duration required

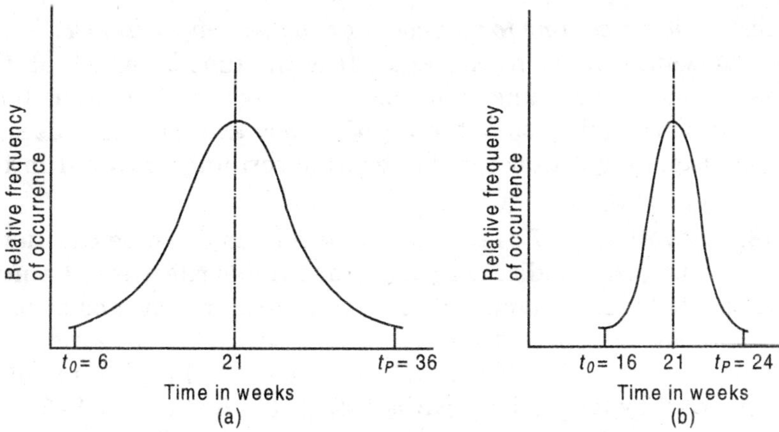

Fig. 7.2 *Time estimate of an activity.*

for the completion of each activity is written along the arrow representing that activity as shown in Fig. 7.3. Thus the time of completion of activity *A* in Fig. 7.3 is $t = 4$ weeks, while for those of activity *B* and activity *C* are 9 and 12 weeks respectively. The total time for the completion of these three activities is 25 weeks.

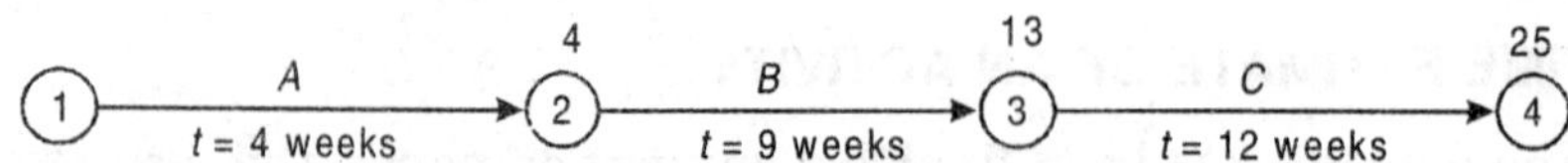

Fig. 7.3 *Time of completion of activities.*

If *i* stands for the predecessor event and *j* stands for the successor event, then *i–j* stands for the activity. In CPM the time of completion of activity *i–j* is represented by t^{ij}. However, in PERT, as indicated in Chapter 4, a similar notation t_E^{ij} is used, where the subscript *E* stand for the *expected time* because of the uncertainty factor being considered.

7.5 EARLIEST OCCURRENCE TIME FOR AN EVENT OR EARLIEST EVENT TIME

An event is defined as the beginning or the end of an activity. In a network since each activity is given a duration, the time when an event can be said to occur can be determined. For example, in the network shown in Fig. 7.3, event 1 stands for the beginning of activity *A* and hence it occurs at time zero. Event 2 stands for the end of activity *A* and also for the beginning of activity *B*. Thus event 2 occurs at time equal to 4 weeks. Similarly event 3 occurs at time 13 weeks and the end event 4 occurs at the end of 25 weeks. These event times are entered on top of the nodes representing the various events.

The *earliest occurrence time for an event* or *earliest event time* T_E is the earliest time at which an event can occur. It is the time by which all the activities leading to an event under consideration are completed. The term earliest event time is analogous to the term *earliest expected time* used in the PERT analysis, except that the degree of uncertainty involved in the word expected is not there.

In a simple network (Fig. 7.3) the earliest event time can be calculated easily as the event times indicated earlier are the earliest event times. However, when a network is complicated and an event is connected by more than one activity path the earliest event time may be calculated as indicated in the following example. Consider a network shown in Fig. 7.4, in which event 6 is connected by two activity paths 1–2, 2–4, 4-6, and 1–3, 3–5, 5–6. By considering the path 1–2–4–6, event 6 can occur at time $T = 31$ weeks. By considering the path 1–3–5–6, event 6 can occur at time $T = 35$ weeks. As indicated earlier no event can be considered to have occurred or reached until all activities leading to it are completed. Therefore, event 6 cannot be considered to have occurred or reached until all the activities along both the paths are completed and hence the earliest time for the occurrence of event 6 will be 35 weeks (i.e., greater of the two times for the two activity paths). Further this earliest time for the occurrence of event 6 will be denoted by T_E^6.

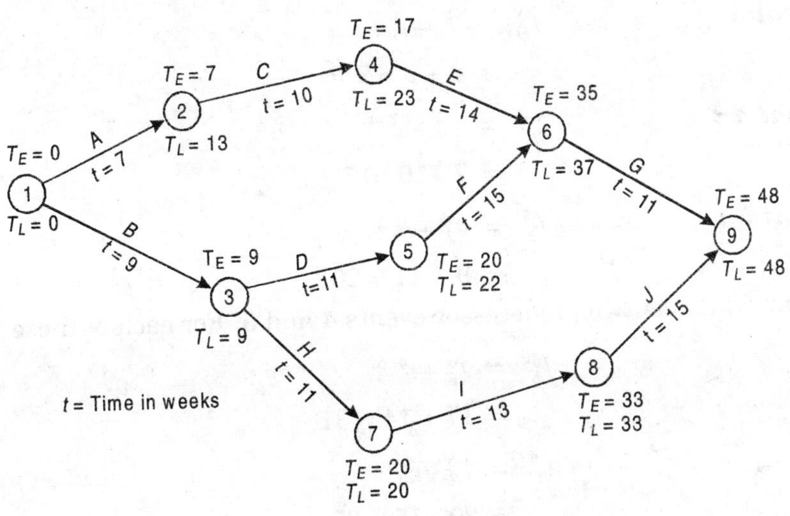

Fig. 7.4 *Network used for computation of earliest event time.*

In the same manner if event 9 is considered then from Fig. 7.4 it may be readily obtained that the earliest time for the occurrence of this event is $T_E^9 = 48$.

7.5.1 Rule for Evaluating T_E

From the above discussion the rule for evaluating the earliest occurrence time for an event or earliest event time can be stated as follows:

To the earliest time of each event that immediately precedes it, add the time of completion of the activity which connects it and choose the highest of the values obtained.

The above rule may be expressed as follows:

$$T_E^j = \text{maximum of } (T_E^i + t^{ij}) \qquad ...(7.1)$$

where T_E^j is the earliest occurrence time for event j; T_E^i is the earliest occurrence time for event i which precedes event j and t^{ij} is the time of completion of activity i–j.

The earliest occurrence time for the various events of network shown in Fig. 7.4 may thus be determined as follows.

Event 1 **:** Since it does not have any predecessor event,

$$T_E^1 = 0$$

Event 2 **:**

$$T_E^2 = T_E^i + t^{1-2}$$
$$= 0 + 7 = 7$$

Event 3 **:**

$$T_E^3 = T_E^i + t^{1-3}$$
$$= 0 + 9 = 9$$

Event 4 **:**

$$T_E^4 = T_E^2 + t^{2-4}$$
$$= 7 + 10 = 17$$

Event 5 **:**

$$T_E^5 = T_E^3 + t^{3-5}$$
$$= 9 + 11 = 20$$

Event 6 **:** It has two predecessor events 4 and 5. For each of these

$$T_E^6 = T_E^4 + t^{4-6}$$
$$= 17 + 14 = 31$$

$$T_E^6 = T_E^5 + t^{5-6}$$
$$= 20 + 15 = 35$$

The maximum of these two is 35 weeks and hence $T_E^6 = 35$ weeks.

Event 7 **:**

$$T_E^7 = T_E^3 + t^{3-7}$$
$$= 9 + 11 = 20$$

Event 8 **:**

$$T_E^8 = T_E^7 + t^{7-8}$$
$$= 20 + 13 = 33$$

Event 9 **:** It has two predecessor events 6 and 8. For each of these

$$T_E^9 = T_E^6 + t^{6-9}$$
$$= 35 + 11 = 46$$

$$T_E^9 = T_E^8 + t^{8-9}$$
$$= 33 + 15 = 48$$

The maximum of these two is 48 weeks and hence $T_E^9 = 48$ weeks.

7.5.2 Forward Pass

It may be noted that in calculating the earliest event time one has to begin the computations from the initial or starting event and come to the end event. This procedure is called *forward pass.*

7.6 LATEST ALLOWABLE OCCURRENCE TIME FOR AN EVENT OR LATEST EVENT TIME

The latest allowable occurrence time for an event or *latest event time* T_L is the latest time by which an event must be completed to keep the project on schedule. Consider the simple network shown in Fig. 7.3 in which the earliest event times are shown on the top of the nodes. For end event 4 the earliest event time $T_E^4 = 25$ weeks which is also the project duration time, hence the latest occurrence time for event 4 is $T_L^4 = 25$ weeks. Since activity 3–4 takes 12 weeks, event 3 cannot occur later than (25 –12) = 13 weeks. Hence, the latest occurrence time for event 3 is $T_L^3 = 13$ weeks. Similarly for event 2, the latest occurrence time $T_L^2 = (13 - 9) = 4$ weeks.

In a network when an event has more than one successor event, the latest occurrence time for the event may be calculated as explained in the following example. Considering the network shown in Fig. 7.4, event 3 has two successor events 5 and 7 and it is connected to the end event 9 by two activity paths viz., 3–5, 5–6, 6–9, and 3–7, 7–8, 8–9. Thus the latest occurrence time for event 3 may be calculated by considering each of these two activity paths. First consider path 3–5–6–9. Since the latest occurrence time for event 9 is 48 weeks and activity 6–9 takes 11 weeks for completion, the latest occurrence time for event 6 is $T_E^6 = (48–11) = 37$ weeks. In the same manner the latest occurrence time for event 5 is $T_L^5 = (37–15) = 22$ weeks and that for event 3 is $T_L^3 = (22–11) = 11$ weeks. Next consider path 3–7–8–9. The latest occurrence time for event 8 is $T_L^8 = (48 - 15) = 33$ weeks, for event 7 it is $T_L^7 = (33–13) =$ 20 weeks and for event 3 it is $T_L^3 = (20 - 11) = 9$ weeks. Thus there are two values of T_L for event 3, which being 9 and 11 weeks. For completion of this project in a schedule of 48 weeks it is obvious that event 3 occurs at an earlier time and therefore the latest time for the occurrence of event 3 is 9 weeks. In the same manner the latest occurrence times for the remaining events have also been calculated and are shown in the figure.

7.6.1 Rule for Evaluation T_L

From the above discussion the rule for evaluating the latest allowable occurrence time for an event or latest event time can be stated as follows :

From the latest allowable occurrence time for each event that immediately succeeds it, subtract the time of completion of the activity which connects it and select the lowest of the values obtained.

The above rule may be expressed as follows:

$$T_L^i = \text{minimum of } (T_L^j - t^{ij}) \qquad \text{... (7.2)}$$

Where T_L^i is the latest allowable occurrence time for event i; T_L^j is the latest allowable occurrence time for event j which succeeds event i; and t^{ij} is the time of completion of activity i–j.

7.6.2 Backward Pass

It may be noted that in calculating the latest event time one has to begin the computations from the end event and come to the initial or starting event. This procedure is called *backward pass.*

7.7 TABULAR COMPUTATIONS FOR T_E AND T_L

The computation of the earliest event time T_E and the latest event time T_L can be conveniently done in a tabular form. For illustration, the network shown in Fig. 7.4 is considered and the computations are shown in Table 7.1. The various steps involved in the computations are as follows.

(i) In column 1 the event numbers, starting from the initial event, are entered.

(ii) In column 2 the predecessor events and in column 6 the successor events to the events of column 1 are entered. An event may have one or more than one predecessor and successor events. Thus against each event of column 1 all the predecessor and successor events should be entered in the respective columns.

(iii) In column 3 the activity time t^{ij} is entered where j is the event under consideration (column 1) and i is the predecessor event (column 2).

(iv) In column 4 the event time T_E^j is entered which is computed by using Eq. 7.1 as

$$T_E^j = T_E^i + t^{ij}$$

When there are more than one predecessor event, several values of T_E^j are obtained, all of which are entered in column 4. For example event 6 (j = 6) has two predecessor events 4 and 5 (i = 4, 5). Considering events 6 and 4, we get

$$\begin{aligned} T_E^6 &= (T_E^4 + t^{4-6}) \\ &= (17 + 14) = 31 \end{aligned}$$

Considering events 6 and 5, we get

$$T_E^6 = (T_E^5 + t^{5-6})$$
$$= (20 + 15) = 35$$

(v) The maximum value of T_E^j is underscored as this is the appropriate value of the earliest event time T_E for the event (column 1) under consideration. This value is entered in column 5 against the event (column 1) under consideration.

Next the latest event time is computed for which the following steps are involved.

(vi) In column 7 the activity time t^{ij} is entered, where i is the event under consideration (column 1) and j is the successor event (column 6).

(vii) In column 8 the latest event time T_L^i is entered which is computed by using Eq. 7.2 as

$$T_L^i = T_L^j - t^{ij}$$

The values of T_L^i are computed by starting from the bottom of the column and moving towards the top of the column. Further when there are more than one successor event, several values of T_L^i are obtained, all of which are entered in column 8.

TABLE 7.1 *Computations of T_E and T_L*

	Earliest event time (↓)				*Latest event time (↑)*			
Event	*Predecessor event (i)*	t^{ij}	T_E^j	T_E	*Successor event (j)*	t^{ij}	T_L^i	T_L
(1)	(2)	(3)	(4)	(5)	(6)	(7)	(8)	(9)
1	—	—	0	0	2	7	6	0
					3	9	$\underline{0}$	
2	1	7	$\underline{7}$	7	4	10	$\underline{13}$	13
3	1	9	$\underline{9}$	9	5	11	11	9
					7	11	$\underline{9}$	
4	2	10	$\underline{17}$	17	6	14	$\underline{23}$	23
5	3	11	$\underline{20}$	20	6	15	$\underline{22}$	22
6	4	14	31	35	9	11	$\underline{37}$	37
	5	15	$\underline{35}$					
7	3	11	$\underline{20}$	20	8	13	$\underline{20}$	20
8	7	13	$\underline{33}$	33	9	15	$\underline{33}$	33
9	6	11	46	48	–	0	$\underline{48}$	48
	8	15	$\underline{48}$					

(viii) The minimum value of T_L^i is underscored as this is the appropriate value of the latest time T_L for the event (column 1) under consideration. This value is entered in column 9 against the event (column 1) under consideration.

Thus for each of the events of column 1, T_E is given in column 5 and T_L is given in column 9.

7.8 START AND FINISH TIMES OF ACTIVITY

In the previous sections two event times viz., *earliest event time* T_E and *latest event time* T_L have been discussed. However, as indicated earlier the CPM networks are activity oriented and hence the following activity times are useful for network analysis.

(i) Earliest start time

(ii) Earliest finish time

(iii) Latest start time

(iv) Latest finish time

The above noted times are defined below.

7.8.1 Earliest Start Times (EST)

The *earliest start time* of an activity is the earliest time by which the activity can commence. This is obviously equal to the earliest event time T_E for the event from which the activity arrow originates, or for the tail event. Thus if the activity is denoted by *i–j*, then

$$(\text{EST})_{ij} = T_E^i \qquad \text{...(7.3)}$$

where T_E^i is the earliest event time for the tail event.

7.8.2 Earliest Finish Time (EFT)

The *earliest finish time* of an activity is the earliest time by which the activity can be finished. This is evidently equal to the earliest start time plus the duration for the activity. Thus for activity *i–j*, we have

$$(\text{EFT})_{ij} = \text{earliest start time} + \text{activity duration}$$

or

$$(\text{EFT})_{ij} = (\text{EST})_{ij} + t^{ij}$$

or

$$(\text{EFT})_{ij} = T_E^i + t^{ij} \qquad \text{...(7.4)}$$

7.8.3 Latest Start Time (LST)

The *latest start time* of an activity is the latest time by which the activity can be started, without delaying the completion of the project. This is evidently equal to the latest occurrence time T_L for the event at which the activity arrow terminates minus the duration for the activity. Thus for activity *i–j*, we have

$$(\text{LST})_{ij} = T_L^j - t^{ij} \quad \text{...(7.5)}$$

7.8.4 Latest Finish Time (LFT)

The *latest finish time* of an activity is the latest time by which the activity can be finished, without delaying the completion of the project Evidently this is equal to the latest occurrence time T_L for the event at which the activity arrow terminates. Thus for activity *i–j*, we have

$$(\text{LFT})_{ij} = T_L^j \quad \text{...(7.6)}$$

A comparison of Eqs. 7.5 and 7.6 indicates that

$$(\text{LFT})_{ij} = (\text{LST})_{ij} + t^{ij} \quad \text{...(7.7)}$$

$$(\text{LST})_{ij} = (\text{LFT})_{ij} - t^{ij} \quad \text{...(7.7 a)}$$

From the above definitions it may be noted that the earliest start time for activity *i–j* coincides with T_E^i and the latest finish time for activity *i–j* coincides with T_L^j The other two terms viz., the earliest finish time and the latest start time are obtained respectively by adding to T_E^i and subtracting from T_L^j the duration for activity *i–j*.

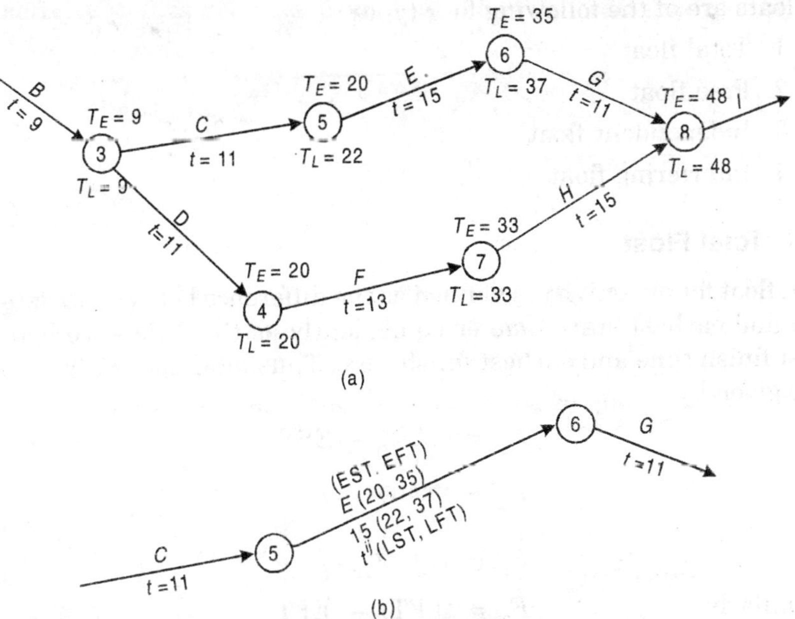

Fig. 7.5 *Network used for computing the four activity times.*

For example, consider a partial network as shown in Fig. 7.5, in which for activity E the values of the above noted four activity times may be obtained as follows.

$$\text{EST} = T_E^j = T_E^5 = 20$$

$$\text{EFT} = T_E^i + t^{ij} = 20 + 15 = 35$$

$$\text{LST} = T_L^j - t^{ij} = 37–15 = 22$$

$$\text{LFT} = T_L^j = 37$$

The above noted four activity times are generally written on the activity arrow along with activity name and activity duration as shown in Fig. 7.5. The activity times, EST and EFT are written above the arrow, while the activity duration, LST and LFT are written below the arrow.

7.9 FLOAT

Float denotes the range within which the start time may fluctuate without affecting the completion of the project. Thus the term float is associated with the activity times and it is analogous to the term slack (defined in Chapter 5) which is associated with the event times. The activities for which float is equal to zero are known as critical activities while those having float are known as non-critical activities.

Floats are of the following four types :

1. Total float
2. Free float
3. Independent float
4. Interfering float

7.9.1 Total Float

Total float for an activity is defined as the difference between its latest start time and earliest start time or equivalently as the difference between its latest finish time and earliest finish time. Thus total float F_T for an activity i–j is given by

$$F_T = (\text{LST})_{ij} - (\text{EST})_{ij} \quad ...(7.8)$$

or

$$F_T = (T_L^j - t^{ij}) - T_E^i \quad ...(7.8\ a)$$

or

$$F_T = (T_L^j - T_E^i) - t^{ij} \quad ....(7.8\ b)$$

Similarly

$$F_T = (\text{LFT})_{ij} - (\text{EFT})_{ij} \quad ....(7.9)$$

from which Eqs. 7.8 (a) and 7.8 (b) may be readily obtained.

For example as shown in Fig. 7.6 the time required for an activity 3–4 is 10 days and it may be started at any time between 16th and 30th days without delaying the project. Thus for this activity EST = 16 and LST = 30 and hence the total float $F_T = (30–16) = 14$ days. Similarly for this activity EFT = (16 + 10) = 26 and LFT = (30 + 10) = 40 and hence the total float $F_T = (40–26) = 14$ days.

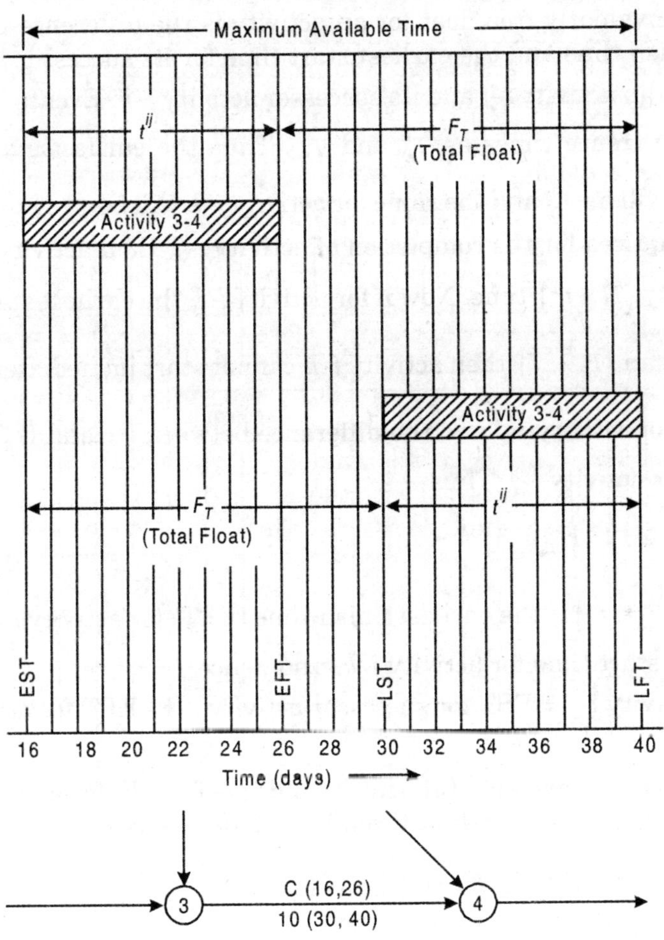

Fig. 7.6 *Network used for computing total float.*

Further for an activity the difference between its latest finish time (LFT) and earliest start time (EST) represents the maximum available time for that activity. Then it may be observed from Fig. 7.6 that total float for an activity is the excess of the maximum available time over the activity time, i.e.,

$$F_T = \text{(Maximum available time)} - t^{ij}$$

or
$$F_T = (T_L^j - T_E^i) - t^{ij}$$
which is same as Eq. 7.8 (b).

7.9.2 Free Float

Free float may be defined as the amount of time by which an activity can be delayed without affecting the earliest start time of any other activity in a project, equivalently free float for an activity is the difference between its earliest finish time and the earliest start time for its successor activity.

Consider an activity *i–j* and its successor activity *j–k*. Events *i* and *j* have earliest occurrence times as T_E^i and T_E^j. Thus the earliest start time for activity *i–j* will be T_E^i and the same for activity *j–k* will be T_E^j. Further if t^{ij} is the time required for the completion of activity *i–j*, then activity *i–j* will be completed by $\left(T_E^i + t^{ij}\right)$ time. Now if for activity *j–k* the earliest start time T_E^j is greater than $\left(T_E^i + t^{ij}\right)$ then activity *j–k* cannot start immediately after the completion of activity *i–j* and the difference between T_E^j and $\left(T_E^i + t^{ij}\right)$ is the free float for activity *i–j*. Thus

$$F_F \text{ for } i\text{–}j = T_E^j - \left(T_E^i + t^{ij}\right) \qquad \text{...(7.10)}$$

Further $\left(T_E^i + t^{ij}\right)$ is the earliest finish time (EFT) for activity *i–j* and T_E^j is the earliest start time for activity *j–k*, and hence

F_F for activity *i–j* = EST for successor activity *j–k* –EFT for activity *i–j* ...(7.11)

A relationship between total float F_T and free float F_F for an activity may be obtained as indicated below. From Eq. 7.8 (b), we have

$$F_T = \left(T_L^j - T_E^i\right) - t^{ij}$$

or
$$F_T = T_L^j - \left(T_E^i + t^{ij}\right)$$

or
$$\left(T_E^i + t^{ij}\right) = T_L^j - F_T$$

Substituting the value of $\left(T_E^i + t^{ij}\right)$ in Eq. 7.10, we get

$$F_F = T_E^j - \left(T_L^j - F_T\right)$$

or
$$F_F = F_T - \left(T_L^j - T_E^j\right) \quad ...(7.12)$$

Further $\left(T_L^i - T_E^j\right) = S_j$

where S_j is the slack for event j or the slack for the head event of activity i–j. Thus
$$F_F = F_T - S_j \quad ...(712a)$$

From Eq. 7.12 (a) it may be observed that free float for an activity is equal to the difference between the total float and the slack for the head event of that activity. However, for an activity if the slack for its head event is equal to zero then free float will be equal to its total float.Fig. 7.7 shows

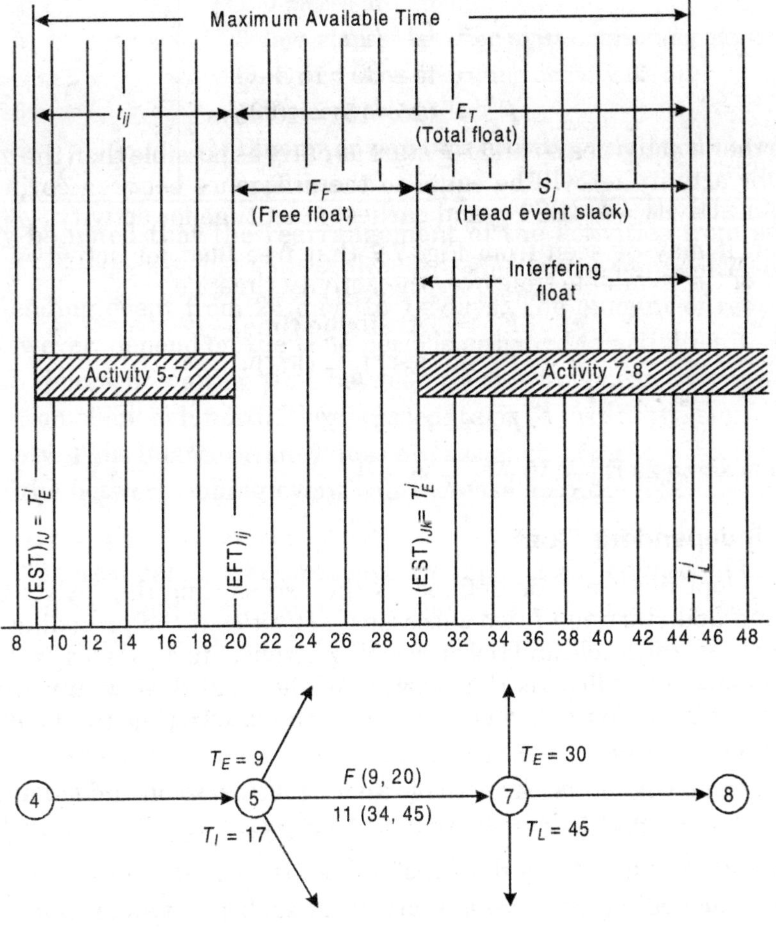

Fig. 7.7 *Relationship between total float and free float of an activity.*

free float and its relationship with total float for an activity 5–7 having an activity time of 11 days. The tail and head event times are marked in the figure. For activity 5–7 free float is given by

$$F_F = T_E^j - T_E^i - t^{ij}$$
$$= 30 - 9 - 11 = 10 \text{ days} \quad \text{...(i)}$$

Also
$$F_F = T_E^j - (\text{EFT})_{ij}$$
$$= 30 - 20 = 10 \text{ days} \quad \text{...(ii)}$$

Also
$$F_F = F_T - S_j$$
$$F_T = \left(T_L^i - T_E^j\right) - t^{ij}$$
$$= 45 - 9 - 11 = 25 \text{ days}$$
$$S_j = T_L^j - T_E^j$$
$$= 45 - 30 = 15 \text{ days}$$

$\therefore$
$$F_F = (25 - 15) = 10 \text{ days} \quad \text{... (iii)}$$

Further if activities *i–j* and *j–k* start as early as possible then the available time for activity *i–j* will be equal to the difference between earliest start time for activity *j–k*, $(\text{EST})_{jk}$ and earliest start time for activity *i–j* $(\text{EST})_{ij}$.

Then it may be seen from Fig. 7.7 that free float for activity *i–j* is the excess of the available time over the activity time, i.e.,

$$F_F = (\text{Available time}) - t^{ij}$$

or
$$F_F = (\text{EST})_{jk} - (\text{EST})_{ij} - t^{ij}$$

or
$$F_F = T_E^j - T_E^i - t^{ij}$$

which is same as Eq. 7.10.

7.9.3 Independent Float

Independent float may be defined as the excess time that exists between finishing and starting of two successive activities if the preceding activity ends as late as possible and the succeeding activity starts as early as possible. Thus independent float is that portion of the total float within which the starting of an activity can be delayed without affecting the floats of the preceding activities.

For example let *i–j* be the activity under consideration and *h–i* and *j–k* be its predecessor and successor activities respectively as shown in Fig. 7.8. Let the preceding activity *h–i* finish at its latest possible time, which is T_L^i and the succeeding activity *j–k* start at its earliest possible time, which is T_E^j. Then activity *i–j* can take up any duration from t^{ij} to $\left(T_E^j - T_L^i\right)$ without in any way affecting the network. The difference between $\left(T_E^j - T_L^i\right)$ and t^{ij} is called the independent float F_{ID} for activity i–j, i.e.,

$$F_{ID} \text{ for } i\text{–}j = \left(T_E^j - T_L^i\right) - t^{ij} \quad \text{...(7.13)}$$

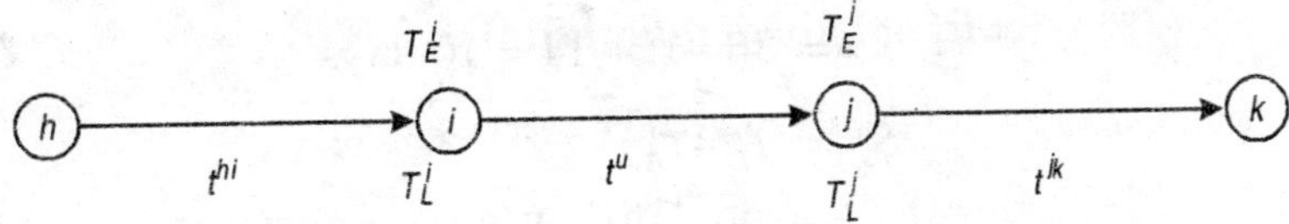

Fig. 7.8 *Network used for computing independent float.*

It may, however, be noted that the independent float for an activity is a part of the free float for the same activity. As such a relationship between independent float and free float for an activity may be obtained as indicated below.

From Eq. 7.10, we have

$$F_F = T_E^j - t^{ij} - T_E^i \quad \text{...(i)}$$

Also from Eq. 7.13, we have

$$T_E^j - t^{ij} = F_{ID} + T_L^i \quad \text{...(ii)}$$

Adding Eqs. (i) and (ii), we get

$$F_F = F_{ID} + T_L^i - T_E^i$$

or

$$F_{ID} = F_F - \left(T_L^i - T_E^i\right) \quad \text{...(7.14)}$$

Further $\left(T_L^i - T_E^i\right) = S_i$

where S_i is the slack for event i or slack for tail event of activity i–j. Thus

$$F_{ID} = F_F - S_i \quad \text{...(7.14 a)}$$

From Eq. 7.14 (a) it may be observed that independent float for an activity is equal to its free float minus the slack for the tail event of that activity. However, for an activity if the slack for its tail event is equal to zero, its independent float and free float are equal. Further if a negative value of independent float is obtained then independent float is taken as zero.

Figure 7.9 shows independent float and its relationship with free float for an activity 15–17 having an activity time of 14 days. The tail and head event times are marked in the figure. For activity 15–17 independent float is given by

$$F_{ID} = \left(T_E^j - T_L^i\right) - t^{ij}$$

$$= (36 - 20) - 14 = 2 \text{ days} \qquad \text{...(i)}$$

Also

$$F_{ID} = F_F - S_i$$

$$F_F = T_E^j - T_E^i - t^{ij}$$

$$= 36 - 12 - 14 = 10 \text{ days}$$

$$S_i = T_L^i - T_E^i$$

$$= (20 - 12) = 8 \text{ days}$$

$$\therefore \quad F_{ID} = (10 - 8) = 2 \text{ days} \qquad \text{...(ii)}$$

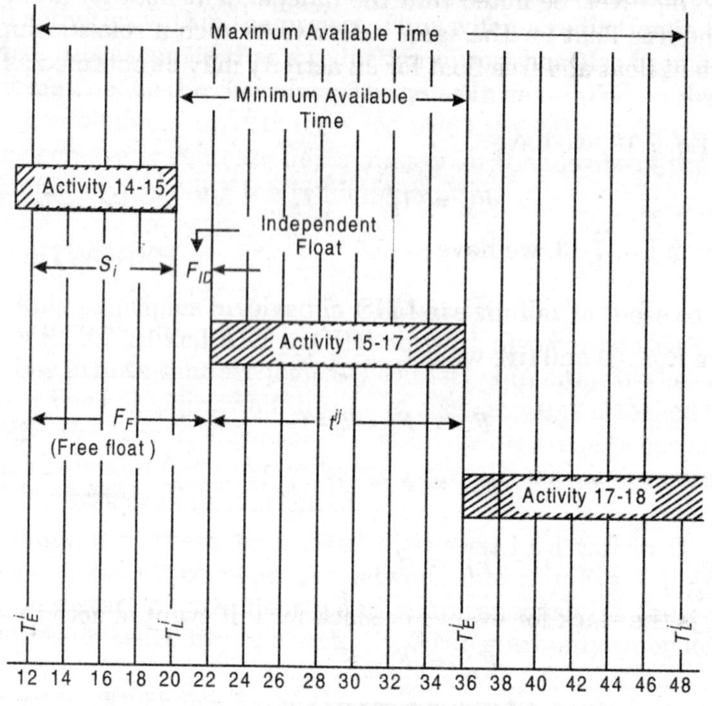

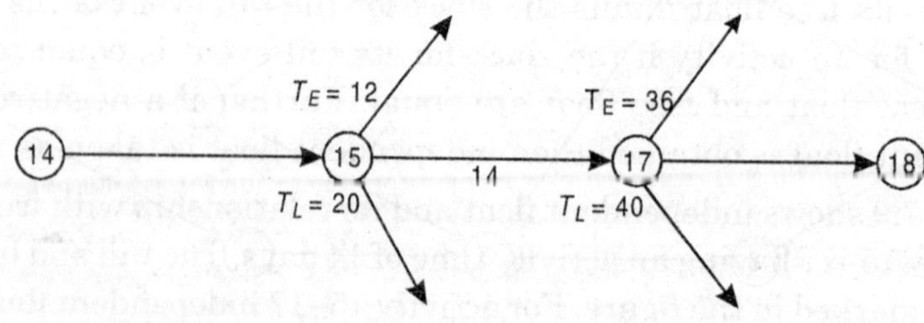

Fig. 7.9 *Relationship between free and independent floats of an activity.*

Further the difference between earliest start time T_E^j for activity j–k and latest start time T_L^i for activity i–j represents the minimum available time for activity i–j. Thus it may be observed from Fig. 7.9 that independent float for an activity is the excess of the minimum available time over the activity time, i.e.,

$$F_{ID} = (\text{Minimum available time}) - t^{ij}$$

$$F_{ID} = \left(T_E^j - T_L^i\right) - t^{ij}$$

which is same as Eq. 7.13.

7.9.4 Interfering Float

Interfering float for an activity may be defined as the difference between its total float and free float. Thus for an activity i–j interfering float is given by

$$F_{IT} = F_T - F_F \qquad \text{...(7.15)}$$

but

$$F_T = \left(T_L^j - T_E^i\right) - t^{ij}$$

and

$$F_F = \left(T_E^j - T_E^i\right) - t^{ij}$$

$$\therefore \quad F_{IT} = \left(T_L^i - T_E^j\right) = S_j \qquad \text{...(7.15 a)}$$

i.e., interfering float for an activity is equal to the slack for the head event of that activity as also shown in Fig. 7.7.

As an example the network shown in Fig. 7.4 is again considered and the values of the activity times, total float, free float and independent float are computed and given in Table 7.2.

TABLE 7.2 *Computations of Activity times and floats*

Activity (*i–j*)	*Duration* t^{ij}	*Earliest* *Start time* (*EST*)	*Earliest* *Finish time* (*LFT*)	*Latest* *Start time* (*LST*)	*Latest* *Finish time* (*LFT*)	*Total float* F_T	*Free float* F_F	*Independent float* F_{ID}
(1)	(2)	(3)	(4)	(5)	(6)	(7)	(8)	(9)
1–2	7	0	7	6	13	6	0	0
1–3	9	0	9	0	9	0	0	0
2–4	10	7	17	13	23	6	0	0
3–5	11	9	20	11	22	2	0	0

Contd.

Contd. Table 7.2

(1)	(2)	(3)	(4)	(5)	(6)	(7)	(8)	(9)
3–7	11	9	20	9	20	0	0	0
4–6	14	17	31	23	37	6	4	0
5–6	15	20	35	22	37	2	0	0
6–9	11	35	46	37	48	2	2	0
7–8	13	20	33	20	33	0	0	0
8–9	15	33	48	33	48	0	0	0

7.10 SUPERCRITICAL, CRITICAL AND SUBCRITICAL ACTIVITIES

As indicated in the previous section the total float for an activity is the difference between maximum available time for the activity and the activity time. Thus depending on the relative magnitudes of the maximum available time and the activity time the value of total float may have three possibilities as described below:

(i) If the maximum available time for an activity is less than the activity time then for this activity the total float will have a negative value. An activity for which total float is negative is known as *supercritical activity.*

(ii) If the maximum available time for an activity is equal to the activity time then for this activity the total float will be equal to zero. An activity for which total float is equal to zero is known as *critical activity.*

(iii) If the maximum available time for an activity is more than the activity time then for this activity the total float will have a positive value. An activity for which total float is positive is known as *subcritical activity.*

In a network activities having negative float or supercritical activities require special attention and action because for such activities available time is less than the time required for the completion of activity or activity time. For such activities efforts would be made to reduce the activity time and thus compress the network so that the total float for an activity is made either equal to zero or positive from the original negative value. Such compression of the network would, however, necessitate employing of more resources and would also mean additional cost.

7.11 CRITICAL PATH

A *critical path* is defined as the path which joins the critical activities or those activities for which total float is equal to zero. In other words critical path connects those events for which the earliest and the latest times are the same, i.e., these events have zero slack time. This path is named as critical path because along this path as soon as the preceding activity is over the succeeding activity has to begin with no slack if the project has to be completed on schedule. Critical path is normally marked with a bold line (Fig. 7.10) or with red ink. Further it may be noted that critical path is the longest path in a network and the time along this path gives the total duration of the project.

Generally there is only one critical path in a network of any project. However, in the same network there could be number of critical paths, each one having the same length equal to the longest path. Sometimes the entire network may consist of critical activities, in which case all the paths will be the critical paths.

Consider the network shown in Fig. 7.10, for which it is desired to determine the critical path. The computed values of the earliest and the latest times as well as those of the floats are given in Table 7.3. Thus the path 1–3–4–6–8–9–10 is the critical path which is shown by thick line. Further the following points may be noted.

1. Critical path starts from the initial event and ends at the end event.
2. All activities lying along the critical path are critical.

TABLE 7.3 *Computation of Critical Path*

Activity (i–j)	*Duration* t^{ij}	*Earliest*		*Latest*		*Total float* F_T	*Free float* F_F	*Indep-pendent* F_{ID}
		Start time (EST)	*Finish time (EFT)*	*Start time (LST)*	*Finish time (LFT)*			
(1)	(2)	(3)	(4)	(5)	(6)	(7)	(8)	(9)
1–2	12	0	12	7	19	7	0	0
1–3	5	0	5	0	5	0	0	0
2–7	14	12	26	19	33	7	0	0
3–4	10	5	15	5	15	0	0	0
3–5	8	5	13	9	17	4	0	0
4–6	12	15	27	15	27	0	0	0
5–8	12	13	25	17	29	4	4	0
6–8	2	27	29	27	29	0	0	0
6–9	10	27	37	31	41	4	4	4
7–9	8	26	34	33	41	7	7	0
8–9	12	29	41	29	41	0	0	0
9–10	9	41	50	41	50	0	0	0

3. All events lying along the critical path have zero slack time. In other words critical path passes through those events for which slack is zero. Although this is a necessary condition but not a sufficient condition for locating the critical path. This is evident from the fact that though events 6

and 9 (see Fig. 7.10) have zero slack but since activity 6–9 (connecting) events 6 and 9) is not a critical activity and hence activity 6–9 does not lie along the critical path.

4. Critical activities have no flexibilities in their start and finish times and hence any delay in any of these activities shall invariably affect the duration of the project. However, non-critical activities have flexibilities in their start and finish times.

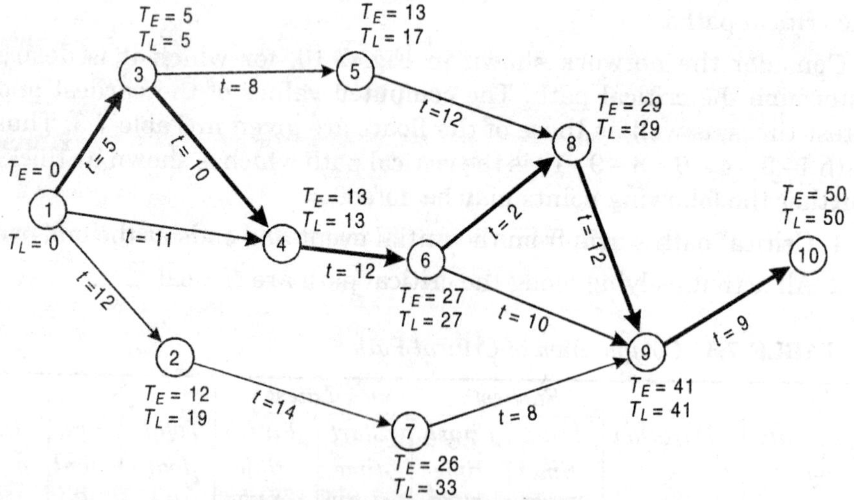

Fig. 7.10 *Network with a critical path.*

7.11.1 Importance of Critical Path

The critical path highlights the activities whose duration determines the duration of the whole project. As such critical path analysis is an important tool in the hands of the management for successful implementation of the project within the expected time. Since it is to be ensured that the activities lying on the critical path are completed as per schedule, the resources such as men, material and money are required to be allocated in such a way that the critical activities are smoothly performed thereby ensuring the timely implementation of the project. The critical path analysis helps the management in taking decision for allocating resources. Thus critical path analysis helps in monitoring the projects. In the subsequent chapters it has been shown that how with the help of critical path analysis optimum utilisation of resources is achieved.

When the project duration is to be reduced, it becomes essential to know which are critical and non-critical activities. It is the duration of the critical activities which determine the completion time of the project. As such if any reduction in the completion time of the project is sought, it is the reduction in the duration time of the critical activities will have to be made which shall reduce the completion time of the project.

ILLUSTRATIVE EXAMPLES

Example 7.1 *Compute the earliest and the latest event times as well as the following activity times for the network shown in Fig. Ex. 7.1.*

(i) Earliest start time

(ii) Latest start time

(iii) Earliest finish time

(iv) Latest finish time

Also compute total float, free float and independent float and determine the critical path.

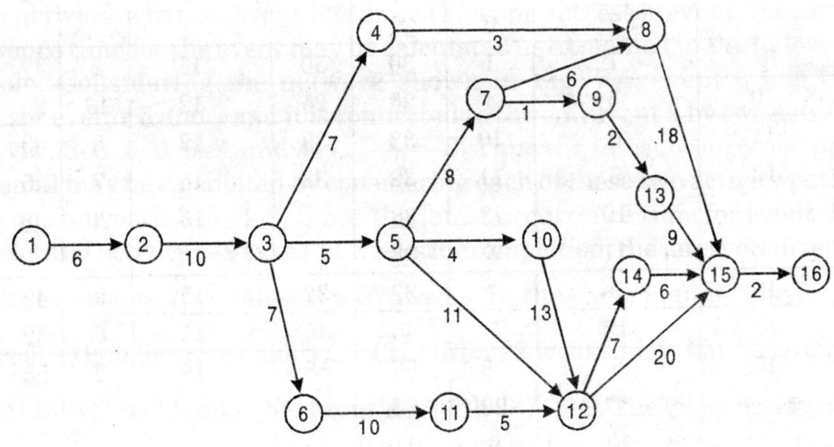

Fig. Ex. 7.1

Solution The computations are shown in the following tables.

TABLE (A) FOR EXAMPLE 7.1

Event	Earliest event time (↓)				Latest event time (↑)			
	Predecessor event (i)	t^{ij}	T_E^j	T_E	*Successor event (j)*	t^{ij}	T_L^i	T_L
(1)	(2)	(3)	(4)	(5)	(6)	(7)	(8)	(9)
1	–	–	0	0	2	6	0	0
2	1	6	6	6	3	10	6	6

Contd.

Contd.

(1)	(2)	(3)	(4)	(5)	(6)	(7)	(8)	(9)
3	2	10	16	16	4	7	30	16
					5	5	16	
					6	7	16	
4	3	7	23	23	8	3	37	37
5	3	5	21	21	7	8	26	21
					10	4	21	
					12	11	27	
6	3	7	23	23	11	10	23	23
7	5	8	29	29	8	6	34	34
						9	46	
8	4	3	26	35	15	18	40	40
	7	6	35					
9	7	1	30	30	13	2	47	47
10	5	4	25	25	12	13	25	25
11	6	10	33	33	12	5	33	33
12	5	11	32	38	14	7	45	38
	10	13	38		15	20	38	
	11	5	38					
13	9	2	32	32	15	9	49	49
14	12	7	45	45	15	6	52	52
15	8	18	53	58	16	2	58	58
	12	20	58					
	13	9	41					
	14	6	51					
16	15	2	60	60	–	0	60	60

TABLE (B) FOR EXAMPLE 7.1

Activity (i–j)	Duration t^{ij}	Earliest		Latest		Total float F_T	Free float F_F	Independent float F_{ID}
		Start time (EST)	Finish time (EFT)	Start time (LST)	Finish time (LFT)			
(1)	(2)	(3)	(4)	(5)	(6)	(7)	(8)	(9)
1–2	6	0	6	0	6	0	0	0
2–3	10	6	16	6	16	0	0	0

Contd.

Contd.

(1)	(2)	(3)	(4)	(5)	(6)	(7)	(8)	(9)
3–4	7	16	23	30	37	14	0	0
3–5	5	16	21	16	21	0	0	0
3–6	7	16	23	16	23	0	0	0
4–8	3	23	26	37	40	14	9	0
5–7	8	21	29	26	34	5	0	0
5–10	4	21	25	21	25	0	0	0
5–12	11	21	32	27	38	6	6	6
6–11	10	23	33	23	33	0	0	0
7–8	6	29	35	34	40	5	0	0
7–9	1	29	30	46	47	17	0	0
8–15	18	35	53	40	58	5	5	0
9–13	2	30	32	47	49	17	0	0
10–12	13	25	38	25	38	0	0	0
11–12	5	33	34	33	38	0	0	0
12–14	7	38	45	45	52	7	0	0
12–15	20	38	58	38	58	0	0	0
13–15	9	32	41	49	58	17	17	0
14–15	6	45	51	52	58	7	0	0
15–16	2	58	60	58	60	0	0	0

In this case there are two critical paths viz., 1–2–3–5–10–12–15–16 and 1–2–3–6–11–12–15–16, which are shown by thick lines in Fig. Sol. Ex. 7.1.

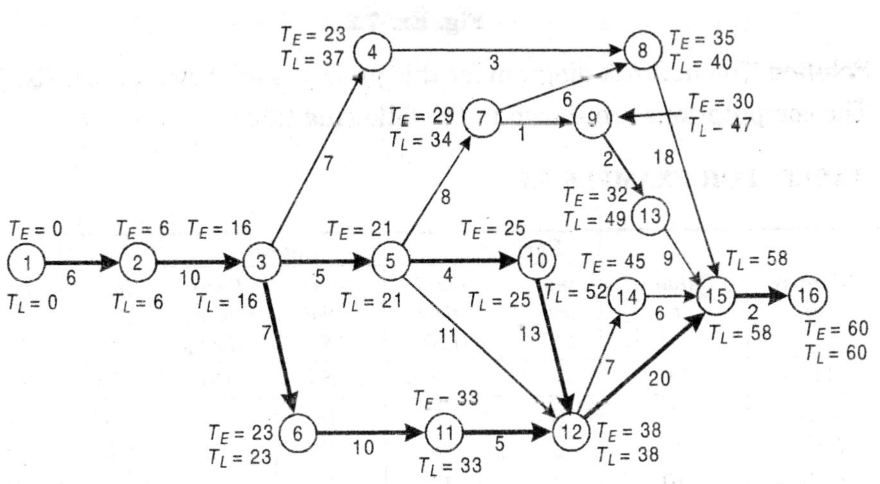

Fig. Sol. Ex. 7.1

Example 7.2. *A building project consists of 12 activities. The normal duration required to perform various activities and the relationship among the activities are given below:*

Activity	*A*	*B*	*C*	*D*	*E*	*F*	*G*	*H*	*I*	*J*	*K*	*L*
Predecessor	—	—	*A*	*A*	*B*	*B*	*C*	*C*	*D, E*	*F*	*G*	*H*
Duration (weeks)	7	5	10	5	8	6	5	4	10	5	8	9

Compute (i) the project completion time; (ii) the critical path; and (iii) the total float and free float for each activity.

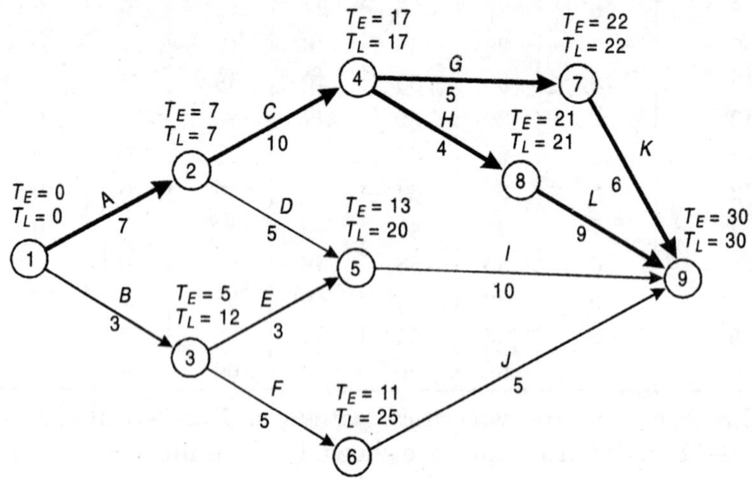

Fig. Ex. 7.2

Solution The network diagram for this project is as shown in Fig. Ex. 7.2. The computations are shown in the following table.

TABLE FOR EXAMPLE 7.2

Activity (i–j)	*Duration* t^{ij}	*Earliest*		*Latest*		*Total float* F_T	*Free float* F_F
		Start time (EST)	*Finish time (EFT)*	*Start time (LST)*	*Finish time (LFT)*		
(1)	(2)	(3)	(4)	(5)	(6)	(7)	(8)
A (1–2)	7	0	7	0	7	0	0
B (1–3)	5	0	5	7	12	7	0
C (2–4)	10	7	17	7	17	0	0

Contd.

Contd.

(1)	(2)	(3)	(4)	(5)	(6)	(7)	(8)
D (2–5)	5	7	12	15	20	8	1
E (3–5)	8	5	13	12	20	7	0
F (3–6)	6	5	11	19	25	14	0
G (4–7)	5	17	22	17	22	0	0
H (4–8)	4	17	21	17	21	0	0
I (5–9)	10	13	23	20	30	7	7
J (6–9)	5	11	16	25	30	14	14
K (7–9)	8	22	30	22	30	0	0
L (8–9)	9	21	30	21	30	0	0

(i) The project completion time is 30 weeks.

(ii) There are two critical paths viz., 1–2–4–7–9 and 1–2–4–8–9 which are shown by thick lines in Fig. Ex. 7.2.

(iii) The total float and free float for each activity are shown in the columns 7 and 8 of the Table.

REVIEW QUESTIONS

7.1 What do you understand by CPM? What is its utility? Illustrate by a simple arrow network diagram.

7.2 Define 'earliest event time' and 'latest event time'. How are these determined ? Explain the tabular form for determining these.

7.3 Distinguish between 'earliest start time' and 'latest start time' of an activity. How are these determined ?

7.4 Distinguish between 'earliest finish time' and 'latest finish time' of an activity. How are these determined ?

7.5 What is the difference between the time estimates of a PERT activity and a CPM activity ?

7.6 What is a float and how is it useful in a CPM network ?

7.7 Differentiate between 'total float', 'free float' and 'independent float'.

7.8 What do you understand by 'independent float' ? Show that independent float for an activity is equal to its free float minus the slack for the tail event of that activity.

7.9 Define 'free float'. How is it determined ? What is its significance ?

7.10 Define critical path. How is it determined ?

7.11 Explain the difference between PERT and CPM networks. Mention the circumstances under which one is preferred to the other.

7.12 **A building project consists of 12 activities. The normal duration required to perform various activities and the relationship among the activities are given below:**

Activity	A	B	C	D	E	F	G	H	I	J	K	L
Predecessor	—	—	A	B	C	B	F	C	D, G	E,I	J,H	K
Duration (weeks)	7	5	10	5	8	6	5	4	10	5	8	9

Compute (i) the project completion time; (ii) the critical path; and (iii) the total float and free float for each activity.

8

Chapter

Project Cost Analysis

8.1 INTRODUCTION

For any project the two important aspects to be considered are the *project time* and the *project cost.* As indicated in the earlier chapters the project time may be determined by locating the critical and subcritical paths in the project network. From the critical path it is also possible to indentify those activities or events that need special attention either in completing the project or in reducing the time for completion. In several cases it would be desirable to reduce the total project time. The reduction in the project time may be achieved in the following ways:

(i) by applying extra resources for early completion of all or some of the activities;

(ii) by relaxing the technical specifications; and

(iii) by changing the arrangement of the activities.

A significant reduction in the project time can be achieved only by applying extra resources for all or some of the activities. This would, however, require the consideration of the additional cost involved on account of extra resources being applied. Besides a few exceptions, the reduction in the project time usually leads to the enhancement of the project cost. As such often it becomes necessary to decide whether to reduce the project time by incurring extra expenditure or not and also on which of the activities or on all of them this extra expenditure is to be incurred. In certain cases the cost is of no consideration but time is most important. In such cases the projects have to be completed at any cost within a shorter duration. For example during war for a project involving the development of a new weapon system, cost considerations are less important as compared to the time factor. Similarly it may be advisable to reduce the project time if such reduction is going to cost less than the benefits earned due to earlier completion of the project. The present chapter deals with the different types of project costs and project times as well as their interrelationships. Further the optimum project duration and optimum time-cost relationship are also discussed subsequently.

8.2 CLASSIFICATION OF PROJECT COSTS AND PROJECT TIMES

(a) Project Costs. The total project cost consists of the sum of two separate costs as noted below:

(i) Direct cost

(ii) Indirect cost

(i) **Direct cost.** Direct cost is the cost which can be calculated activity-wise. This includes the cost of material, labour, equipment, etc.

(ii) **Indirect cost.** Indirect cost is the cost associated with the project as a whole. This cost cannot be calculated activity-wise but it is spread over a group of activities or project as a whole. This cost includes *overheads* or *overhead charges* such as establishment charges of organisation, expenditure on a central store organisation, supervision charges, insurance charges, expenditure for maintenance of services during construction, etc. Indirect cost may also include *outage loss* such as loss of benefits for the period during which the project has not been completed, penalty for delay in the completion of the project, etc.

The total cost of performing (or completing) a particular activity is usually termed as *activity cost*.

The project costs may also be classified as

(i) Normal cost

(ii) Crash cost

(i) **Normal cost.** Normal cost is the cost required to complete a project in normal time duration. This is usually the minimum possible cost required to complete a project.

(ii) **Crash cost.** Crash cost is the cost required to complete a project in the minimum possible time which is known as crash time.

(b) Project times. The project times may be classified as

(i) Normal time

(ii) Crash time

(i) **Normal time.** Normal time is the time required to complete a project at normal cost.

(ii) **Crash time.** Crash time is the minimum possible time in which a project can be completed by applying extra resources. It may, however, be noted that it would not be possible to reduce the completion time of a project beyond the crash time by any amount of increase in resources.

8.3 PROJECT TIME-COST RELATIONSHIP

The project cost and project time are closely related to each other. However, the direct and indirect costs depict an altogether different type of variation with time as indicated below.

(a) Variation of Direct Cost with Time. It has been observed that in general the direct cost increases as the time decreases and it decreases as the time increases as shown in Fig. 8.1 (a). However, for the sake of

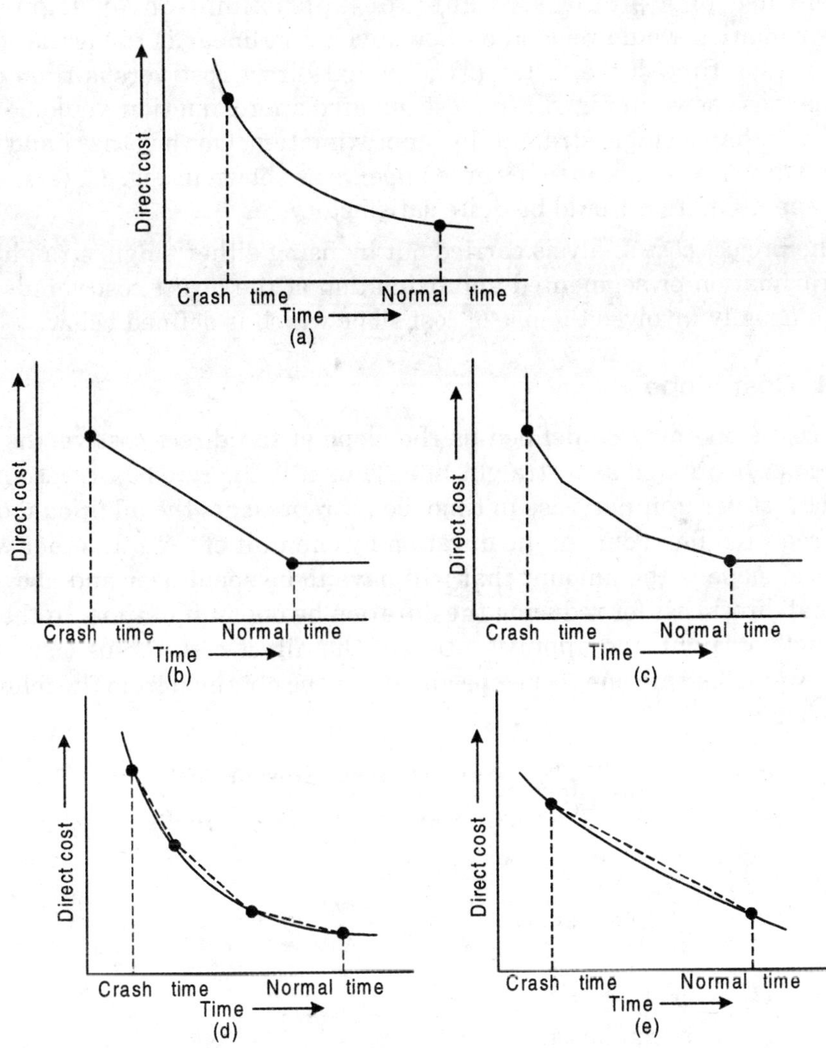

Fig. 8.1 *Variation of direct cost with time.*

convenience the direct cost versus time curve may be approximately represented by straight line plots as shown in Fig. 8.1 (b) and 8.1 (c). If it is assumed that the direct cost varies linearly with time at a constant rate then a single straight line would be obtained as shown in Fig. 8.1 (b). On the other hand if it is assumed that the direct cost varies with time linearly but at different rates then a series of interconnected straight lines representing a segmented approximation would be obtained as shown in Fig. 8.1 (c). Though the segmented approximation may be more accurate, it makes the calculations more complicated.

The use of a single straight line approximation or segmented approximation would depend on how much non-linear is the actual direct cost versus time curve. Thus if the actual direct cost versus time curve appears as shown in Fig. 8.1 (d), a segmented approximation would be more accurate than a single straight line approximation. On the other hand if the actual direct cost versus time curve appears as shown in Fig. 8.1 (e) a single line approximation would be quite satisfactory.

The project cost analysis carried out by using either single straight line approximation or segmented approximation of the direct cost versus time curve usually involves the use of cost slope which is defined below.

8.3.1 Cost Slope

The cost slope may be defined as the slope of the direct cost versus time curve approximated as a straight line. Thus it is the rate of increase in the direct cost per unit decrease in time, i.e., it represents the additional direct cost required for reducing the duration by one unit of time. In other words the cost slope is the amount that will have to be spent over and above the normal direct cost for reducing the duration by one unit of time. In the case of single straight line approximation of the direct cost versus time curve there would be only one cost slope and it may be obtained from the following equation :

$$\text{Cost slope} = \frac{\text{Crash cost} - \text{Normal cost}}{\text{Normal time} - \text{Crash time}}$$

or

$$\text{Cost slope} = \frac{C_c - C_n}{T_n - T_c} = \frac{\Delta C}{\Delta T} \qquad \text{...(8.1)}$$

where C_c = crash cost;

C_n = normal cost;

T_n = normal time;

T_c = crash time;

ΔC = increase in cost; and

ΔT = decrease in time

In the case of segmented approximation of the direct cost versus time curve there would be more than one cost slope.

For reducing the duration extra expenditure is required to be incurred, but it would be desirable to keep this extra expenditure to a minimum. As such the decision about the crashing or expediting of only those activities should be taken which will involve minimum extra cost. Further these activities should be crashed or expedited to such an extent that the corresponding values of the cost slopes would fulfill the criteria of minimum extra cost.

8.3.2 Variation of Indirect Cost with Time

The indirect cost always increases with time. As indicated earlier the indirect cost consists of overheads or overhead charges and outage loss. The overheads increase linearly with time at a constant rate. On the other hand the outage

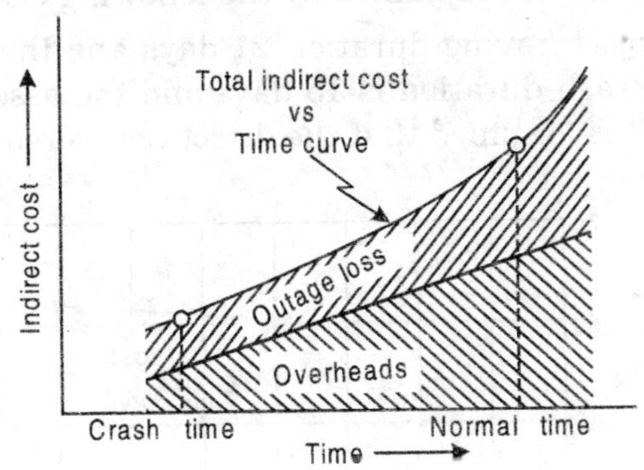

Fig. 8.2 *Variation of indirect cost with time.*

loss increases non-linearly with time. Thus the total indirect cost increases non-linearly with time as shown in Fig. 8.2. However, as an approximation it may be assumed that the indirect cost varies linearly with time.

8.4 OPTIMUM COST AND OPTIMUM DURATION

For any project if the direct and indirect costs vary with time as shown in Fig. 8.3, the total project cost versus time curve would have the shape as indicated in this figure. Such a curve will have a point A where the tangent drawn to the curve would be horizontal. At this point the total cost of the project will be minimum which is known as the *optimum cost* for the project. The time corresponding to this point is called the optimum duration for the project. In the process of reducing the project time efforts should be made to

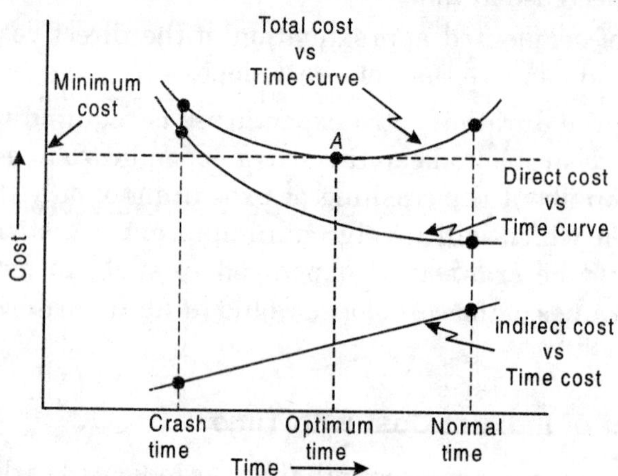

Fig. 8.3 *Optimum cost and optimum duration for a project.*

achieve optimum duration so that the project cost would be minimum (or optimum).This is further explained by the following example.

Consider a project having duration 21 days and the normal direct cost Rs. 37,500. The crash duration is 15 days and the associated direct crash cost Rs. 50,100. It is assumed that the direct cost versus time curve for the

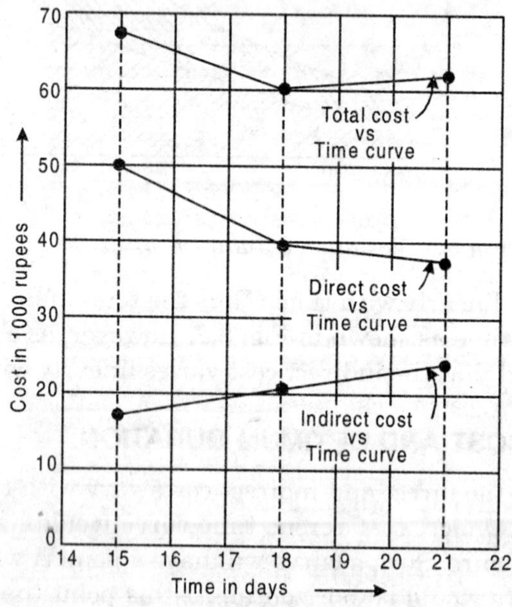

Fig. 8.4 *Cost versus time curves with linear variations for determining optimum cost and optimum time for a project.*

project consists of two straight lines as shown in Fig. 8.4 which indicates that corresponding to a duration of 18 days the direct cost is Rs. 39,900. Thus in this case there would be two cost slopes the values of which may be calculated as indicated below.

(i) If the duration of the project is reduced from 21 days to 18 days the direct cost would increase from Rs. 37,500 to Rs. 39,900. Hence the cost slope $\left(\frac{39{,}900-37{,}500}{21-18}\right)$ or Rs. 800 per day, i.e., the direct cost would increase at the rate of Rs. 800 per day.

(ii) If the duration of the project is reduced from 18 days to 15 days the direct cost would increase from Rs. 39,900 to Rs. 50,100. Hence the cost slope is equal to $\left(\frac{50{,}100-39{,}900}{21-18}\right)$ or Rs. 3,400 per day, i.e., the direct cost would increase at the rate of Rs. 3,400 per day.

The indirect cost is taken as Rs. 1,150 per day.

For the normal duration of 21 days, the sum of the direct and indirect costs is 37,500 + (1150 × 21) = Rs. 61,650.

During the reduction in the project time from 21 days to 18 days the direct cost increases at the rate of Rs. 800 per day and the indirect cost decreases at the rate of Rs. 1,150 per day. Hence the net decrease is (1150 – 800) = Rs. 350 per day. The total cost for completion of the project in 18 days is

$$61{,}650 - (3 \times 350) = \text{Rs. } 60{,}600$$

During the subsequent reduction in the project time from 18 days to 15 days the direct cost increases at the rate of Rs. 3,400 per day and the indirect cost decreases at the same rate as before, i.e., Rs. 1,150 per day. Hence the net increase is (3,400 – 1,150) = Rs. 2,250 per day. The total cost for completion of the project in 15 days is 60,600 + (3 × 2,250) = Rs. 67,350.

Therefore the optimum project time is 18 days and the optimum project cost is Rs. 60,600.

8.5 CONTRACTING THE NETWORK FOR OPTIMIZATION OF PROJECT COST AND PROJECT DURATION

As indicated in the earlier chapters the critical path in a project network represents the longest duration for the project The critical path in a network is usually based on the normal durations of the activities. As such in order to reduce the duration of a project and consequently contract the network it would be necessary to crash or expedite the critical activities (i.e., the activities along the critical path). However, it would be essential to know how much reduction in the project duration would be achieved and what would be the additional cost by such crashing or expediting of activities. In addition to critical activities the non-critical activities may also be crashed or expedited but the additional cost would be very high without any additional advantage over and above the one obtained by crashing only the critical activities. Moreover, the non-critical activities need not be crashed because their crashing is not going to reduce the project duration. In this section a systematic method of contracting a given network by crashing or expediting the activities and the consequent change in the project cost are discussed.

Figure 8.5 shows the network for a particular project which consists of 9 activities. The number indicated along the activity arrows are the normal durations in days. Table 8.1 lists the activities, their normal durations (in days) and their corresponding costs (in rupees), the crash durations (in days) and their corresponding costs (in rupees). The cost versus time curves are

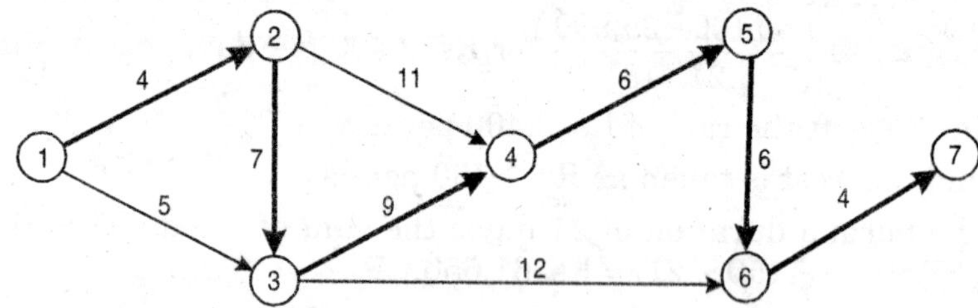

Fig. 8.5 *A project network.*

assumed to be straight lines so that for each activity the cost slope is constant. There cost slopes are also indicated in this table. The indirect costs work out to Rs. 1,600 per day.

TABLE 8.1 *Values of normal and crash times and costs and cost slopes for the activities shown in Fig. 8.5*

Activity	*Normal*		*Crash*		*Cost slope*		
	Time (days)	*Cost (Rs.)*	*Time (days)*	*Cost (Rs.)*	ΔT	ΔC	$(\Delta C/\Delta T)$
1–2	4	3,500	3	4,000	1	500	500
1–3	5	14,500	3	16,200	2	1,700	850
2–3	7	22,000	5	24,000	2	2,000	1000
2–4	11	11,200	7	16,000	4	4,800	1200
3–4	9	4,000	5	9,600	4	5,600	1400
3–6	12	16,000	9	18,100	3	2,100	700
4–5	6	4,500	4	6,100	2	1,600	800
5–6	6	12,000	4	14,400	2	2,400	1200
6–7	4	5,000	3	8,600	1	3,600	3600
		92,700		1,17,000			

The critical path is found to be 1–2–3–4–5–6–7 which is shown in Fig. 8.5 from which the normal duration for the project is found to be 36 days. For the sake of convenience a time-scaled version of the project network is drawn as shown in Fig. 8.6 in which the critical path is shown by a straight (thick) line.

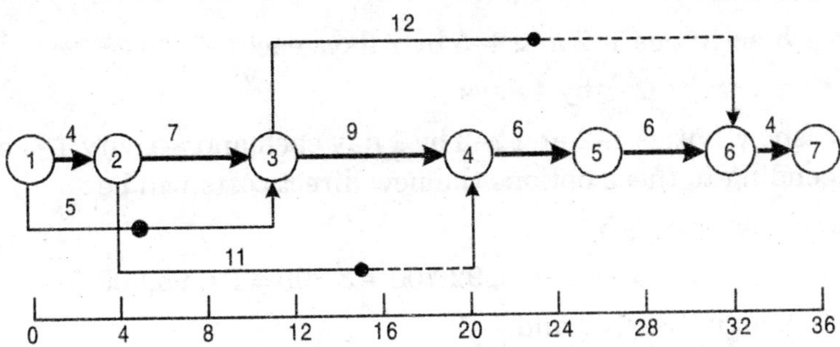

Fig. 8.6 *Time-scaled version of the project network of Fig. 8.5*

The overall normal duration for the project is 36 days and the total direct cost Rs. 92,700. According to the crash time given in Table 8.1 the critical path still appears to be 1–2–3–4–5–6–7 and the crash duration is 24 days. Hence the project may take anywhere from 24 to 36 days depending on the additional expenditure that may be incurred. If it is decided to complete the project in 24 days then as shown in the table the direct cost would be Rs. 1,17,000. In arriving at this result every activity in the project would be required to be expedited. However, as indicated earlier the non-critical activities of the project need not be expedited in order to reduce the project duration. Expediting the non-critical activities at extra cost would be a mere waste unless these activities become critical activities during the process of reduction in the project duration.

In general there are two reasons for reducing the project duration as indicated below:

(i) To complete the project before a certain target date. For this some of the activities may be crashed or expedited and the extra cost involved to complete the project in the desired shorter duration is determined. In this case the indirect cost is not taken into account but the analysis is carried out on the basis of the direct cost only.

(ii) To reduce the overall cost of the project. This would be possible if the indirect cost per day is greater than some of the cost slopes. In this case by crashing or expediting some of the activities the project duration is reduced thereby decreasing the total indirect cost. The optimum project duration as well as the optimum project cost are thus determined.

Both the above noted cases of project cost analysis are explained by means of an example.

(i) Consider the project network shown in Fig. 8.5. The normal duration of the project is 36 days and the total direct cost of the project is Rs. 92,700. If it is desired that the project be completed in 32 days, then the various options may be as follows :

(a) crash activity 4–5 by 4 days.

(b) crash activities 1–2 and 4–5 by 2 days each.

(c) crash activity 2–3 by 4 days.

(d) crash activities 1–2 and 2–3 by 1 day each and activity 4–5 by 2 days.

Corresponding to these options the new direct costs will be :

(a) crash activity 4–5 :

$$= 92{,}700 + 3{,}200 = \text{Rs. } 95{,}900$$

(b) crash activities 1–2 and 4–5 :

$$= 92{,}700 + 1{,}000 + 1{,}600 = \text{Rs. } 95{,}300$$

(c) crash activities 2–3 :

$$= 92{,}700 + 4{,}000 = \text{Rs. } 96{,}700$$

(d) crash activities 1–2, 2–3 and 4–5 :

$$= 92{,}700 + 500 + 1{,}000 + 1{,}600 = \text{Rs. } 95{,}800$$

Hence the best solution would be to crash activities 1–2 and 4–5 by 2 days each. In this case since the indirect cost is not considered, the project cost is a minimum when the activities are completed in their normal durations, and increases as the number of activities crashed increases.

(ii) In this case the first step is to indentify those activities along the critical path whose cost slopes are less than the indirect cost per day. Thus again considering the project network shown in Fig. 8.5, the cost slopes of activities 1–2, 2–3, 3–4, 4–5 and 5–6 are less than the indirect cost per day. These activities are taken in the order of increasing cost slopes. Activity 1–2 has a cost slope of Rs. 500 per day. This activity can be crashed or expedited by 1 day at the cost of Rs. 500. The next activity in the order is 4–5, which can be crashed or expedited by 2 days at the cost of Rs. 1,600. Next activity 2–3 is taken whose cost slope is Rs. 1,000 per day. This activity can be crashed or expedited by 2 days at the cost of Rs. 2,000. A new time-scaled version of the modified network may be drawn (see Fig. 8.7) to see whether during these time contraction process a new critical path has come-up or a sub-critical path established.

The next activity in the order of increasing cost slope is 5–6 which can be crashed or expedited by 2 days at the cost of Rs. 2 400. The next activity in the order is 3–4. From Table 8.1 it may be seen that activity 3–4 can be crashed or expedited by 4 days, but a look at the new time-scaled version

(Fig. 8.7) shows that activity 2–4 has a slack of only 3 days. Hence activity 3–4 cannot be crashed or expedited by more than 3 days without affecting activity 2–4. Thus activity 3–4 may be crashed or expedited by 3 days at the cost of Rs. 4,200. By this a new sub-critical path has been established. The

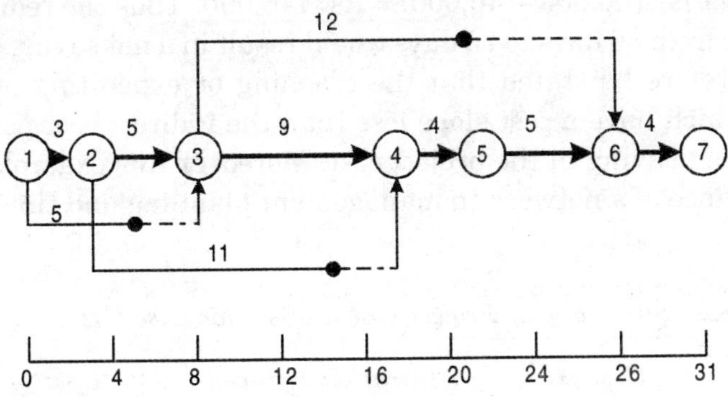

Fig. 8.7 *New time-scaled version of the modified network.*

new time-scaled version of the modified network will be as shown in Fig. 8.8 which shows that the project duration has been reduced to 26 days.

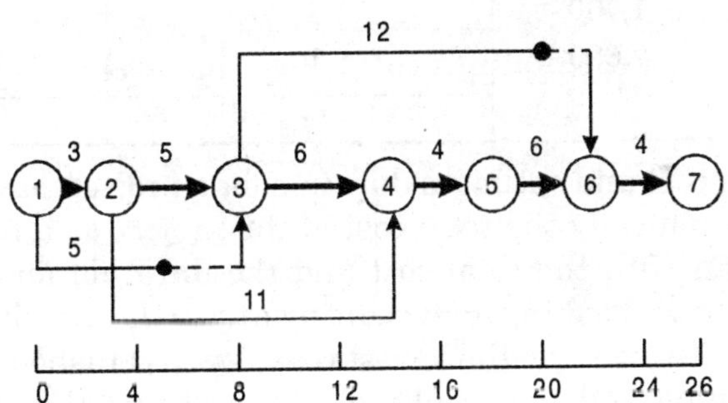

Fig. 8.8 *New time-scaled version of the modified network.*

Table 8.1 shows that activity 3–4 can be further crashed or expedited by 1 day. But this cannot be achieved without contracting activity 2–4. Therefore the cost slope must include both the cost slope of activity 2–4 and of 3–4. The combined cost slope is (1,200 + 1,400) = 2,600. The project duration would then be reduced to (26–1) = 25 days. A summary of what has been achieved so far by the project cost analysis for this case is given in Table 8.2.

From Table 8.2 it is seen that a total reduction of 11 days in the project duration has been achieved at an additional direct cost of Rs. 13,300, but for this period the indirect cost of Rs. 1,600 per day resulting in Rs. 17,600 has been saved. Further for the normal project time of 36 days the direct cost is

Rs. 92,700, the indirect cost is (1600 × 36) = Rs. 57,600, and hence the total cost of the project is (92,700 + 57,600) = Rs. 150,300. Similarly for the crashed or reduced project time of 25 days the direct cost is (92,700 +13,300) = Rs. 106,000, the indirect cost is (1600 ×25) = Rs. 40,000, and hence the total cost of the project is (106,000 + 40,000) = Rs. 146,000. Thus the reduction in the project time from 36 days to 25 days would result in a net saving of Rs. 4,300. It may therefore be stated that the crashing or expediting of only those activities which have a cost slope less than the indirect cost per day would result in a net saving in the project cost. Moreover this example illustrates the significance of a network in management planning and time scheduling of a project.

TABLE 8.2 *Summary of Project cost analsis for case (II)*

Activity	*Cost slope (Rs. per day)*	*Duration reduced by (days)*	*Cost of contraction (Rs.)*
1–2	500	1	500
4–5	800	2	1,600
2–3	1,000	2	2,000
5–6	1,200	2	2,400
3–4	1,400	3	4,200
3–4, 2–4	2,600	1	2,600
		11	13,300

The optimum cost and optimum duration for a project may be obtained by representing graphically the total cost of the project as a function of time. For this to begin with the total cost and the duration for the project are determined without crashing or expediting any of the activities. Next one of the critical activities having the lowest cost slope is crashed or expedited by a suitable duration and the resulting total cost and the duration for the project are determined. In the next step the two critical activities having respectively the lowest and the next higher cost slopes are crashed or expedited by suitable durations and the resulting total cost and the duration for the project are determined. The same process is repeated by crashing or expediting three, four, five, etc., critical activities taken in the ascending order of their cost slopes and the resulting total cost and the duration for the project are determined for each case. These values of the total cost of the project are plotted against the corresponding values of the duration and the plotted points are joined by a smooth curve. The same example is again considered to illustrate the process of cost optimization.

Table 8.3 shows the various computations carried out to obtain the total project cost and the corresponding project duration. Figure 8.9 shows the plot of total project cost versus duration curve in respect of the values given in Table 8.3. The optimum project cost is found to be Rs. 145,000, and the optimum project duration is 26 days.

TABLE 8.3 *Comutations for total Project cost versus project duration curve*

Activity crashed	*Days saved*	*Project duration (days)*	*Direct project cost (Rs.)*	*Indirect cost (Rs.)*	*Total project cost (Rs.)*
None	0	36	92,700	57,600	1,50,300
1–2	1	35	93,200	56,000	1,49,200
4–5	2	33	94,800	52,800	1,47,600
2–3	2	31	96,800	49,600	1,46,400
5–6	2	29	99,200	46,400	1,45,600
3–4	3	26	1,03,400	41,600	1,45,000
3–4, 2–4	1	25	1,06,000	40,000	1,46,000
6–7	1	24	1,09,600	38,400	1,48,000

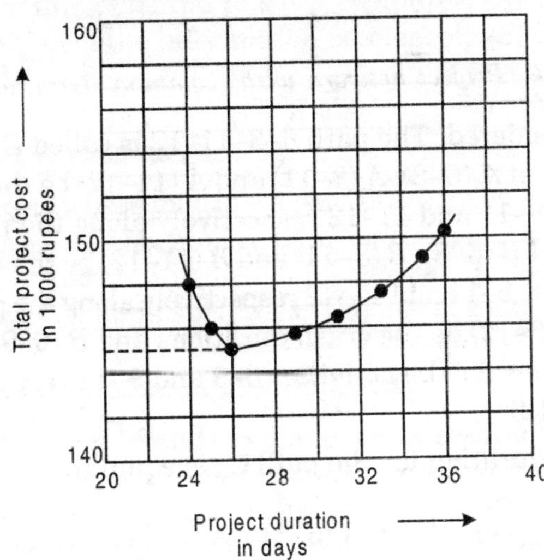

Fig. 8.9 *Total project cost v/s project duration curve.*

8.6 GRAPH REDUCTION THEOREM

In the analysis of large networks the problem would be very much simplified if the activities which do not contribute to the analysis could be identified and neglected. Such activities can be easily identified by applying a rule which is discussed in this section.

Consider a network shown in Fig. 8.10 from which it may be seen that the nodes 6 and 12 are interconnected through two paths viz., 6–8–11–12 and 6–9–12. These paths are called common terminal paths, since the two paths have common terminals or end-nodes 6 and 12. Similarly paths 9–12–14–15 and 9–10–13–15 are another pair of common terminal paths with the common end-nodes 9 and 15. One pair of common terminal paths, say, 6–8–11–12

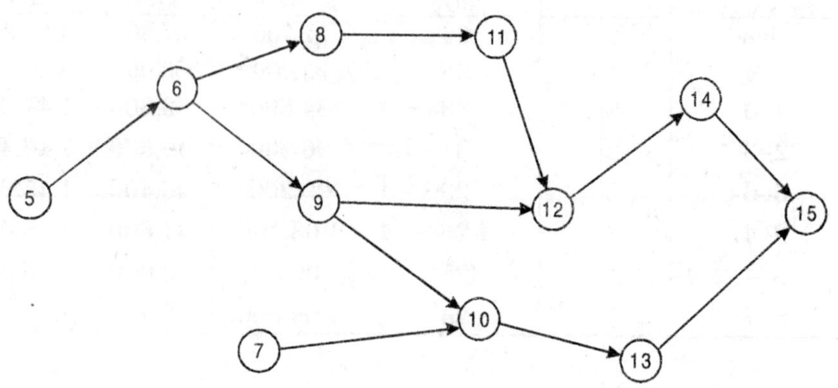

Fig. 8.10 *Project network with common terminal paths.*

and 6–9–12 is considered. The path 6–8–11–12 is called C_1 and the path 6–9–12 is called C_2. Let A (6–8), A (8–11) and A (11–12) be the crash durations for activities 6–8, 8–11 and 11–12 respectively along the path C_t (i.e., 6–8–11– 12). Further let B (6–8), B (8–11) and B (11–12) be the normal durations for the activities 6–8, 8–11 and 11–12 respectively along the path C_1. Similarly let A (6–9) and A (9–12) be the crash durations and B (6–9) and B (9–12) be the normal durations for the activities 6–9 and 9–12 respectively along the path C_2 (i.e., 6–9–12).

The total crash duration for the path C_x is equal to

$$\sum_{C_1} A(i-j) = A\,(6\text{–}8) + A\,(8\text{–}11) + A\,(11\text{–}12)$$

$$= (\lambda_A)_{C_1}$$

Similarly the total normal duration for the path C_1 is equal to

$$\sum_{C_1} B(i-j) = B\,(6\text{–}8) + B\,(8\text{–}11) + B\,(11\text{–}12)$$

$$= (\lambda_B)_{C_1}$$

Also the total crash duration for the path C_2 is equal to

$$\sum_{C_1} A(i-j) = A\ (6\text{–}9) + A\ (9\text{–}12)$$

$$= (\lambda_A)_{C_2}$$

and the total normal duration for the path C_2 is equal to

$$\sum_{C_2} B(i-j) = B\ (6\text{–}9) + B\ (9\text{–}12)$$

$$= (\lambda_B)_{C_2}$$

If it is assumed that the crash duration for the path C_2 is greater than or equal to the normal duration for the path C_1, i.e.,

$$(\lambda_A)_{C_2} \geq (\lambda_B)_{C_1}$$

Therefore,

$$(\lambda_B)_{C_2} \geq (\lambda_B)_{C_1}$$

since the normal duration for path C_2 will always be greater than or equal* to the crash duration for same path. Thus in the process of reducing the duration from node 6 to node 12, the activities along the path C_1 do not contribute to the analysis because even the crash duration for the path C_2 is greater than (or at the most equal to) the normal duration for the path C_1. Under such conditions if the path C_2 is made a part of the critical path, then the activities of the path C_1 can be neglected. It may, however, be noted that if the activities such as those occurring in path C_1 are also a part of other common terminal paths then these activities can be neglected only when they satisfy the above condition for all the common terminal paths of which they are a part.

8.7 PERT/COST

In a PERT/Cost system the estimated cost of each activity is introduced in the network in adition to the estimated time as ordinarily done in PERT/Time system. Thus PERT/Cost system is an extension of the basic PERT/Time system for the management of complex research and development projects. This is necessary because cost and time are closely interrelated in any network operation and cannot be considered independently. The basic objectives of PERT/Cost system are (i) to achieve a more realistic estimate of

* The normal duration and the crash duration will be equal when no activity in that path can be crashed.

the total cost of a project; and (ii) to have a better control against the original estimate after the project has begun.

The PERT/Cost system was developed in 1962 by the Department of Defence (DOD) U.S. Government and NASA. In this system both schedule and cost are available on a common network which permits better control on the progress as well as the cost of the project.

8.8 AGGREGATE COST ANALYSIS (OR AGGREGATE PLANNING) AND COST CONTROL

Normally during the execution of any project the management periodically compares the actual cost of the project with the estimated cost at different stages of completion of the project. Such a comparison in respect of the actual and the estimated costs of the project as a whole is known as aggregate cost analysis or aggregate planning, which is carried out to exercise cost control. However, besides the aggregate cost analysis the cost analysis of the individual activities of the project is also essential to exercise a better cost control on the project. This is explained by the following example.

Let there be six activities involved in a certain project with their estimated costs as indicated in Table 8.4. The status of the project is reviewed on 31st July. At the time of reviewing it is found that the activities 1 and 2 are completed and the remaining four activities are in progress. The actual costs for these activities at the time of review are also given in Table 8.4. According to the figures given the estimated cost of the project is Rs. 6,60,000 and the actual cost upto the date of review is Rs. 6,20,000. Thus as per the aggregate cost analysis upto the date of review there is under spending of Rs. 40,000 and hence the project appears to be under good cost control. However, this type of cost analysis does not give a true picture of the situation. This is so because the cost analysis of the individual activities shows that the actual cost of activity 1 has been Rs. 20,000 more than its estimated cost and the actual cost of activity 2 has been just the double of the estimated cost. The activities 3, 4 and 5 have consumed less than what was allotted to them individually and activity 6 has consumed the allotted amount The under-run in the three activities 3, 4 and 5 may be due to their late starting or the delay in their progress. Thus even if these activities were to consume as much as was originally estimated (which may in all probability be not true and the actual cost may be much higher when the activities are completed), the six activities would consume Rs. 1,20,000 more than their estimated cost. Further the actual cost may be higher than this because the activities 3, 4 and 5 are being delayed and if the time schedule is to be maintained they may have to be executed on a crash basis.

It is thus evident that instead of an aggregate cost analysis, the cost analysis of the individual activities in respect of their costs and time spans is more desirable for better cost control on a project.

TABLE 8.4 *Project status as on July 31st*

Activity	*Estimated cost (Rs.)*	*Actual (Rs.)*	*Over-run (Rs.)*	*Under-run (Rs.)*
1	1,50,000	1,70,000	20,000	—
2	1,00,000	2,00,000	1,00,000	—
3	2,00,000	1,00,000	—	1,00,000
4	1,00,000	50,000	—	50,000
5	60,000	50,000	—	10,000
6	50,000	50,000	—	—
Total	6,60,000	6,20,000	+1,20,000	–1,60,000

Activity 1 completed on May 31st
Activity 2 completed on July 31st

ILLUSTRATIVE EXAMPLES

Example 8.1 *The following information is available about the various activities of a network.*

Activity	*Normal duration in weeks*	*Normal cost in rupees*	*Crash duration in weeks*	*Crash cost in rupees*
1–2	4	*4,000*	3	*7,000*
1–3	8	*5,000*	7	*8,000*
2–3	5	*8,000*	3	*10,000*

Project overhead costs are at Rs. 2,000 per week.

Determine (i) direct cost-duration relationship; (ii) total cost-duration relationship.

Also draw the least cost network.

Solution The network for the given data of the various activities is shown in Fig. Ex. 8.1 (a). The critical path is found to be 1–2–3 which is shown by a thick line from which the normal duration for the project is found to be 9 weeks.

A time-scaled version of the network is drawn as shown in Fig. Ex. 8.1 (b) in which the critical path is shown by a straight (thick) line.

Table (A) lists the activities, their normal and crash durations and costs and their cost slopes.

TABLE (A) *For Example 8.1*

Activity	*Normal*		*Crash*		*Cost slope*		
	Duration (weeks)	*Cost (Rs.)*	*Duration (weeks)*	*Cost (Rs.)*	ΔT	ΔC	$(\Delta C/\Delta T)$
1–2	4	4,000	3	7,000	1	3,000	3,000
1–3	8	5,000	7	8,000	1	3,000	3,000
2–3	5	8,000	3	10,000	2	2,000	1,000
		17,000		25,000			

The critical activity 2–3 has the lowest cost slope of Rs. 1,000 per week. From Table (A) it may be seen that activity 2–3 may be crashed by 2 weeks, but a look at the time-scaled version (Fig. Ex. 8.1b) shows that activity 1–3 has

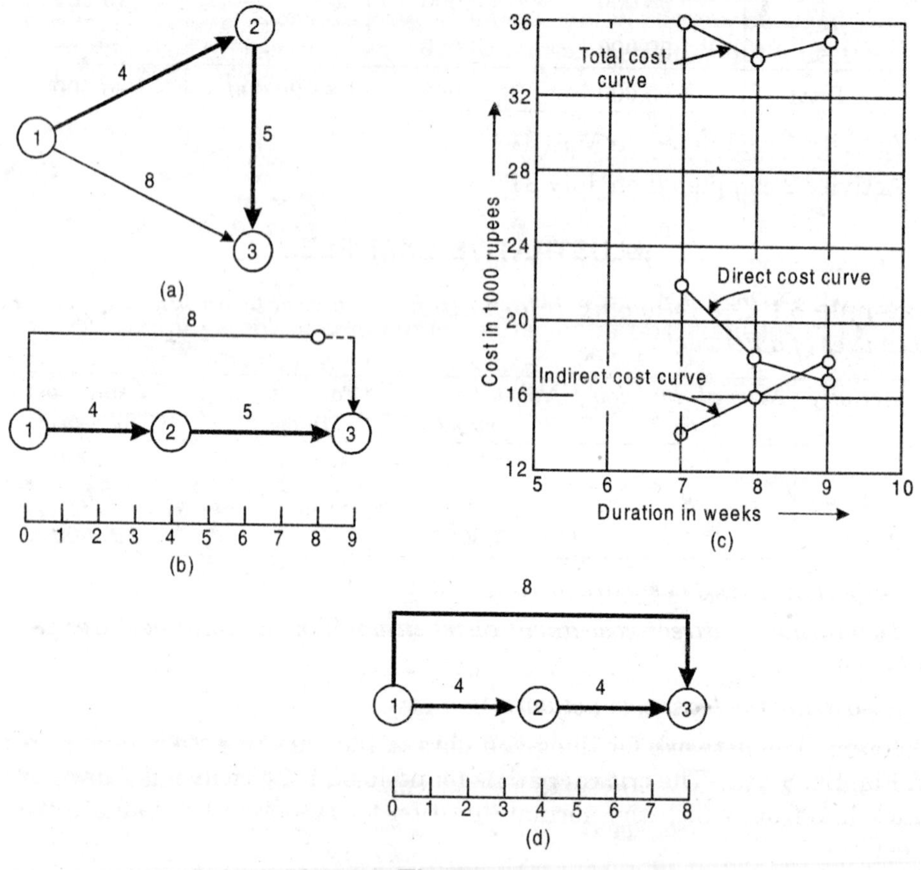

Fig. Ex. 8.1

a slack of only 1 week and hence activity 2–3 cannot be crashed by more than 1 week without affecting activity 1–3. Thus if activity 2–3 is crashed by 1 week the extra cost will be = (1 × 1,000) = Rs. 1,000.

The direct cost of the project will then be = (17,000 + 1,000) = Rs. 18,000 and the duration of the project will be = (9–1) = 8 days.

With the crashing of activity 2–3 by 1 week, activity 1–3 would also become critical.

Activity 2–3 has still 1 week of crashing left, but it cannot be crashed unless activity 1–3 is also crashed by 1 week. Thus both the activities 2–3 and 1–3 are crashed simultaneously by 1 week for which the combined cost slope would be (1,000 + 3,000) = Rs. 4,000 per week. The extra cost for crashing activities 2–3 and 1–3 simultaneously by 1 week = (1×4,000) = Rs. 4,000.

The direct cost of the project will then be = (18,000 + 4,000) = Rs. 22,000 and the project duration will be = (8–1) = 7 weeks.

Activity 1–2 may also be crashed by 1 week but since its cost slope is more than the rate of overhead costs, its crashing will result in increasing the total cost of the project and hence activity 1–2 is not crashed.

The total cost of the project for any duration is obtained by adding the overhead costs to the corresponding direct costs. Table (B) shows the total project cost and the corresponding project duration.

TABLE (B) *For Example 8.1*

Activity crashed	*Weeks saved*	*Project duration (weeks)*	*Extra cost due to crashing (Rs.)*	*Direct project cost (Rs.)*	*Overhead cost (Rs.)*	*Total project cost*
None	0	9	–	17,000	18,000	35,000
2–3	1	8	1,000	18,000	16,000	34,000
2–3, 1–3	1	7	4,000	22,000	14,000	36,000

Figure Ex. 8.1(c) shows the direct cost-duration curve and the total cost-duration curve. From Table (B) as well as from Fig. Ex. 8.1(c) it is evident that the optimum (or minimum) cost of the project is Rs. 34,000 and the corresponding optimum duration is 8 weeks.

The time-scaled version of the least cost network is shown in Fig. Ex. 8.1 (d).

Example 8.2 *The following information applies to a particular project:*

Event 0 is the initial event

Event 1 is preceded by event 0

Event 3 is preceded by event 1

Event 4 is preceded by event 1

Event 2 is preceded by event 1

Event 3 is preceded by events 2 and 1

Event 4 is preceded by events 3 and 1

Event 5 is preceded by event 4

The values of the expected times, crash times, normal costs and crash costs for the various activities in the project are as follows:

Activity	*0–1*	*1–3*	*1–2*	*2–3*	*1–4*	*3–4*	*4–5*
Expected time (days)	*3*	*16*	*6*	*8*	*10*	*5*	*3*
Crash time (days)	*2*	*11*	*4*	*6*	*6*	*3*	
Normal cost (Rs.)	*5,000*	*10,000*	*8,000*	*12,000*	*15,000*	*9,000*	*6,000*
Crash cost (Rs.)	*5,500*	*12,000*	*9,500*	*16,000*	*19,000*	*12,000*	*7,800*

(i) Draw the arrow diagram for the project.

(ii) If the project overhead costs are Rs. 1,700 per day find the optimum cost and optimum duration for the project. Also draw the least cost network.

Solution The arrow diagram (or network diagram) for the project is as shown in the Fig. Ex. 8.2 (a).

The critical path is found to be 0–1–3–4–5 which is shown in Fig. Ex. 8.2 (a) by a thick line form which the normal duration for the project is found to be 27 days.

A time-scaled version of the project network is drawn as shown in Fig. Ex. 8.2 (b) in which the critical path is shown by a straight (thick) line.

Table (A) lists the activities, their expected or normal times (in days) and their corresponding costs (in rupees), the crash times (in days) and their corresponding costs (in rupees). The cost versus time curves are assumed to be straight lines so that for each activity the cost slope is constant. These cost slopes are also indicated in this table.

TABLE (A) *For Example 8.2*

Activity	*Normal*		*Crash*		*Cost slope*		
	Time (days)	*Cost (Rs.)*	*Time (days)*	*Cost (Rs.)*	ΔT	ΔC	$(\Delta C/\Delta T)$
0–1	3	5,000	2	5,500	1	500	500
1–3	16	10,000	11	12,000	5	2,000	400
1–2	6	8,000	4	9,500	2	1,500	750
2–3	8	12,000	6	16,000	2	4,000	2,000
1–4	10	15,000	6	19,000	4	4,000	1,000
3–4	5	9,000	3	12,000	2	3,000	1,500
4–5	3	6,000	2	7,800	1	1,800	1,800
		65,000		81,800			

The overall normal duration for the project is 27 days and the total direct cost Rs. 65,000. According to the crash time given in Table A the critical path still appears to be 0–1–3–4–5 and the crash duration is 18 days. Hence the project may take anywhere from 18 to 27 days depending on the additional expenditure that may be incurred.

Out of the various critical activities, activity 1–3 has the lowest cost slope of Rs. 400 per day. From Table (A) it may be seen that activity 1–3 can be crashed by 5 days, but a look at the time-scaled version of the network (Fig. Ex. 8.2 (b) shows that activity 2–3 has a slack of only 2 days and hence activity 1–3

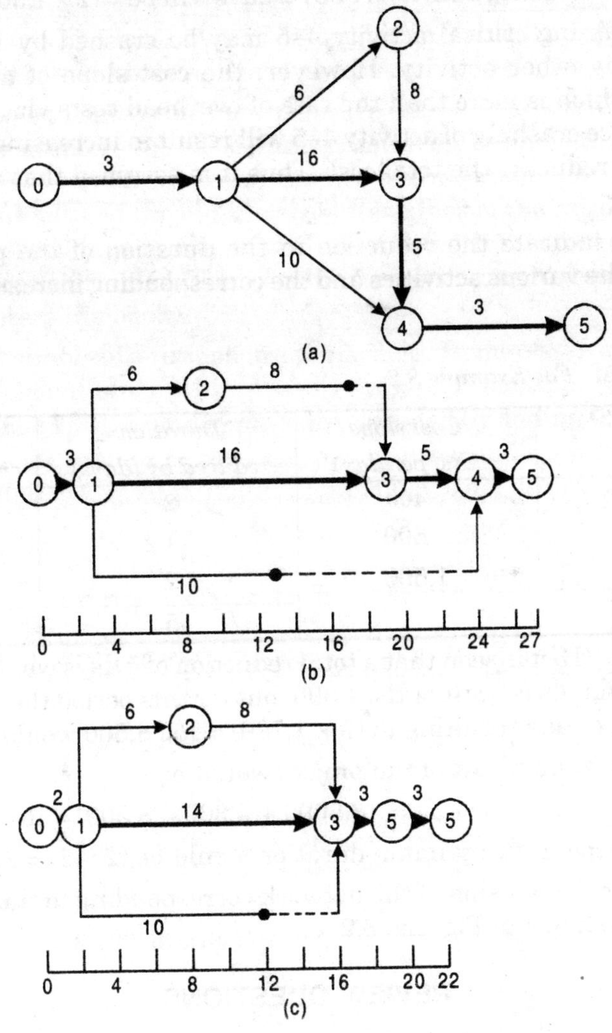

Fig. Ex. 8.2

cannot be crashed by more than 2 days without affecting activity 2–3. Moreover the cost slope of activity 2–3 is more than the rate of overhead costs and hence no advantage would be derived in crashing activity 2–3.

Thus if activity 1–3 is crashed by 2 days, the extra cost will be = (2 × 400) = Rs. 800.

The next critical activity in the order of increasing cost slope is activity 0–1, which can be crashed by 1 day without affecting any other activity. The extra cost for crashing activity 0–1 by 1 day will be = (1 × 500) = Rs. 500.

The next critical activity in the order of increasing cost slope is activity 3–4 which can be crashed by 2 days without affecting any other activity. The extra cost for crashing activity 3–4 by 2 days will be = (2 × 1,500) = Rs. 3,000.

The remaining critical activity 4–5 may be crashed by 1 day without affecting any other activity. However, the cost slope of activity 4–5 is Rs. 1,800, which is more than the rate of overhead costs viz., Rs. 1,700 per day and hence crashing of activity 4–5 will result in increasing the total cost rather than reducing the total cost. Thus it is assumed that activity 4–5 is not crashed.

Table (B) indicate the reduction in the duration of the project due to crashing of the various activities and the corresponding increase in the direct cost.

TABLE (B) *For Example 8.2*

Activity	*Cost slope (Rs. per day)*	*Duration reduced by (days)*	*Cost of crashing (Rs.)*
1–3	400	2	800
0–1	500	1	500
3–4	1,500	2	3,000
		5	4,300

From Table (B) it is seen that a total reduction of 5 days would be achieved at an additional direct cost of Rs. 4,300, but for this period the overhead cost of Rs. 1,700 per day resulting in (5 × 1,700) = Rs. 8,500 would be saved.

Thus the optimum cost of the project would be

= (6,5000 + 4,300 – 8,500) = Rs. 60,800

and the corresponding optimum duration would be (27–5) = 22 days.

The time-scaled version of the network corresponding to this least cost to the project is shown in Fig. Ex. 8.2 (c).

REVIEW QUESTIONS

8.1. Define the terms 'direct cost' and 'indirect cost'.

8.2. Define the terms 'normal cost' and 'crash cost'; 'normal time' and 'crash time'.

8.3. Define the terms 'overheads'and 'outage loss'.

8.4. What do you understand by 'cost slope'? How is it determined?

8.5. What do you understand by optimum cost and optimum duration? Draw a typical cost—duration curve and show on it optimum cost and optimum duration.

8.6. Write a brief note on optimization of project cost and project duration. Support your answer by an example.

8.7. Explain 'Graph reduction theorem'.

8.8. The following data pertains to a project network.

Activity	*Normal duration (weeks)*	*Normal cost (Rs.)*	*Crash duration (weeks)*	*Crash cost (Rs.)*
1–2	4	8,000	3	15,500
1–3	8	5,000	5	9,500
2–3	6	7,000	4	9,000
2–4	9	9,000	7	16,000
3–4	5	6,000	3	12,000

The indirect cost of the project is Rs. 3,000 per week.

Determine the optimum cost and the optimum duration of the project. Also draw the least cost network.

8.9. The following table gives the information about various activities of a project network.

Activity	*Normal duration (days)*	*Normal cost (Rs.)*	*Crash duration (days)*	*Crash cost (Rs.)*
1–2	9	8,000	7	10,000
1–3	5	5,000	3	8,000
2–3	7	7,000	5	8,600
2–4	8	6,000	6	7,000
3–4	6	9,000	4	11,400

The overhead costs are Rs. 1,300 per day. Determine (a) direct cost-duration relationship; (b) total cost-duration relationship and the corresponding least cost network.

8.10. Write a brief note on PERT/Cost.

8.11. What do you understand by aggregate cost analysis and cost control? Explain why instead of aggregate cost analysis, cost analysis of individual activities is more essential?

9
Chapter

Resource Allocation and Multi Project Scheduling

9.1 INTRODUCTION

For completion of projects in time and within the estimated cost proper allocation and utilisation of resources such as manpower, money, materials and machinery are essential. Unless resources are made available at right time and in right quantity work cannot proceed. In the network analysis for PERT/CPM, there is implicit assumption that the resources required to perform activities are available in unlimited supply, or at least sufficient resources are available for each activity to be scheduled sometime between its earliest and latest start dates. In other words it is assumed that the activities will not be delayed beyond their estimated duration for the reasons of resources limitations. However, in actual practice the assumption of unlimited resources may be justified only in some cases and in most cases the resources are limited. When the resources are limited and the demands are made for the same type of resource by several activities at the same time, then it would be essential to adopt a systematic method for the allocation of resources. For proper management of resources it is essential to assess the requirement of various resources and also to know the times at which they are needed on various activities. Further the various activities of a project should be scheduled in such a way that the demand for various resources is more or less uniform for the entire duration of the project. Large fluctuations in the demand of the resources may cause problems in the execution of the project. In the following sections the various aspects of allocation and scheduling of resources for various activities of a project are presented.

9.2 PROJECT RESOURCES

The various kinds of resources required to be used for the implementation of a project are indicated in Chapter 1 section 1.2 and the same are again listed below.

(a) Manpower resources

(b) Equipment resources or plant and machinery resources

(c) Financial resources

(d) Material resources

(e) Space resources

(f) Time resources

Out of the various resources the manpower is considered to be a more important resource. This is so because manpower resource is an active resource whereas the other resources are passive resources. Money, machines or materials do not do any work by themselves. These resources are used by men. As such it is generally believed that if men are utilized in proper way, then to a greater extent, other resources are also used in a proper way. On the other hand if utilization of men is not proper then other resources are also not very well utilized.

Further manpower is a non-pool type of resource because if men are not used in time then since mandays do not accumulate they are lost for ever and are required to be paid for. On the other hand the other resources such as money or materials are not lost when not used in time but they remain in balance for being used later.

Manpower may also be considered as an inflexible resource because it cannot be extended to any desired number. In several cases the required type of manpower may not be available in sufficient number, which may lead to considerable delay in project

Although manpower resource is important but it does not mean that the other resources are to be neglected. In fact man cannot produce anything without the use of other resources. In the following sections for the sake of convenience the entire discussion regarding the allocation of resources has been illustrated by using manpower resource. The allocation of other resources may, however, be treated in exactly the same manner.

9.3 OBJECTIVES OF RESOURCE ALLOCATION

The first objective of resource allocation is to reduce the frequent variation in resource requirement. In general these variations would cost in terms of effort, time and money. Moreover in the case of manpower resources such variations may lead to several problems. Due to labour unions being quite strong the laying off of men is very difficult, especially in Indian conditions where jobs are scarce. In respect of skilled manpower there is a risk that the laid off men may find job elsewhere, and may not come back when they are needed again. This may need fresh recruitment and training which means extra cost and time. The only alternative in such situations would be to retain them on pay roll and utilize their services in a best possible manner.

Secondly, when requirement of resources exceeds the supply, it would not be possible to satisfy the demand of all the activities simultaneously. When some of the activities are denied resources their start would be delayed. In other words the peak requirements of resources will have to be reduced until they no longer exceed the availability limits. In general this should be accomplished within the float range of activities without increasing the project duration. However, if it is inevitable to extend the project duration, it must be extended by the absolute minimum.

Thirdly, whenever there is a surplus resource it should be made available to other activities which need it most, may be within the same project or in other project. Such shifting of resources would be essential to maximise their utilization and also to avoid their under-utilization.

9.4 GENERAL APPROACH TO RESOURCE ALLOCATION-CRITERIA FOR RESOURCE ALLOCATION

The network with the calculated values of T_E's and T_L's and the critical path provides a base for resource allocation and scheduling. In the process of allocating the resources amongst the various activities certain priorities need to be decided. Obviously the activities with lesser float being relatively more critical are given a higher priority for allocation of resources. However, where two activities are equally critical the one which needs more of overall resources may be given higher priority. This is with a view to allocate resources to an activity which involves more quantum of work and in turn needs more of overall resources. With this guideline and network as a base the allocation of resources may be made by the method of trial and error. However, the trial and error method may provide solution for the problem of resource allocation and scheduling only for small projects. For large complex projects where resources of many kinds are required to be used it may not be possible to solve the problem only by trial and error method. In such cases instead of trial and error certain other methods such as MAP technique (Multiple Resource Allocation Procedure) and RAMPS (Resource Allocation and Multi Project Scheduling) may be used to solve the resource allocation and scheduling problem.

9.5 QUEUING INTERPRETATION OF THE RESOURCE ALLOCATION PROBLEM

The resource allocation problem may be considered similar to a queuing problem for exposition. The resources such as men, machines, materials, etc., constitute what is service station in the queuing theory terminology. Activities arrive in queues with certain discipline. The discipline is determined by the logical activity-dependency relationship on the basis of which the network is constructed. The float provides the play on the basis of which priorities are assigned for serving the activities. There may be time when the service stations, i.e., resources are idle and there is no activity in the queue. At other times there may be too many activities in the queue to be serviced simultaneously. As a consequence some of the activities might have to be delayed. If the delay is within the free float this would not affect the following activities. However, if free float is exceeded it would affect the following activities. As such at each time period it is to be ascertained if there are activities in the queue and resources idle to service these. If so, a particular service station can be booked for the duration of the, activity. If during any time period either no activity is queuing or all the stations are already booked, then one can simply skip to the next time period.

9.6 ASSESSMENT OF RESOURCES REQUIREMENTS

The requirement of resources for various activities of a project are usually assessed on the basis of early start time of each activity. Alternatively the latest start times of activities may also be used for assessing the requirement of resources. There may be several activities which may be required to be performed simultaneously and which may require the same type of resources. In such cases the total requirements of resources at any time to execute all

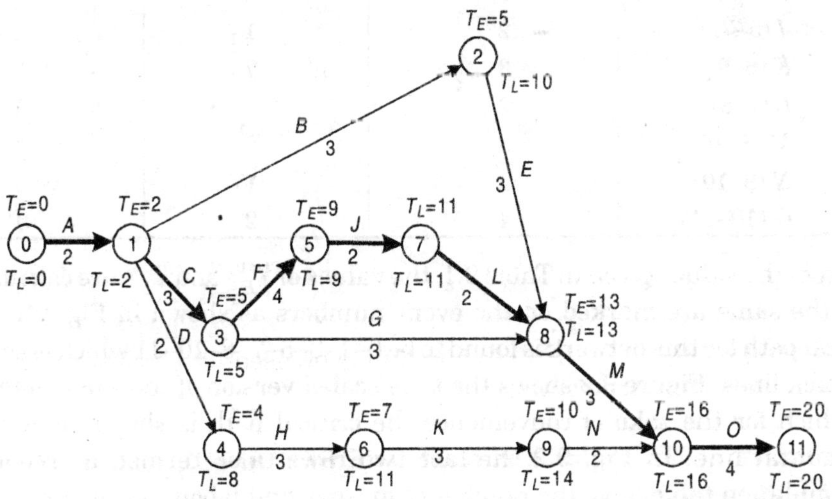

Fig. 9.1 *Project network used for the assessment of resources.*

these activities simultaneously may exceed the available resources. On the other hand at some other time during the execution of the same project there may be only a few activities which may require these resources. Hence there may not be a uniform requirement of a particular type of resource during the project time. The requirement of a particular type of resource for the various activities of a project may be represented by *resource usage profiles* or *histograms* or *loading charts* as indicated in the following example.

Consider a project network consisting of fourteen activities as shown in Fig. 9.1. The duration of each activity is marked under its activity arrow and also shown in Table 9.1. The resources required for these activities are identified in terms of say mason (marked by *M*) and labourers (marked by *L*) as the craftsman required for each activity as shown in Table 9.1. The problem is analyzed from the point of view of requirement of these resources.

TABLE 9.1 *Values of duration and resources required for activities of Fig 9.1*

Activity	*Duration (days)*	*Masons (M)*	*Labourers (L)*
A (0–1)	2	1	1
B (1–2)	3	2	2
C (1–3)	3	3	2
D (1–4)	2	2	2
E (2–8)	3	2	2
F (3–5)	4	3	2
G (3–8)	3	2	2
H (4–6)	3	2	2
J (5–7)	2	1	1
K (6–9)	3	2	2
L (7–8)	2	1	1
M (8–10)	3	2	1
N (9–10)	2	1	1
O (10–11)	4	2	1

From the values given in Table 9.1, the values of T_E's and T_L's are calculated and the same are marked on the event numbers as shown in Fig. 9.1. The critical path for this network is found to be 0–1–3–5–7–8–10–11 which is shown by thick lines. Figure 9.2 shows the time scaled version of the same network in which for the sake of convenience the critical path is shown by a thick horizontal line. In Fig. 9.2 the last two rows (also termed as resource accumulation table) give the number of masons and labourers required each day. It may be noted that the time-scaled version (also sometimes known as *activity-time schedule* or *squared network*) of Fig. 9.2 has been prepared by using the earliest start time for each event but as an alternative the same may also be prepared by using the latest start time for each event.

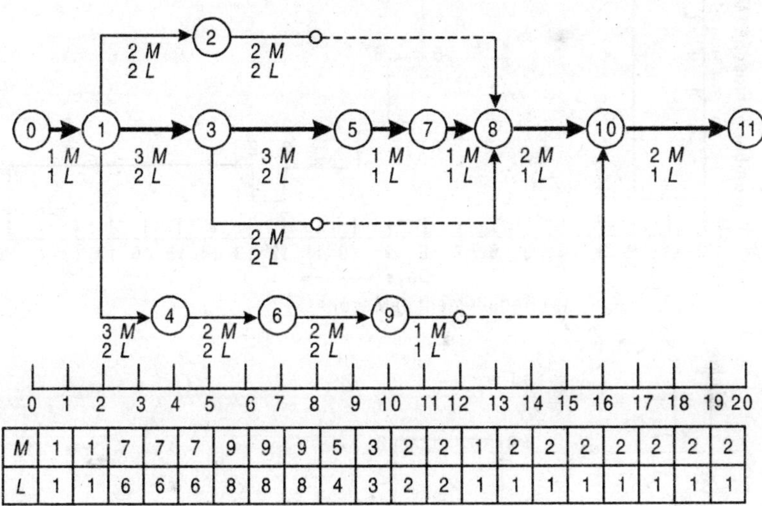

M	1	1	7	7	7	9	9	9	5	3	2	2	1	2	2	2	2	2	2	2
L	1	1	6	6	6	8	8	8	4	3	2	2	1	1	1	1	1	1	1	1

Fig. 9.2 *Time-scaled version of the network of Fig. 9.1.*

The resources viz., masons and labourers required every day are also shown in Figs. 9.3 (a) and (b) which are known as *resource usage profiles* or *histograms.* It may be noted from Figs. 9.3 (a) and (b) that the demand for masons and labourers is not uniform along the project duration. On 6th, 7th and 8th days the demand for masons is as high as 9, whereas from 14th day onwards it comes down to 2. Similarly on 6th, 7th and 8th days the demand for labourers is as high as 8 which from 13th day onwards comes down to 1. Thus if 9 masons and 8 labourers are employed for the entire project duration of 20 days, then during most of the days they will be idler. The problem may not be serious as long as the resources happen to be casual and can be employed on per day basis. However, when dealing with staff such as foreman, supervisor, etc., which have to be employed on a permanent or semi-permanent basis, it would be advisable to utilize the resources in a fairly uniform manner by rescheduling some of the activities. This can be achieved by the following two approaches:

1. Resource smoothing
2. Resource levelling

which are discussed in the next sections.

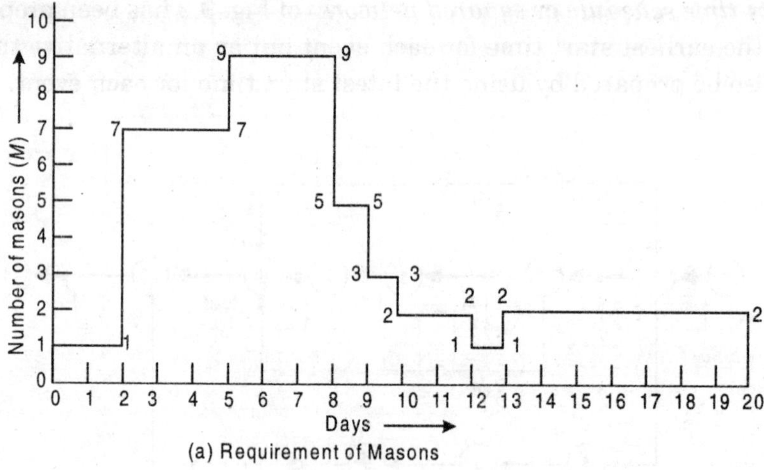

(a) Requirement of Masons

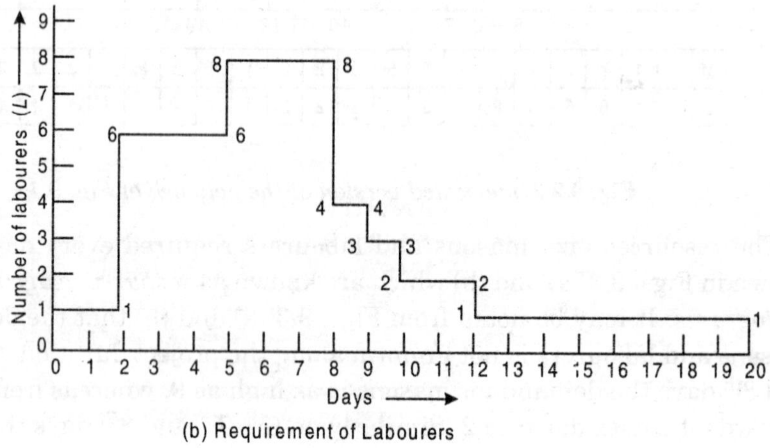

(b) Requirement of Labourers

Fig. 9.3 *Resource usage profiles in respect of resource accumulation table of Fig. 9.1.*

9.7 RESOURCE SMOOTHING

In resource smoothing the total project duration is not changed but the activities having floats are rescheduled so that a uniform demand for the resources is achieved. Thus in this case there is constraint on the project duration. There is, however, no constraint on the resources. The procedure is illustrated by considering the same project network shown in Fig. 9.1. The duration of the project in this case is 20 days. From the time-scaled version (Fig. 9.2) of this network it may be noted that activities 2–8, 3–8, 1–4, 4–6, 6–9 and 9–10 possess floats of different magnitudes. In the first instance activity 3–8 may be shifted so that it starts on the 11th day instead of on the 6th day. This would reduce the demand for masons from 9 to 7 on the 6th, 7th and 8th days so that the maximum demand for the masons on any day is now 7 and not 9. The corresponding demand for the labourers on these days would also be reduced from 8 to 6. The modified resource accumulation table and the time-scaled version of the project would be as shown in Fig. 9.4. For further smoothening of the resources activities 4–6, 6–9 and 9–10 may be delayed by their entire float of 4 days. The time-scaled

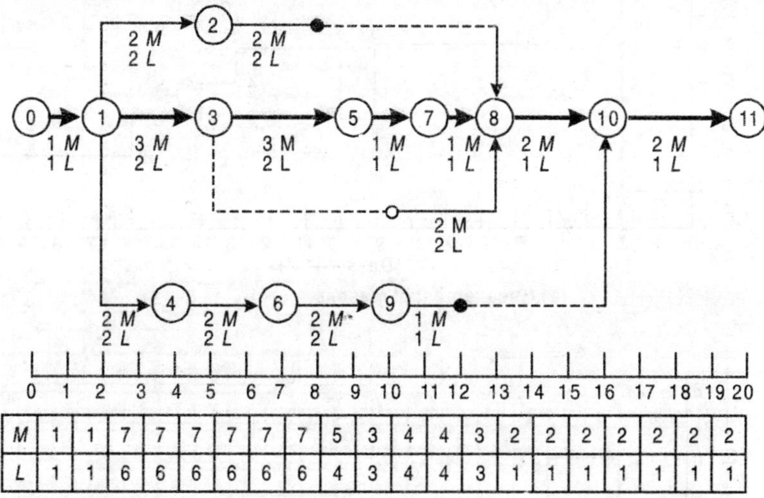

M	1	1	7	7	7	7	7	7	5	3	4	4	3	2	2	2	2	2	2	2
L	1	1	6	6	6	6	6	6	4	3	4	4	3	1	1	1	1	1	1	1

Fig. 9.4 *Modified time-scaled version of the network of Fig. 9.1.*

version of the network and the resource accumulation table will then appear as shown in Fig. 9.5. Although by this modification the maximum number of

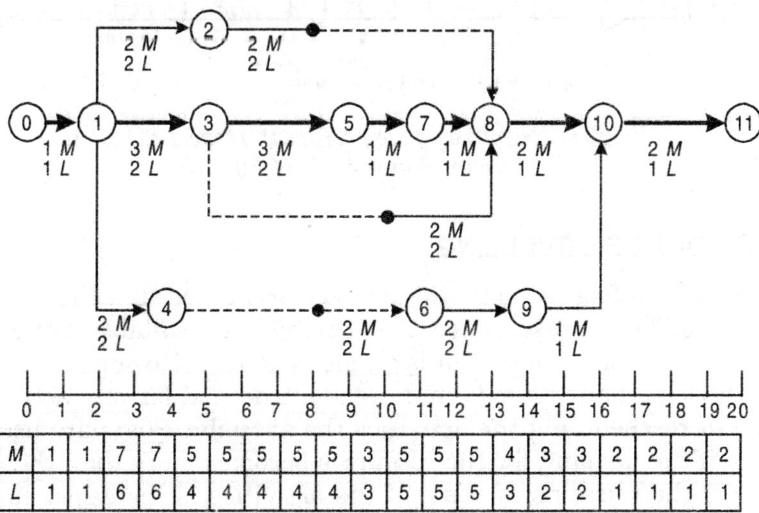

M	1	1	7	7	5	5	5	5	5	3	5	5	5	4	3	3	2	2	2	2
L	1	1	6	6	4	4	4	4	4	3	5	5	5	3	2	2	1	1	1	1

Fig. 9.5 *Modified time-scaled version of the network of Fig. 9.1.*

masons and labourers required is again 7 and 6 respectively as in the previous case but by judiciously utilizing the floats of the various activities it has been possible to smoothen the demand for the resources. This fact is also indicated by the resource usage profiles for this case as shown in Fig. 9.6.

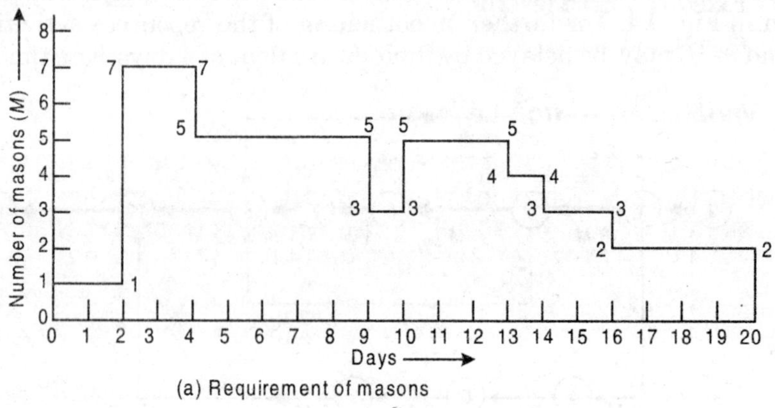

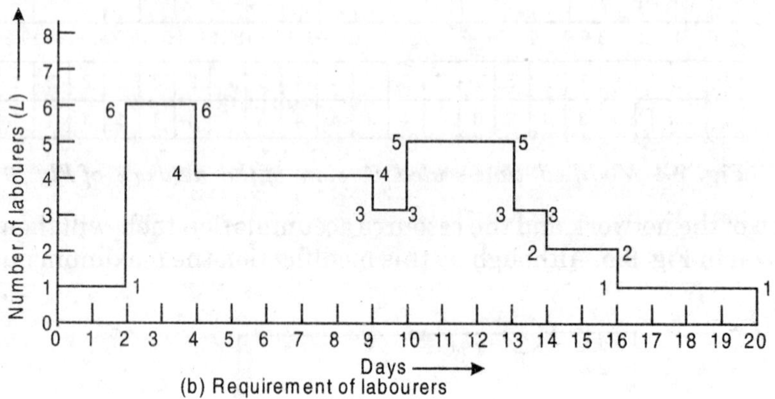

Fig. 9.6 *Resource usage profiles in respect of resource accumulation table of Fig. 9.5.*

9.8 RESOURCE LEVELLING

In resource levelling the activities are so rescheduled that the maximum or peak demand for the resources does not exceed the available resources. Thus in this case the main constraint is on the resources. However, the resources cannot be less than the maximum amount needed for any activity of the project. In rescheduling the activities the available floats are used and in doing so if the demand for the resources becomes more than the available resources, the duration of some of the activities is increased so that the demand for the resources for these activities is decreased. Thus in the process of resource levelling the project duration may change. In other words in this case there is no constraint on the project duration.

Resource levelling may be classified as follows:

1 Variable resource levelling
2. Fixed resource levelling
3. Combined resource levelling

9.8.1 Variable Resource Levelling

In this case manpower is built-up as per requirements and once the maximum is reached there is a gradual reduction of the manpower and hence it is known as variable resource levelling. Since management cannot employ and terminate its personnel as and when desired, the build-up of labour and termination of their services has to be gradual. Moreover even with fluctuating requirements a more uniform manpower utilisation pattern would always be desired. From this consideration also it would be advisable to establish a gradual build-up of personnel with a peak preferably reaching near the end of the project.

9.8.2 Fixed Resource Levelling

In this case a fixed number of personnel would be employed and the same would be available for any project. This may, however, result both in excessive overtime as well as idle or standby labour force. As such the aim would be to select the optimum number of personnel to minimise both overtime and unproductive standby personnel. For example if an organisation is handling several projects simultaneously and its design department has engineers of different specialisation under fixed levelling, the problem would be to find tho best limit of engineers of each specialisation and assign the projects appropriately.

9.8.3 Combined Resource Levelling

It involves a combination of fixed and variable levelling. In this a fixed set of manpower is assigned to each project. However, in order to satisfy its increasing needs a variable set of manpower is also assigned. The aim in this case is to determine an optimum combination of fixed and variable manpower resources.

9.9 RESOURCE ALLOCATION AND SCHEDULING IN PROJECTS OF LONG DURATION

Projects with long duration involve a large number of activities some of which need to be taken up in near future while others are to be taken up in distant future. While the scheduling of resources for activities to be taken up in near future may be done with a fair degree of accuracy the same for activities to be taken up in distant future is always doubtful. This is so because if there is any deviation in the actual progress from the scheduled progress, the entire schedule of resources for activities in distant future will be disturbed. As a result the entire effort made in scheduling of these activities would be wasted. It may, therefore, be concluded that detailed resource scheduling may be attempted for only those activities which are to be taken up in near future say for about a month or so. However, tentative scheduling for only key or controlling resources may be done for all the activities of a network of a project of long duration.

The total network of a project of long duration may be divided into sub-networks and for each sub-network the same methods of resource allocation and scheduling as dealt with earlier may be used for achieving the optimum utilisation of resources. The entire master control network is, however, examined in respect of the constraints of key resources which are governing the project completion. This would facilitate strategic planning of resources and to decide the level of resources to be procured for the project. This would also help in taking decision about the number of a particular equipment which may be expensive, need to be procured for any project. With this approach it would be possible for the management to visualize the requirement of resources for any project in advance and also to generate alternative feasible solutions to select the best one. However, if the availability of any of the resources is less than that arrived at from the above indicated analysis, it would result in prolongation of project period. This would be known to the management very much in advance thereby enabling them to take corrective action before it would be too late.

9.10 MULTI-PROJECT- MULTI-RESOURCE ALLOCATION

Simultaneous implementation of multiple projects with resources drawn from a central pool is a usual phenomenon. For example in a minor irrigation programme, several irrigation projects are executed by a Division or Circle, which allocates resources such as tractors, dumpers, rollers, skilled manpower, etc., to various ongoing projects as per the need at each project site and availability in common pool. Similarly there may be a contracting organisation executing works of several clients at different sites with its common pool of resources serving the various works in progress. However, in almost all such cases most of the common type of resources are drawn by the projects from their own pools and only some scarce resources, which are to be shared by several projects, are supplied from the central pool. When projects draw resources from their own pools, the problem of allocation of resources is relatively simple. For such situations the same procedures as described earlier can be used for resource allocation. In the case of resources drawn by the projects from a common pool, a coordinated effort is necessary to avoid any conflict arising during the allocation of these resources. In order to meet the requirement of the scarce resources at all the work sites, one has to decide the number of such units to be procured and then allocate them to work places in such a way that the best use of these units is made. Moreover the resources should be allocated in a manner that would benefit the overall programme and not only any individual project.

In the process of allocation of scarce resources from a central pool it is implied that the resources will have to be shifted from one project site to another. However, the usual tendency is to shift the resources only when the same are no longer required, in which case they would remain idle at one project site, while the works on other projects which need them badly would be held up and in turn the overall programme would be badly affected. Since the shifting of resources from one site to another involves expenditure, effort and time, the decision regarding the shifting of resources should be based on a systematic analysis of costs in transferring resources from one site to another vis-a-vis costs of delays on account of not transferring resources. Merely because of the fear that the resources may not become available when needed again the same should not be retained at the same project site.

Basically the problem of multi project resource allocation is the same as that of a single project. The various networks of multi projects which share resources can be treated as sub-networks and can be combined into a single master network for the entire programme. Once these networks are integrated into a single network the procedure of single project can be applied. However, the problem of resource allocation for multi projects is not so simple. The procedures of single project resource allocation have to be modified to take care of the problems which may arise in the case of multi-projects. For some of these problems standard methods are available to obtain solutions, while for others there are no such solutions available. In the later case each problem will have to handled separately.

In the case of multi projects the resources are allocated on the basis of priorities assigned to each project. Priorities are usually assigned to the projects in view of either purely economic or socio-economic or political considerations. From economic point of view a project which gives higher return deserves earlier completion and hence higher priority. Similarly a project deserves higher priority if delay in its commissioning and completion leads to heavy loss of production and profit and higher indirect cost. There may be social and political considerations, which are difficult to quantify, yet may affect the priority to be assigned to a project. Further a project whose delay may seriously affect the implementation of overall programme may have to be given a higher priority.

Another difficulty experienced in the allocation of resources in the case of multi projects is that of mobility of resources between the projects. The mobility of resources may cost considerably in terms of effort, time and money. For example transferring heavy equipment from site to site involves expense as well as time, and this has got to be considered while scheduling resources.

ILLUSTRATIVE EXAMPLE

Example 9.1 *Prepare manpower loading charts based on early start and late start times for the project network shown in Fig. Ex. 9.1. Compute the optimum crew size and prepare a loading chart satisfying constraint of 7 men.*

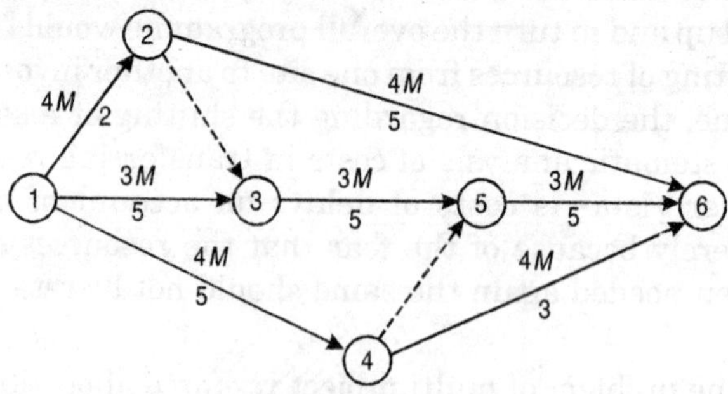

Fig. Ex. 9.1

Solution The solution is presented in a tabular form for which the activity details from the network are transferred on to the various columns in the table. In column 1 activities are entered. In column 2 durations of activities are entered. Required number of men for each activity are entered in column 3. Column 4 represents manday requirement of each activity, which is obtained by multiplying number of men and duration, i.e., column 2 × column 3. In columns 5 and 6 respectively earliest start time (EST) and earliest finish time (EFT) of each activity are entered. However, in the case of resource allocation based on the latest start time, in columns 5 and 6 respectively latest start time (LST) and latest finish time (LFT) of each activity are entered. In column 7 total float of each activity is entered.

(a) Resource Allocation Based on Earliest Start Time. The solution of the problem for this case is shown in Table (A) in which the various details of all the activities are entered as indicated earlier. The aggregation of resources at the bottom of the table indicates the requirement of men on various days. A time-scaled version of network for this case is shown in Fig. Ex. 9.1 (a) (ii) from which also aggregation of resources may be made. Thus this solution requires 11 men on the first 7 days, then 7 men for one day and 3 men for the remaining period. This requirement of men is shown in the Fig. Ex. 9.1 (a).

TABLE (A)

Activity	D	M	M×D	EST	EFT	F_T	Allocation Table														
(1)	(2)	(3)	(4)	(5)	(6)	(7)	0 1	2	3	4	5	6	7	8	9	10	11	12	13	14	15
1-2	2	4	8	0	2	3	4	4													
1-3	5	3	15	0	5	0	3	3	3	3	3										
1-4	5	4	20	0	5	5	4	4	4	4	4										
2-3	0	0	0	2	2	3															
2-6	5	4	20	2	7	5			4	4	4	4	4								
3-5	5	3	15	5	10	0						3	3	3	3	3					
4-5	0	0	0	5	5	5															
4-6	3	4	12	5	8	7						4	4	4							
5-6	5	3	15	10	15	0											3	3	3	3	3
						Total	11	11	11	11	11	11	11	7	3	3	3	3	3	3	3

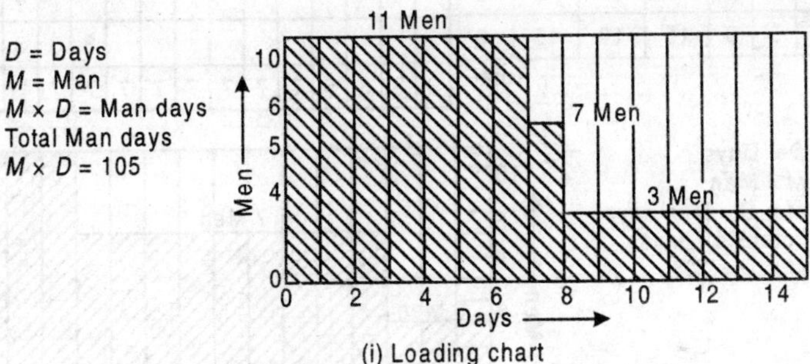

(i) Loading chart

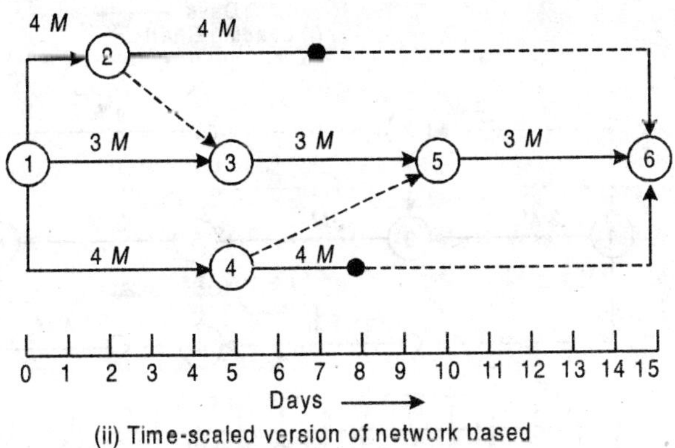

(ii) Time-scaled version of network based on earliest start time

Fig Ex. 9.1 (a)

(b) Resource Allocation Based on Latest Start Times. Another alternative solution of the problem may be obtained by performing all the activities at their latest times. The solution of the problem for this

TABLE (B)

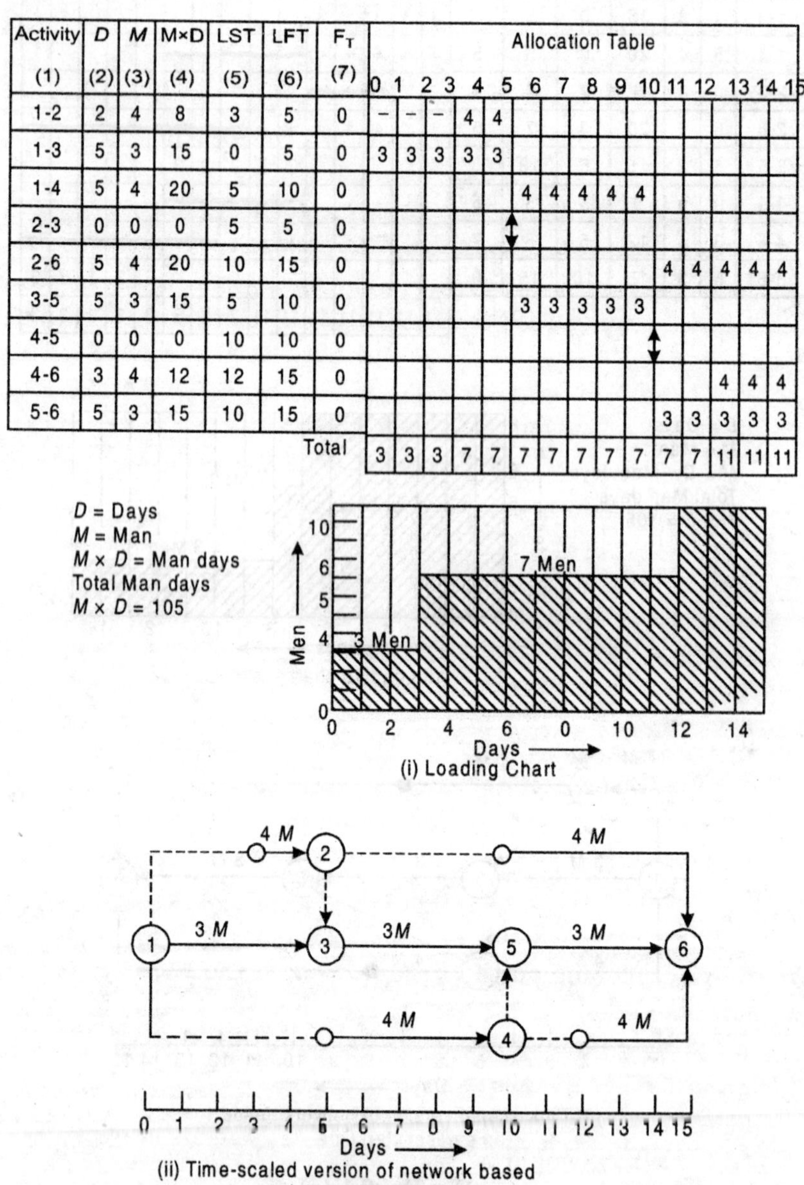

Activity (1)	D (2)	M (3)	M×D (4)	LST (5)	LFT (6)	F_T (7)	Allocation Table 0 1 2 3 4 5 6 7 8 9 10 11 12 13 14 15														
1-2	2	4	8	3	5	0	–	–	–	4	4										
1-3	5	3	15	0	5	0	3	3	3	3	3										
1-4	5	4	20	5	10	0						4	4	4	4	4					
2-3	0	0	0	5	5	0															
2-6	5	4	20	10	15	0											4	4	4	4	4
3-5	5	3	15	5	10	0						3	3	3	3	3					
4-5	0	0	0	10	10	0															
4-6	3	4	12	12	15	0													4	4	4
5-6	5	3	15	10	15	0											3	3	3	3	3
						Total	3	3	3	7	7	7	7	7	7	7	7	7	11	11	11

(i) Loading Chart

(ii) Time-scaled version of network based on latest start time

Fig. Ex. 9.1 (b)

case is shown in Table (B). In this case since starting of each activity is delayed to the maximum no float is left for any of the activities, and hence every activity becomes critical. The aggregation of resources at the bottom of the table indicates the requirement of men on various days. Again a time-scaled version of network for this case is shown in Fig. Ex. 9.1 (b) from which also aggregation of resources may be made. Thus this solution requires 3 men on the first 3 days, then 7 men for 9 days and 11 men for the remaining 3 days.

Optimum crew size is obtained by dividing the total mandays required by the duration of the project. Thus

$$\text{Optimum crew size} = \frac{\text{Mandays required}}{\text{Duration}} \qquad \text{... (i)}$$

This is based on the consideration that the employment of men is as less as possible and utilisation is as high as possible. If the result obtained by Eq. (i) is a fraction, select the next higher figure for optimum crew size.

Thus in this case from Eq. (i), we have

$$\text{Optimum crew size} = \frac{105}{15} = 7 \text{ men}$$

(c) Resource Allocation for Limited Availability of Only 7 Men. On the first day there are 3 activities, viz., 1–2, 1–3, and 1–4 which are eligible to start. These activities require 4, 3 and 4 men respectively, and hence total requirement is of 11 men whereas availability is only 7 men. As such one activity requiring 4 men will have to be delayed by a few days. For this priorities may be assigned to these three activities. Activity 1–3 being critical it gets the first priority and hence it cannot be delayed. Second priority goes to activity 1–2 which has a float equal to 3 and third priority goes to activity 1–4 which has a float equal to 5. Activity 1–4 cannot be scheduled on the first day for want of men. Therefore as shown in allocation Table (C) activity 1–4 instead of starting on the first day would start on the third day and instead of finishing on the fifth day would finish on the seventh day, i.e., starting and finishing times of activity 1–4 are delayed by 2 days which results in reducing its float by 2 days (i.e., from 5 to 3 days).

The effect of delayed start and finish of activity 1–4 on the activities 4–5 and 4–6 needs to be examined, since these activities can start only on finish of activity 1–4 which would be completing on the 7th day. Activity 4–5 is a dummy activity and it can start only on the 7th day. Similarly activity 4–6 can start only from 8th day, i.e., after the completion of activity 1–4 on the 7th day.

At the end of the 2nd day, 4 men would become free from activity 1–2. From 3rd day activities 1–4 and 2–6 would make demand on these 4 men. Thus there is a conflict on resources because demand is of 8 men whereas availability is only of 4 men. Again criterion of float may be applied to decide the allocation. From Table (C) it may be observed that activity 1–4 is

TABLE (C)

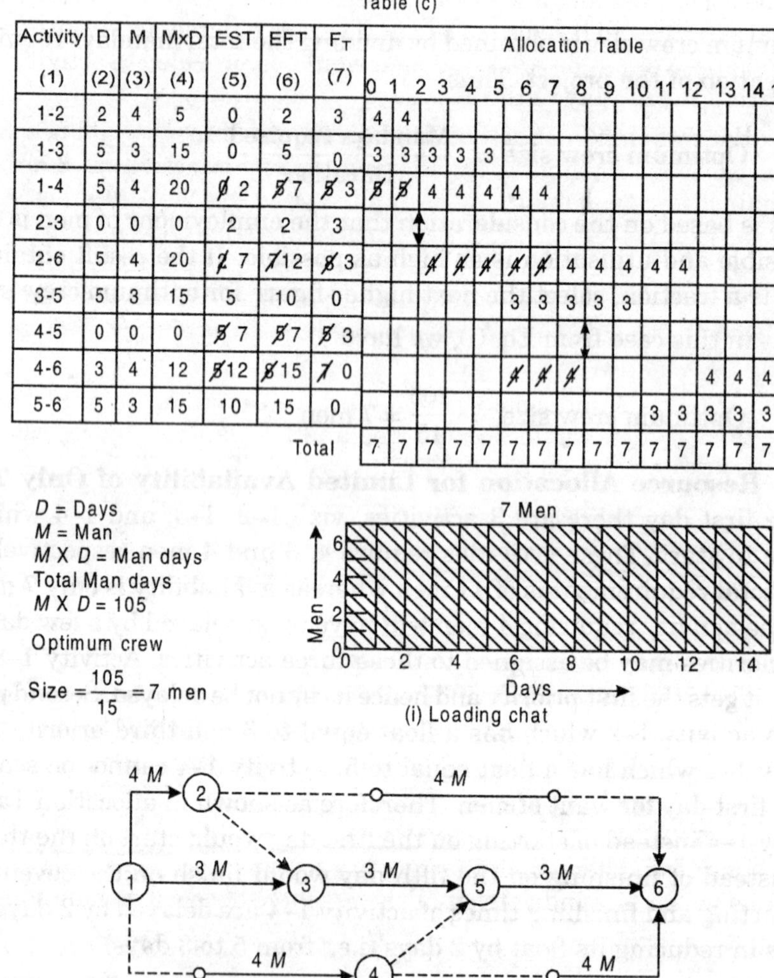

Table (c)

Activity (1)	D (2)	M (3)	MxD (4)	EST (5)	EFT (6)	F_T (7)	Allocation Table 0–1	1–2	2–3	3–4	4–5	5–6	6–7	7–8	8–9	9–10	10–11	11–12	12–13	13–14	14–15
1-2	2	4	5	0	2	3	4	4													
1-3	5	3	15	0	5	0	3	3	3	3	3										
1-4	5	4	20	~~0~~ 2	~~5~~ 7	~~5~~ 3	~~5~~	~~5~~	4	4	4	4	4								
2-3	0	0	0	2	2	3															
2-6	5	4	20	~~2~~ 7	~~7~~ 12	~~8~~ 3			~~4~~	~~4~~	~~4~~	~~4~~	~~4~~	4	4	4	4	4			
3-5	5	3	15	5	10	0						3	3	3	3	3					
4-5	0	0	0	~~5~~ 7	~~5~~ 7	~~5~~ 3															
4-6	3	4	12	~~5~~ 12	~~8~~ 15	~~7~~ 0						~~4~~	~~4~~	~~4~~					4	4	4
5-6	5	3	15	10	15	0											3	3	3	3	3
						Total	7	7	7	7	7	7	7	7	7	7	7	7	7	7	7

D = Days
M = Man
$M \times D$ = Man days
Total Man days
$M \times D = 105$
Optimum crew

$$\text{Size} = \frac{105}{15} = 7 \text{ men}$$

(i) Loading chat

(ii) Time-scaled version of resource based netwok

Fig. Ex. 9.1 (c)

scheduled now from 3rd to 7th day leaving a balance float of 3 days. On the other hand activity 2–6 has a float of 8 days. Thus a higher priority goes to activity 1–4. Thus 4 men relieved from activity 1–2 would be provided for activity 1–4.

Activity 2–3 is a dummy activity which requires no resource. The constraint on event 3 from event 2 is represented by dummy activity 2–3 on the 2nd day. Again activity 2–6 cannot be started till the 5th day when activity 1–3 would be completed and 3 men would become free. Moreover activity 3–5 is a critical activity and it requires 3 men. Therefore immediately after activity 1–3 would be over on the 5th day, 3 men would be provided to activity 3–5 for 5 days from the 6th day to the 10th day.

After the completion of activity 1–4 on 7th day 4 men would become free and they could be considered for allotment to either activity 2–6 or activity 4–6. Again criterion of float may be applied to decide the allocation. Activity 2–6 has a float of (15–5–7) = 3 days whereas activity 4–6 has a float of (15–3–7) = 5 days. Thus activity 2–6 would be allotted 4 men for 5 days form 8th day to 12th day. After the completion of activity 2–6 on 12th day, 4 men would become free and the same would be allotted to activity 4–6 for 3 days form the 13th day to the 15th day.

Lastly with the same consideration after the completion of activity 3–5 on the 10th day, 3 men would become free and the same would be allotted to activity 5–6 for 5 days from the 11th day to the 15th day.

Thus it may be observed that with only 7 men the project could be completed within 15 days. All the 7 men are utilised throughout thus indicating 100 percent utilisation of effective force ratio (EFR) which is defined as follows :

$$\text{EFR} = \frac{\text{Scheduled force}}{\text{Available force}} \qquad \text{... (ii)}$$

In this case from the loading chart for Table (C), we have

$$\text{EFR} = \frac{15 \times 7}{15 \times 7} = 1.0 \text{ or } 100\%$$

The time-scaled version of the network for this case is also shown in Fig. Ex. 9.1 (c) which also indicates that the resource does not remain idle at any time.

REVIEW QUESTIONS

9.1 What are the objectives of resource allocation?

9.2 Explain how resource allocation problem may be considered similar to a queuing problem?

9.3 What do you understand by 'resource smoothing' and 'resource levelling'?

9.4 Explain briefly 'variable resource levelling' and 'fixed resource levelling'.

9.5 Write a brief note on resource allocation and scheduling in projects of long duration.

9.6 Write an explanatory note on multi-project-multi-resource-allocation.

9.7 Discuss in brief the problem of resource allocation. How is this problem solved?

9.8 A project consists of twelve activities. Table below shows the duration for each activity and the corresponding manpower required. Draw a network and number the events according to Fulkerson's rule. Establish the critical path. Draw a time-scaled version of the network assuming that all the activities begin at (i) the earliest start times, (ii) the latest start times. Adjust the project network such that a balanced crew operates, i.e., carry out the process of resource smoothing.

Activity	*Preceded by*	*Duration (days)*	*Manpower required*
A	–	5	2C, 2L
B	A	9	2C, 1L
C	A	7	4C, 4L
D	A	9	2C
E	C	5	4C
F	C	12	4C, 2L
G	E	9	2C
H	E	3	2L
J	A	9	3C, 1L
K	H	7	2C, 2L
L	F	5	2C
M	G, K	5	2L

C : Carpenter; L : Labour.

9.9 Prepare manpower plan based on early start and late start times for a project consisting of ten activities the details of which are given in the table below. Compute the optimum crew-size and prepare a time-scaled version of the network satisfying the constraint of 10 men.

Activity	*Duration (days)*	*Manpower required*
1–2	3	10M
2–3	5	5M
2–4	9	5M
2–5	10	5M
3 1	0	0
3–7	6	2M
4–6	6	3M
5–8	4	3M
6–7	4	7M
7–8	3	10M

9.10 A housing project comprises nine activities the details of which are given in the following table. Compute the cement requirement based on early start and latest start times. Also prepare a graph for cumulative cement requirement. What is the minimum and maximum requirement of cement up to the 8th week.

Activity	*Duration (days)*	*Cement required*
1–2	4	20T
2–3	4	24T
2–4	6	18T
2–5	2	10T
3–6	2	20T
4-6	8	24T
5-6	4	20T
5-7	6	30T
6-7	8	40T

10

Chapter

Use of Computer in PERT/ CPM Network Analysis

10.1 INTRODUCTION

The analysis of a project network can be done either manually or with the help of a computer. When a project network consists of very few activities or when all the activities are very well-known to the manager supervising the same then the network analysis can be done manually. In such cases decisions concerning rearrangement, rescheduling, reduction of project time, etc., are usually quite simple and the same may be taken without much difficulty. Further in the initial stages till good understanding of the logic of CPM/ PERT is developed it is desirable to carry out the network analysis manually. However, manual analysis of a project network is time and effort consuming and it is susceptible to mathematical errors. Moreover the analysis of complex networks involving a large number of activities may not be possible manually. In such cases the use of computer would be of considerable assistance. Some of the aspects of the use of computers in the analysis of project networks are discussed in the following sections.

10.2 FACTORS DECIDING THE USE OF COMPUTERS IN NETWORK ANALYSIS

The various factors which may help to decide whether a computer should be used or not in network analysis are described below.

10.2.1 Size of Network

Usually when the project network is of big size the use of computer in the network analysis is necessary. This is so because even the time analysis for a big network would take long time when done manually. It has been established on the basis of experience that when the number of activities is more than two hundred it is necessary to use computer.

10.2.2 Frequency of Updating

If the network is to be prepared only once and no updating is required, it may not be necessary to use a computer. This is so because in such a case the time and effort consumed in preparing the programme for computer will not be worth it. As such when networks are used in only initial planning, no computer is necessary. On the other hand when updatings are required to be made at quick frequency say daily, weekly, or so, then even with small networks, use of computer is desirable.

10.2.3 Timely Information

If the time available for analysing the progress of a project is short and timely information about the progress of the project is frequently required to be given, then it is essential to use a computer. On the other hand if any delay in submission of the information is tolerable then the use of computer may be avoided.

10.2.4 Multiple Agencies

In complex projects where multiple agencies are involved and the information about the progress of the project is to be collected from all the agencies, analysed and conclusions drawn and the revised plan is to be again circulated to all the agencies, then in such cases the use of computer is justifiable.

10.2.5 Use of Sophisticated Techniques

When an organization intends to make use of techniques such as *time cost trade off, PERT/CPM, multi-project multi-resource allocation technique,* etc., it is essential to use computer. This is so because in these techniques the computations involved are so large that for large size projects it is almost impossible to do them manually. The projects would, however, be deprived of the benefits from the use of these techniques if the computers are not used. For example, in deciding the resource allocation of say manpower or machinery the management may like to assess the effect of a particular allocation on both project cost and project time. For this a number of alternative allocations are required to be tried so that the best out of these may be selected. This is possible only by the use of computers which simulate the conditions quickly and give results. In general computer is an asset in preparing manpower loading charts, manpower levelling, equipment levelling, financial allocation, computations of cost overruns, etc.

10.2.6 Availability of Computer Facility

These days computers are being installed for several other purposes, such as pay roll, cost accounting, etc. Thus if computer is available within the organisation, it may be beneficially used in network analysis also.

10.2.7 Size of Organization

Some of the organizations may be so large that persons making decisions in one part of the project know little or nothing about what is going on in other parts of the project. In such cases if alterations are made in the arrangement of some of the activities of one part of the project then the management may be interested in knowing the effect of such alterations on some of the other parts of the project or on the entire project. With the help of computer the desired information may be readily obtained in such situations.

10.2.8 Quick Generation of Information

The computers are used for network analysis due to their ability to generate masses of information quickly. In projects containing thousands of interconnected activities, information and data cannot be complete and accurate without the use of computers. If the data is obtained in time it would be possible to determine the slack time available in the network during any project time which would enable the management to shift resources and take other decisions to complete the project in the shortest feasible time.

Further management's lack of up-to-date knowledge about certain part of a project may result in considerable expense. For instance, if management learns well in advance that a particular activity in a project is behind schedule, some arrangements may be made to reschedule the activities that would follow it in such a way that the project cost is not affected. On the other hand if the information about any activity falling behind schedule is known only a day or two before the next activity is to commence, it may involve some additional expense thus resulting in a higher project cost. Thus it is only the use of computer that would provide adequate, accurate and current information for the management to act quickly.

10.2.9 Combining Networks

Computers can help in combining small networks together to form project networks or master networks. As indicated in section 3.11 the process of combining networks involves first the identification of interface events, i.e., events common to more than one network. For small networks this identification is not difficult. For large, involved networks, the use of computers can help in reducing the time necessary to prepare the master network.

10.2.10 Presentation of Data in a Compact Form

Computers help to present the network data in a more compact form. For example, a network consisting of 1000 activities occupies so much space on paper that it is quite awkward and unwieldy to handle. A computer can digest the whole network, analyze it, pick out the salient information required by the management, and prepare and present the data in the desired form.

10.2.11 Cost of Using a Computer

Cost of using a computer is around 0.1 percent of the project cost, but the benefits are much more than the cost As such use of computer in network analysis results on the whole in saving of money, provided computer is used intelligently.

The decision regarding the use of computer in network analysis will, however, depend on the combined analysis of all the above mentioned factors.

10.3 PROCEDURE OF COMPUTER PROCESSING

For the use of computer in network analysis it is necessary to prepare the activity data in a specific manner as prescribed in the computer manual brought out by the manufacturer of the computer. This data along with the computer programme is then fed to the computer. Computer prepares a master file (on tape) which contains activity code no., description, estimated duration, cost, up-to-date status, etc. Then following the instructions given in the programme computer does the processing of data to provide the output in the desired fashion. Figure 10.1 illustrates the procedure of computer processing.

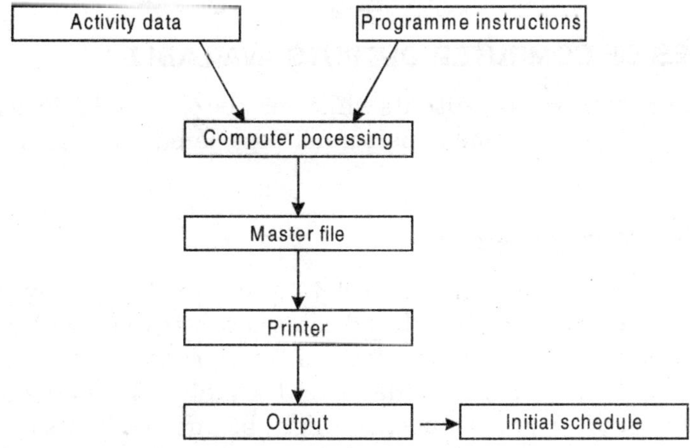

Fig. 10.1 *Procedure of computer processing.*

The masterfile which may be in the form of punched cards or tape contains all the information of initial planning. It is this file which can be fed back to computer for control purpose. As the project is progressing its review is taken in which the management may like to apply the actual progress on

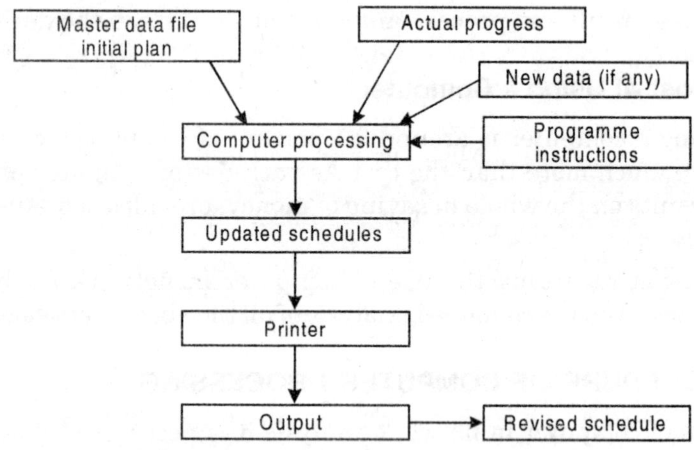

Fig. 10.2 *Procedure of progress control.*

initial plan, make a comparison between scheduled and actually accomplished, and evaluate the effect on the project as a whole. At this stage it is necessary to incorporate the new data, if any, such as change in logic of activities, revised activity durations, costs, new activities, etc., on the original plan. Computer accepts this actual progress with new data and does synthesis according to instructions in the programme to provide revised schedules. Figure 10.2 shows the procedure of progress control.

10.4 TYPES OF COMPUTER OUTPUTS AVAILABLE

The various general types of outputs which may be obtained from a computer and are useful to management personnel associated with projects are as follows.

10.4.1 Event Number Report

The event number report helps in isolating and analyzing any particular event and the activities lead to it. It indicates how many and which activities lead to a particular event. The analysis of the reported information on the activities that lead to a particular event enables the management to understand how the event in question might be affected by its current and future position in the network.

The event number report also provides the earliest expected date for each of the ending events of each of the activities leading into the event. By analyzing this information the management can know which of the activities has the ending event with the latest expect date of completion and can thus be in a position to know which activity will be most likely to affect the accomplishment of the event in question.

The report provides the latest allowable date for each event. From the latest allowable date and the earliest expected dates of events leading up to the event in question, management is able to recognize probable critical spots in advance. Further when the latest allowable dates of events on the network are compared periodically with information concerning degree of completion and the current calender date, the time of completion of the entire project may be estimated.

Finally, the event number report makes available for each event the slack time associated with that event. The significance of slack time is that management, in replanning or readjusting the network, can be properly apprised of the availability of surplus resources, the degree of criticality of each event, and where slippage in the network can most likely be made up. By analyzing successive reports, management can easily observe the movement of any event in question from the critical to other non-critical events and vice-versa.

10.4.2 Slack Time Report

The slack time report lists the various paths through the network beginning with the critical path and going all the way down to the path with the greatest amount of slack time. The amount of slack time associated with each path is noted on it. Using this report the management can see at a glance the problems connected with each path. For instance, if the slack associated with a path is positive, the activities along that path can easily be delayed without increasing the earliest expected date of the network ending event. Further if a path has a higher positive slack value it is possible to divert the resources from that path to other more critical paths without interfering with previously scheduled completion dates for the network. On the other hand a negative slack for a path indicates how much one must speed up completion of the activities on this path in order to not to interfere with scheduled completion dates for the network. In many cases replanning may take the form of reapplying resources from the paths having positive slack to those having negative slack. For this a slack time report for the network must be available so that quick decisions may be taken in this regard.

With the help of a computer it is possible to generate slack value reports for various alternative solutions of the network problem. Analysis of these reports indicates which of the solutions is most appropriate and the same may be adopted by the management.

The use of a computer to generate the slack time report generally allows the management to foresee problems and to take action which will prevent these problems from actually happening. In this respect the slack time report is not only a control device but also an excellent method of intermediate-range planning.

10.4.3 Latest Allowable Date Report

The latest allowable date report provides the latest allowable dates for each of the events yet to occur in the network. The use of latest allowable date report in conjunction with the slack time report constitutes a very effective planning tool for the management. Comparison of latest allowable dates of events with current calender dates is a method of determining the current position of the various events.

10.4.4 Departmental Report

The departmental report provides planning and control information for the departmental heads to enable them to observe how their respective parts of the network are progressing. If the various departmental heads are given the current performance information about each activity for which they are responsible, a much better degree of coordination between the various departments and better overall project performance may be expected.

In general these four types of reports are usually obtained for any project. However, in some cases the information contained in one or more of these reports may not be sufficient for the purpose of managerial decision-making. In such cases with the help of computer additional information needed by the management may be obtained.

In general the management is interested in certain information that allows the managers to plan, to direct and to control effectively. In many cases a computer is able to yield this information more economically than hand computing. However, the types of information required, the time constraints imposed upon the generation and reporting of this information, the duration of the project, the availability of computer and the magnitude of the project all go together to decide whether computer is to be used or not.

APPENDIX–A

Linear Programming and Critical Path Scheduling

Linear programming deals with maximizing or minimizing (that is optimizing) of an objective function subjected to some restrictions (or constraints) in those situations where the objective function and the associated restrictions can be expressed in terms of linear expressions. The technique of linear programming can be applied to the identification of the critical path for an activity based or event-oriented network. The problem of finding the critical path as a linear programming problem may be formulated as explained below.

Let variable x_i represent the early occurrence time of node i, $i = 1, 2,...., m$, where m = the number of nodes in the network. The objective is to minimize the difference between x_i and x_m, where 1 is the first node and m is the last node in the network. (It is assumed that there is only one initial and one final node.) The constraints being that the time difference between any two adjacent nodes, x_i and x_j, is at least as great as the duration t_{ij}, of the connecting activity i–j. Thus the general formulation of the problem is :

Minimize $\quad x_0 = x_m - x_1$

subject to $\quad x_j - x_i \geq t_{ij}$, all activities i–j.

x_i unconstrained in sign, $i = 1, 2,....., m$.

The usual solution would be in which x_1 =0, unless some other value is specified initially. Actually, any other x_i including x_m, may be arbitrarily assigned an initial value without affecting the value of the minimizing function, since the later measures only the difference between x_m and x_1 and the two vary directly with each other.

A basic linear programming formulation of critical path calculations is illustrated in the following example.

Consider a network whose details are as given below :

Activity	(1–2)	(1–3)	(2–3)	(2–4)	(3–5)	(4–5)
Duration	3	2	4	3	5	4

Since there are six activities there will be six constraints and the linear programming problem becomes:

Minimize $x_0 = x_5 - x_1$

subjected to $x_2 - x_1 \geq t_{1-2} = 3$

$x_3 - x_1 \geq t_{1-3} = 2$

$x_3 - x_2 \geq t_{2-3} = 4$

$x_4 - x_2 \geq t_{2-4} = 3$

$x_5 - x_3 \geq t_{3-5} = 5$

$x_5 - x_4 \geq t_{4-5} = 4$

As stated earlier if $x_1 = 0$ the problem becomes

Minimize $x_0 = x_5$

subjected to $x_2 \geq 3$

$x_3 \geq 2$

$x_3 - x_2 \geq 4$

$x_4 - x_2 \geq 3$

$x_5 - x_3 \geq 5$

$x_5 - x_4 \geq 4$

The problem is solved by dual simplex method as given below. Let $y = x_2 - 3 \geq 0$. The above expressions may be written as

Minimize $x_0 = x_5$; or $x_0 - x_5 = 0$

subjected to $-x_3 + y + s_1 = -7$

$-x_4 + y + s_2 = -6$

$-x_5 + x_3 + s_3 = -5$

$-x_5 + x_4 + s_4 = -4$

The starting dual simplex table is as shown Table App. A.1

TABLE App. A.1

Basic	x_3	x_4	x_5	s_1	s_2	s_3	s_4	*Solution*
x_0	0	0	–1	0	0	0	0	0
s_1	–1	0	0	1	0	0	0	–7
s_2	0	–1	0	0	1	0	0	–6
s_3	1	0	–1	0	0	1	0	–5
s_4	0	1	–1	0	0	0	1	–4

Leaving variable : The most negative variable in Table App. A. 1 under solution column is s_1 and hence s_1 leaves the basic.

Entering variable : There is only one negative entry in $s_1$row which is in x_3 column and hence x_3 enters the basic. It may, however, be noted that if there are more than one negative entries in the row of the leaving variable then all these entries are picked up and the absolute values of the ratios of these entries with corresponding entries in the x_0 – row (with x_0 – row entries in the numerator) are determined. The variable corresponding to the minimum of these ratios enters the basic.

Now the usual simplex iterations are performed. Divide s_t – row by –1 to make the pivot element unity. This gives x_3 – row of Table App. A. 2, which is the pivot row. The x_0, s_2, s_3 and s_4 rows are obtained by adding 0, 0, –1 and 0 times the pivot row to the x_0 – row, s_2,– row, s_3 –row and s_4 – row of Table App. A. 1. This gives Table App. A. 2. This completes one iteration.

TABLE App. A. 2

Basic	x_3	x_4	x_5	s_1	s_2	s_3	s_4	*Solution*
x_0	0	0	–1	0	0	0	0	0
x_3	1	0	0	–1	0	0	0	7
s_2	0	–1	0	0	1	0	0	6
s_3	0	0	–1	1	0	1	0	–12
s_4	0	1	–1	0	0	0	1	–4

Leaving variable : In Table App. A. 2 the most negative variable is s_3 and hence s_3 leaves the basic.

Entering variable : There is only one negative entry in s_3 – row which is in x_5 column and hence x_5 enters the basic.

The s_3 – row is divided by –1 to make the pivot element unity. This gives the x_5 – row of Table App. A. 3, which is the pivot row. The x_0, s_2 and s_4 rows are obtained by adding 1, 0 and 1 times the pivot row to the x_0 – row, s_2 – row and s_4 – row of Table App. A. 2. This gives Table App. A. 3. This is second iteration.

TABLE App. A. 3

Basic	x_3	x_4	x_5	s_1	s_2	s_3	s_4	*Solution*
x_0	0	0	0	–1	0	–1	0	12
x_3	1	0	0	–1	0	0	0	7
s_2	0	–1	0	0	1	0	0	–6
s_3	0	0	1	–1	0	–1	0	12
s_4	0	1	0	–1	0	–1	1	8

Leaving variable **: In Table App. A. 3 the most negative variable is s_2 and hence s_2 leaves the basic.**

Entering variable **: There is only one negative entry in s_2 – row which is in x_4 column and hence x_4 enters the basic.**

The s_2 – row is divided by –1 to make the pivot element unit. This gives the x_4 – row of Table App. A. 4, which is the pivot row. Thus all the values of the variables under solution column are positive and hence optimal solution is reached as shown in Table App. A. 4.

TABLE App. A. 4

Basic	x_3	x_4	x_5	s_1	s_2	s_3	s_4	*Solution*
x_0	0	0	0	–1	0	–1	0	12
x_3	1	0	0	–1	0	0	0	7
s_2	0	1	0	0	–1	0	0	6
s_3	0	0	1	–1	0	–1	0	12
s_4	0	1	0	–1	0	–1	1	8

The optimal solution is

$x_3 = 7, x_4 = 6, x_5 = 12, s_4 = 8$

Further since $y = 0$, $x_2 = 3$. The rest of the variables are zero being non-basic. Thus complete solution of the problem is

$x_1 = 0, x_2 = 3\ x_3 = 7, x_4 = 6\ x_5 = 12.$

The critical path is the path along which all s_i are zero. In this case except s_4 all other values of s_i are zero and hence the critical path is 1–2–3–5 with duration $x_0 = x_5$=12.

Multiple Choice Questions

1. The various phases involved in the project management are
   (a) planning and scheduling.
   (b) planning and controlling.
   (c) scheduling and controlling.
   (d) planning, scheduling and controlling.
2. Which of the following are the limitations of a bar chart?
   (a) Lack of degree of details and no information about interdependencies between activities.
   (b) Lack of degree of details and no information about the progress of the project.
   (c) Lack of degree of details and inability to reflect the time uncertainties.
   (d) Lack of degree of details, no information about interdependencies between activities as well as about the progress of the project and inability to reflect the time uncertainties.
3. PERT (Programme Evaluation and Review Technique) is mainly useful for
   (a) any small or large project
   (b) only large projects.
   (c) research and development projects.
   (d) only large and complex projects.
4. In a CPM network
   (a) activity arrows are drawn to a scale.

(b) the tail of an arrow represents the start of an activity and the arrow head represents the finish of an activity.

(c) the tail of an arrow represents the finish of an activity.

(d) the arrow head represents the start of an activity.

5. A CPM network is

(a) activity oriented.

(b) event oriented.

(c) both activity as well as event oriented.

(d) neither activity nor event oriented.

6. A PERT network is

(a) activity oriented.

(b) event oriented.

(c) both activity as well as event oriented.

(d) neither activity nor event oriented.

7. Check which of the following is not a PERT event.

(a) List of required equipment completed.

(b) Income tax form completed.

(c) Assembly of units started.

(d) Assemble units.

8. Check which of the following is a PERT event.

(a) Write a report.

(b) Report is being written.

(c) Blueprints started.

(d) Blueprints are being prepared.

9. In CPM activity times are

(a) deterministic.

(b) non-deterministic.

(c) probabilistic or stochastic.

(d) probabilistic following a particular distribution.

10. In PERT the time estimates of activities and probability of their occurrence follow

(a) normal distribution.

(b) Poisson's distribution.

(c) β-distribution.

(d) binomial distribution.

11. In the network shown in Fig. MCQ. 1, activity 3–6 can be started only when

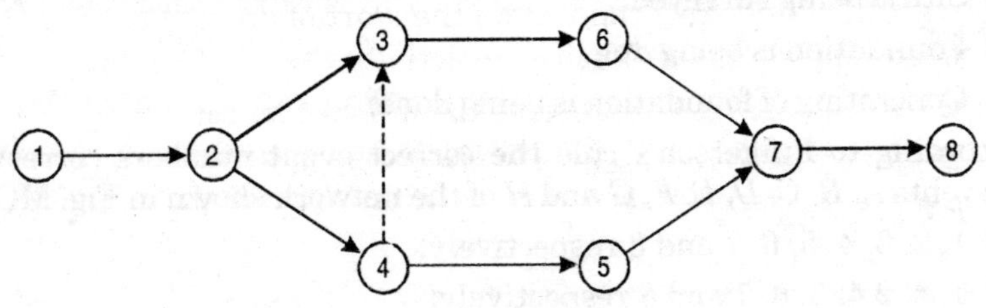

MCQ. Fig. 11

(a) activity 2–3 is completed.

(b) activity 2–4 is completed.

(c) activities 1–2 and 2–3 are completed.

(d) activities 2–3 and 2–4 are completed.

12. In the network shown in Fig. MCQ. 1, event 6 is preceded by

(a) event 3 only (b) events 3 and 4

(c) event 4 only (d) events 2 and 3

13. The area under the β-distribution curve is divided into two equal halves by a vertical ordinate through

(a) optimistic time (b) most likely time

(c) pessimistic time (d) expected time

14. In the network shown in Fig. MCQ. 14, activity 6–7 can be started only when

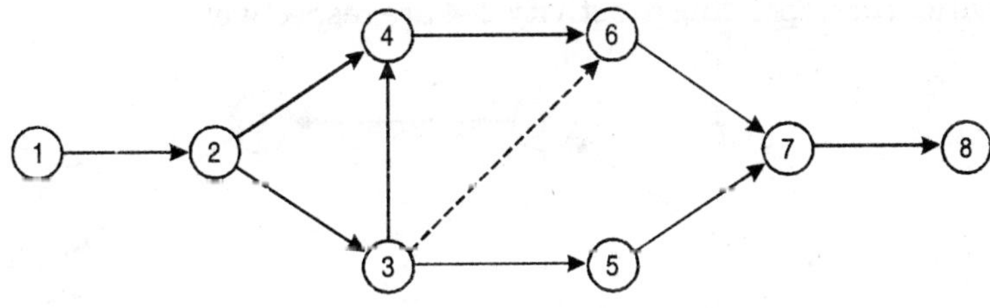

Fig. MCQ. 14

(a) activity 2–3 is completed.

(b) activity 4–6 is completed.

(c) activities 3–4 and 4–6 are completed.

(d) activities 2–4 and 4–6 are completed.

15. In the network shown in Fig. MCQ. 14, event 7 succeeds

(a) event 6 only. (b) events 3 and 5.

(c) events 3, 5 and 6. (d) events 5 and 6.

16. Check which of the following does not represent an activity

(a) Site clearance completed.

(b) Site is being surveyed.

(c) Foundation is being dug.

(d) Concreting of foundation is being done.

17. According to Fulkerson's rule the correct event numbers corresponding to events *A, B, C, D, E, F, G* and *H* of the network shown in Fig. MCQ. 17 is

(a) 1, 2, 3, 4, 5, 6, 7 and 8 respectively.

(b) 1, 3, 2,4, 5, 6, 7 and 8 respectively.

(c) 1, 4, 3, 2, 7, 6, 5 and 8 respectively.

(d) 1, 3, 2, 5,4,6, 7 and 8 respectively.

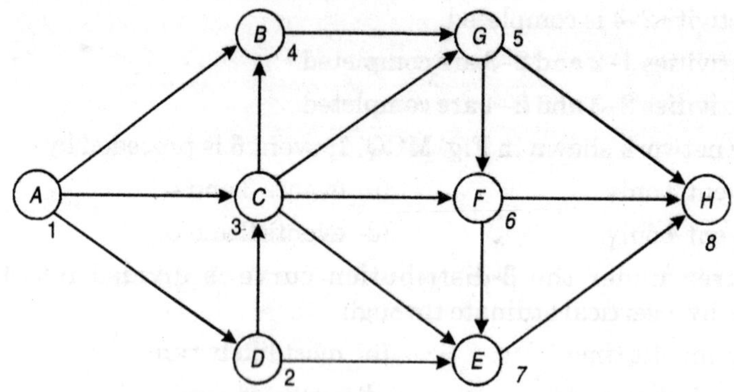

Fig. MCQ. 17

18. In the network shown in Fig. MCQ. 18 the concurrent and succeeding activities corresponding to activity 2–4 are respectively

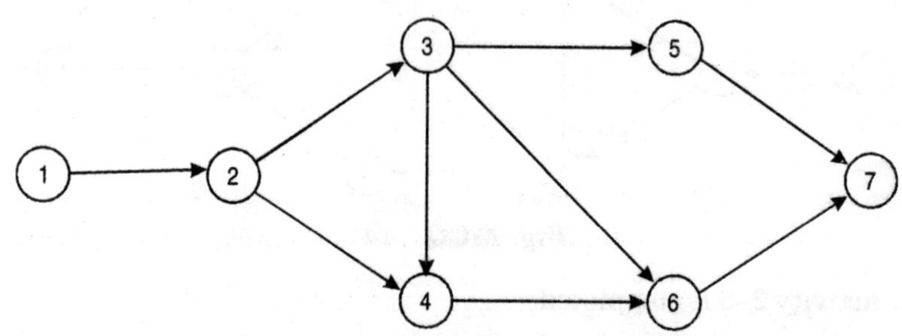

Fig. MCQ. 18

(a) 2–3 and 4–6. (b) 4–6 and 2–3.

(c) 2–3 and 1–2. (d) 1–2 and 2–3.

19. In the network shown in Fig. MCQ. 18 the concurrent and preceding activities corresponding to activity 2–4 are respectively

(a) 2–3 and 3–4. (b) 2–3 and 1–2.

(c) 1–2 and 2–3. (d) 3–4 and 2–3.

20. Check which of the following represent an activity.
    (a) Site survey completed.
    (b) Foundation excavation completed.
    (c) Concreting in foundation completed.
    (d) Masonry work in foundations is being done.
21. The earliest finish time (EFT) of an activity is
    (a) equal to the earliest start time of activity plus the activity duration.
    (b) equal to the earliest start time of activity minus the activity duration.
    (c) equal to earliest event time for the node from which the activity arrow originates.
    (d) less than earliest event time for the node at which the activity arrow terminates.
22. The latest start time (LST) of an activity is
    (a) equal to the latest occurrence time for the event at which the activity arrow terminates.
    (b) equal to the latest occurrence time for the event at which the activity arrow terminates minus the activity duration.
    (c) equal to the latest occurrence time for the event at which the activity arrow terminates plus the activity duration.
    (d) more than the latest occurrence time for the event at which the activity arrow terminates.
23. The latest finish time (LFT) of an activity is
    (a) less than the latest occurrence time for the event at which the activity arrow terminates.
    (b) more than the latest occurrence time for the event at which the activity arrow terminates.
    (c) equal to the latest occurrence time for the event at which the activity arrow terminates.
    (d) equal to the latest occurrence time for the event from which the activity arrow originates.
24. In the network shown in Fig. MCQ 24 the earliest start time (EST) of activity 6–7 is (the number on the arrow shows duration of the activity)

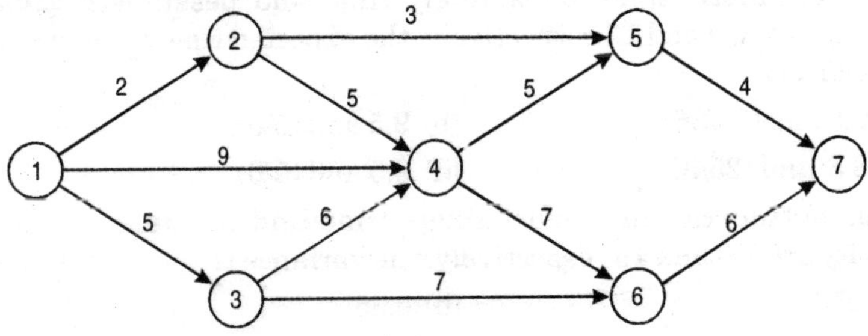

Fig. MCQ. 24

(a) 12 (b) 14
(c) 16 (d) 18

25. In the network shown in Fig. MCQ 24 the earliest finish time (EFT) of activity 6–7 is
(a) 24 (b) 22
(c) 20 (d) 18

26. In the network shown in Fig. MCQ 24 the latest start time (LST) of activity 6–7 is
(a) 12 (b) 14
(c) 18 (d) 20

27. in the network shown in Fig. MCQ 24 the latest finish time (LFT) of activity 6–7 is
(a) 14 (b) 16
(c) 20 (d) 24

28. In the network shown in Fig. MCQ 24 event 4 occurs after
(a) event 2 only. (b) events 1 and 2 only.
(c) events 1,2 and 3 only. (d) events 2 and 3 only.

29. In the network shown in Fig. MCQ 24 latest start time (LST) and latest finish time (LFT) of activity 4–6 are respectively
(a) 18 and 11 (b) 11 and 18
(c) 9 and 16 (d) 16 and 9

30. In the network shown in Fig. MCQ 24 earliest start time (EST) and earliest finish time (EFT) of activity 4–6 are respectively
(a) 11 and 18 (b) 9 and 16
(c) 7 and 14 (d) 18 and 11

31. If the optimistic time, most likely time and pessimistic time for an activity are 5,7 and 9 respectively, the expected time t_E for the activity is
(a) 6.5 (b) 7.0
(c) 7.5 (d) 8.0

32. If the optmistic time, most likely time and pessimistic time for an activity are 8, 9 and 13 respectively, the expected time t_E and variance are respectively
(a) 9.5 and (25/36) (b) 9.5 and (5/6)
(c) 8.5 and (25/36) (d) 8.5 and (5/6)

33. If the optimistic time, most likely time and pessimistic time for an activity are 7.8 and 10 respectively, the variance is
(a) 0.50 (b) 0.35
(c) 0.25 (d) 0.20

34. Total float for an activity is defined as
   (a) the difference between the latest start time and the earliest start time of the activity.
   (b) the difference between its earliest finish time and the earliest start time of its successor activity.
   (c) the excess time that exists between finishing and starting of two successive activities.
   (d) the difference between the latest allowable occurrence time and the earliest occurrence time for the head event of the activity.

35. Free float for an activity is defined as
   (a) the difference between the latest start time and the earliest start time of the activity.
   (b) the difference between its earliest finish time and the earliest start time of its successor activity.
   (c) the excess time that exists between finishing and starting of two successive activities.
   (d) the difference between the latest allowable occurrence time and the earliest occurrence time for the head event of the activity.

36. Independent float for an activity is defined as
   (a) the difference between the latest start time and the earliest start time of the activity
   (b) the difference between its earliest finish time and the earliest start time of its successor activity.
   (c) the excess time that exists between finishing and starting of two successive activities.
   (d) the difference between the latest allowable occurrence time and the earliest occurrence time for the head event of the activity.

37. Interfering float for an activity is defined as
   (a) the difference between the latest start time and the earliest start time of the activity.
   (b) the difference between its earliest finish time and the earliest start time of its successor activity.
   (c) the excess time that exists between finishing and starting of two successive activities.
   (d) the difference between the latest allowable occurrence time and the earliest occurrence time for the head event of the activity.

38. Free float is determined to
   (a) identify the activities which can be delayed without affecting the total float of succeeding activity
   (b) identify the activities which can be delayed without affecting the total

float of preceding activity.

(c) identify the activities which can be delayed without affecting the total float of both preceding as well as succeeding activities.

(d) establish priorities.

39. Whenever an activity has zero total float, then

(a) Free float of the activity is also zero but its independent float need not be zero.

(b) independent float of the activity is also zero but its free float need not be zero.

(c) both free float and independent float of the activity are zero.

(d) both free float and independent float of the activity need not be zero.

40. Total float for any activity is given by the difference between

(a) its latest finish time (LFT) and earliest start time (EST) of its successor activity.

(b) its latest start time (LST) and earliest start time (EST).

(c) its latest start time (LST) and earliest finish time (EFT).

(d) its earliest finish time (EFT) and earliest start time (EST) of its successor activity.

41. In the network shown in Fig. MCQ 41 total float for activity 3–5 is (the number on the arrow shows duration of the activity)

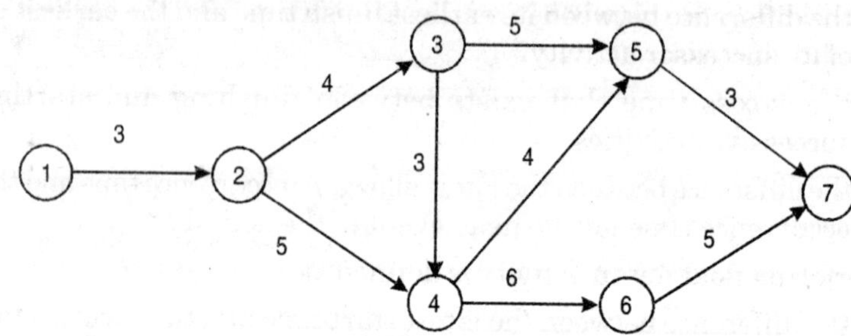

Fig. MCQ. 41

(a) 0 (b) 2

(c) 4 (d) 6

42. In the network shown in Fig. MCQ 41, free float for activity 3–5 is

(a) 0 (b) 2

(c) 4 (d) 6

43. In the network shown in Fig. MCQ 41, independent float for activity 3-5 is

(a) 0 (b) 2

(c) 4 (d) 6

44. In the network shown in Fig. MCQ 41, interfering float for activity 3–5 is
(a) 0 (b) 2
(c) 4 (d) 6

45. In the network shown in Fig. MCQ 41, the critical path is
(a) 1–2–3–5–7 (b) 1–2–3–4–6–7
(c) 1–2–4–6–7 (d) 1–2–4–5–7

46. Free float for an activity is given by the difference between
(a) its earliest finish time (EFT) and earliest start time (EST) for its successor activity.
(b) its latest start time (LST) and earliest start time (EST).
(c) its latest finish time (LFT) and earliest start time (EST).
(d) its earliest finish time (EFT) and latest start time (LST) for its successor activity.

47. In a network critical path
(a) is always the shortest path.
(b) is always the longest path.
(c) may be the shortest path.
(d) may be the longest path.

48. A critical path
(a) always begins at the initial (or first) event and terminates at the final (or last) event.
(b) always begins at the initial (or first) event but does not terminate at the final (or last) event.
(c) does not begin at the initial (or first) event but terminates at the final (or last) event.
(d) neither begins at the initial (or first) event nor terminates at the final (or last) event.

49. The independent float affects
(a) only preceding activities.
(b) only succeeding activities.
(c) only the particular activity involved.
(d) both the preceding and succeeding activities.

50. If the total float for the various activities are as follow

Activity	*Total float*
1–2	3
2–3	5
3–4	6
4–5	4

the most critical activity is

(a) 1–2 (b) 2–3

(c) 3–4 (d) 4–5

51. The minimum and maximum time taken by a telephone operator for maturing a call are 6 minutes and half an hour respectively. However, in most cases the time taken is 12 minutes. The expected time for maturing a call will be

(a) 12 minutes (b) 13 minutes

(c) 14 minutes (d) 15 minutes

52. The variance in the case of MCQ 51 is

(a) 16 (b) 24

(c) 30 (d) 36

53. Which of the networks shown in Fig. MCQ 53 represents correctly oriented activity arrows ?

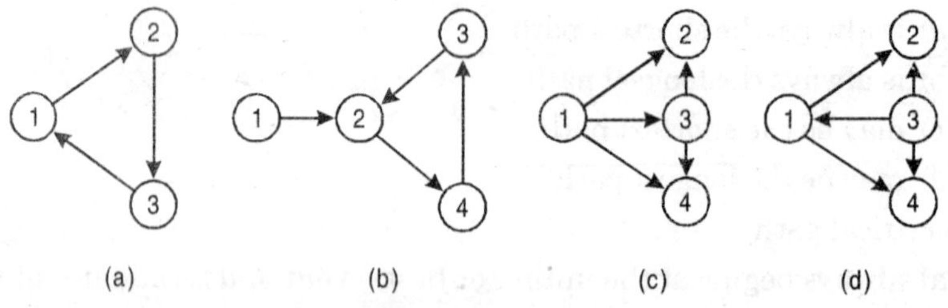

Fig. MCQ. 53

54. The time by which a particular activity can be delayed without affecting its preceding and succeeding activities is known as

(a) total float. (b) free float.

(c) interfering float (d) independent float

55. In general direct cost

(a) increases as the time decreases

(b) decreases as the time decreases

(c) is independent of time

(d) varies erratically with time.

56. The cost slope is defined as

(a) $\dfrac{\text{Crash cost–Normal cost}}{\text{Normal time}}$ (b) $\dfrac{\text{Crash cost–Normal cost}}{\text{Crash time}}$

(c) $\dfrac{\text{Crash cost–Normal cost}}{\text{Normal time–Crash time}}$ (d) $\dfrac{\text{Normal cost–Crash cost}}{\text{Normal time–Crash time}}$

57. The time corresponding to minimum total project cost is called

(a) normal time. (b) optimistic time.
(c) crash time. (d) optimum time.

58. The direct cost of a project with respect to normal time is
(a) maximum (b) minimum
(c) zero (d) infinite

59. The time beyond which the direct cost will not be reduced with the increase in time is known as
(a) crash time. (b) optimistic time.
(c) normal time. (d) optimum time.

60. The reduction in project time normally results in
(a) decreasing the direct cost and increasing the indirect cost.
(b) increasing the direct cost and decreasing the indirect cost.
(c) increasing both the direct cost and the indirect cost.
(d) decreasing both the direct cost and the indirect cost.

61. Economic saving of project time would result by crashing
(a) costliest critical activity.
(b) costliest non-critical activity.
(c) cheapest critical activity.
(d) cheapest non-critical activity.

62. Slack or Slack time refers to
(a) an activity.
(b) an event.
(c) both activity and event.
(d) neither activity nor event.

63. The process of incorporating changes in a network by replanning and rescheduling is called
(a) resource levelling.
(b) resource smoothing.
(c) updating.
(d) scheduling of critical path.

64. Updating a network may result in
(a) changing the critical path.
(b) decreasing the project completion time.
(c) increasing the project completion time.
(d) changing the critical path and increasing or decreasing the project completion time.

65. Normal time and crash time for each of the activities of a network shown in Fig. MCQ 65 are given below.

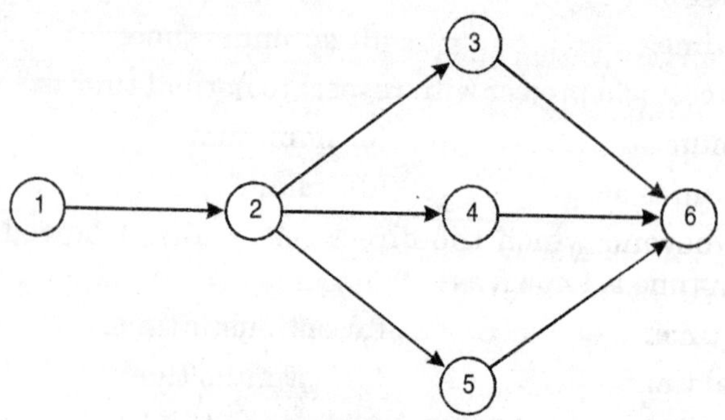

Fig. MCQ. 65

Activity	*Normal time (weeks)*	*Crash time (weeks)*
1–2	3	2
2–3	4	2
2–4	5	3
2–5	6	4
3–6	7	6
4–6	8	7
5–6	9	8

The minimum time required for the completion of project is

(a) 10 weeks (b) 12 weeks

(c) 14 weeks (d) 16 weeks

66. The normal time required for the completion of project represented by network shown in Fig. MCQ 65 is

(a) 20 weeks (b) 18 weeks

(c) 16 weeks (d) 14 weeks

67. Crash duration for the project is obtained by summing up the

(a) normal durations for all the activities.

(b) crash durations for all the activities.

(c) crash durations for all the activities along the critical path obtained by taking into account the crash duration for all the activities.

(d) crash durations for all the activities along the critical path obtained by taking into account the normal duration for all the activities.

68. In the case of resource smoothing operation for rescheduling of activities the constraint is on

(a) project duration.

(b) resources.

(c) both project duration and resources.

(d) neither project duration nor resources.

69. In the case of resource levelling operation for rescheduling of activities the constraint is on

(a) project duration.

(b) resources.

(c) both project duration and resources.

(d) neither project duration nor resources.

70. Slack or Slack time.

(a) can never be greater than zero.

(b) is always zero for critical activities.

(c) can never be less than zero.

(d) is minimum for critical activities.

71. The table below shows the activity, normal time, normal cost, crash time, crash cost and cost slope for the project network shown in Fig. MCQ 71.

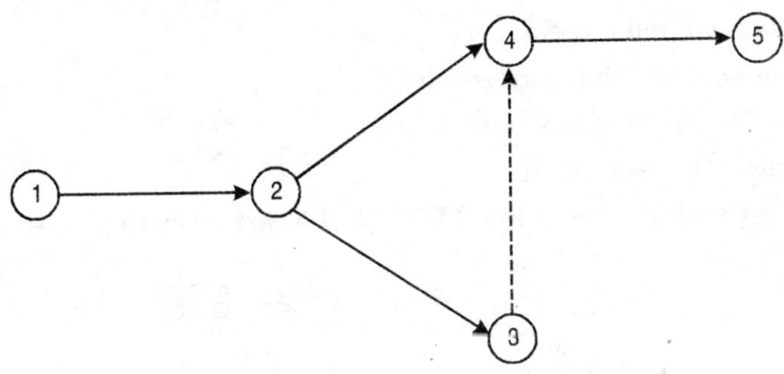

Fig. MCQ. 71

Activity	*Normal*		*Crash*		*Cost slope*		
	Time (days)	*Cost (Rs.)*	*Time (days)*	*Cost (Rs.)*	ΔT	ΔC	$\Delta C/\Delta T$
1–2	5	500	3	560	2	60	30
2–3	4	430	3	480	1	50	50
2–4	3	360	2	380	1	20	20
3–4	0	–	–	–	–	–	–
4–5	8	660	5	840	3	180	60

The normal cost and crash cost for the entire project are respectively

(a) Rs. 1590 and Rs. 1880.

(b) Rs. 1520 and Rs. 1780.

(c) Rs. 1450 and Rs. 1700.

(d) Rs. 1290 and Rs. 1420.

72. If the management decides to complete the project represented by the network shown in Fig. MCQ 71 in 15 days instead of 17 days then the crashing may be done for

(a) activity 4–5 by 2 days.

(b) activity 1–2 by 2 days.

(c) activity 1–2 by 1 day and activity 2–3 by 1 day.

(d) activity 1–2 by 1 day and activity 2–4 by 1 day.

73. If the earliest expected time for the completion of a project is 24 weeks but the desired (or latest) completion time for the project is 22 weeks, then the slack or slack time for the project is

(a) 2 weeks (b) 0

(c) –2 weeks (d) 1 week

74. Interfering float for an activity is the difference between its

(a) total float and free float.

(b) total float and independent float

(c) free float and independent float.

(d) none of the other floats.

75. In the network shown in Fig. MCQ 75 the correct critical path is

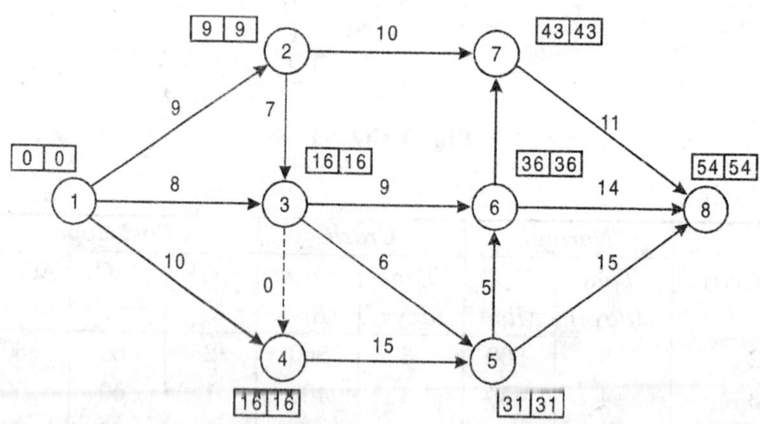

The box shows for each event earliest expected Time T_E and latest allowable time T_L in days on left side and right side respectively

Fig. MCQ. 75

(a) 1–2–3–6–7–8 (b) 1–2–3–5–6–7–8

(c) 1–3–5–6–7–8 (d) 1–2–3–6–8

76. In the network shown in Fig. MCQ 75 the number of critical activities is

(a) 4 (b) 5

(c) 6 (d) 7

77. In the network shown in Fig. MCQ 75 the total float is maximum for

(a) activity 1–3 (b) activity 2–7

(c) activity 5–8 (d) activity 3–6

78. In the network shown in Fig. MCQ 75 the total float for activity 6–8 is

(a) 4 (b) 6

(c) 8 (d) 9

79. In the network shown in Fig. MCQ 75 the free float for activity 6–8 is

(a) 9 (b) 8

(c) 6 (d) 4

80. In the network shown in Fig. MCQ 75 the number of noncritical activities is

(a) 4 (b) 5

(c) 7 (d) 8

81. If for an activity two engineers John Smith and Jack Doe gave the following time estimates

	Optimistic	*Most likely*	*Pessimistic*
Smith	2	4	6
Doe	8	10	11

then

(a) Doe was more uncertain about, the activity then Smith.

(b) Smith was more uncertain about the activity than Doe.

(c) both Smith and Doe had same degree of uncertainty.

(d) it cannot be known who was more uncertain.

82. In the network shown in Fig. MCQ 75 for event 3 the number of predecessor events is

(a) 1 (b) 2

(c) 3 (d) 4

83. In the network shown in Fig. MCQ 75 for event 3 the number of successor events is

(a) 1 (b) 2

(c) 3 (d) 4

84. *Dual role events* are those events which are

(a) head events for more than one activity.

(b) tail events for more than one activity.

(c) head events for some activities and tail events for other activities.

(d) neither tail events nor head events.

85. ***Assertion* (A) :** In the network shown in Fig. MCQ 75 activity 2–3 is critical.

***Reason* (R) :** For activity 2–3 the earliest finish time (EFT) and the latest finish time (LFT) are same and hence total float is equal to zero. Select the correct answer.

(a) A is true but R is not the correct explanation.

(b) A is true and R is the correct explanation.

(c) Both A and R are false.

(d) A is false but R is true.

86. ***Assertion* (A) :** In the network shown in Fig. MCQ 75 for event 6 slack or slack time is zero.

***Reason* (R) :** For event 6 the earliest expected time T_E and the latest allowable occurrence time T_L are equal. Select the correct answer.

(a) A is true but R is not the correct explanation of A.

(b) A is true and R is the correct explanation of A.

(c) Both A and R are false.

(d) A is false but R is true.

87. ***Assertion* (A) :** 'Engine assembly ordered from manufacturer' is a PERT event.

***Reason* (R) :** An event as used in PERT is the *start* or *completion* of a task and it is not the actual performance of the task.

Select the correct answer.

(a) Both A and R are false.

(b) A is false but R is true.

(c) A is true and R is the correct explanation of A.

(d) A is true but R is not the correct explanation of A.

88. ***Assertion* (A):** 'Engine is being assembled' is a PERT activity.

***Reason* (R) :** A PERT activity is the actual performance of a task which is a time consuming portion of the PERT network and requires manpower, material, space, facilities, or other resources.

Select the correct answer.

(a) Both A and R are false.

(b) A is false but R is true.

(c) A is true but R is not the correct explanation of A.

(d) A is true and R is the correct explanation of A.

89. A PERT network is
   (a) activity oriented.
   (b) event oriented.
   (c) time oriented.
   (d) resource oriented.
90. Select the incorrect statement
   (a) Critical activity is one for which free float is zero.
   (b) Critical path always begins at the very first event.
   (c) A critical path always terminates at the last event.
   (d) Critical activities control the project duration.
91. Which of the following is an example of parallel activities:
   (a) Construction of walls and casting of roofs.
   (b) Construction of walls and carpentry work of doors and windows.
   (c) Casting of roof and construction of parapet wall.
   (d) Digging of a septic tank pit and construction of septic tank.
92. Dummy activity is
   (a) a zero time activity.
   (b) a critical activity.
   (c) a parallel activity.
   (d) an activity having maximum expected time.
93. A network of seven activities is shown in Fig. MCQ 93. The respective activity durations are shown beside the arrows. Which one of the following is the total float in *AB*, the total float in *CE* and the free float in *EF* respectively ?

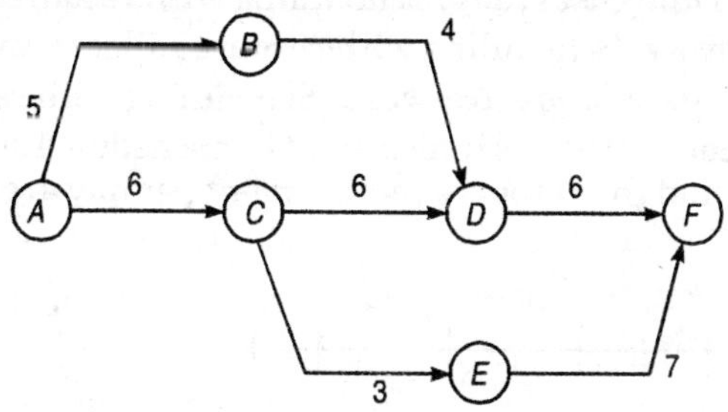

Fig. MCQ. 93

(a) 2, 2, 3 (b) 3, 3, 2
(c) 3, 2, 2 (d) 2, 3, 2

94. Consider the *AON* diagram MCQ 94. What is the minimum number of dummy arrows required for conversion into *AOA* diagram ?

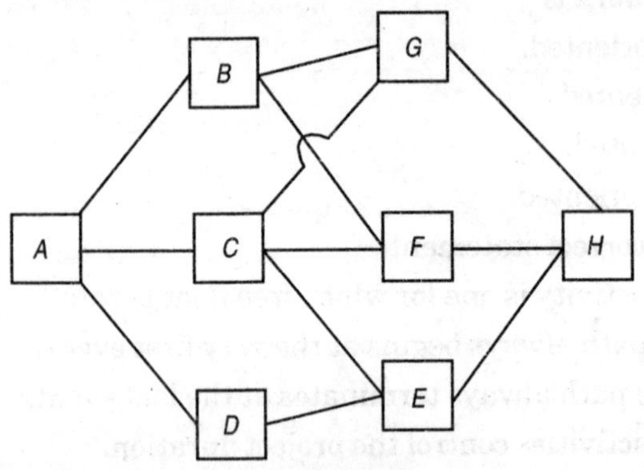

Fig. MCQ. 94

(a) 3
(b) 4
(c) 5
(d) 6

95. The line of a PERT network is shown in the diagram MCQ 95 with t_O, t_L, t_p (or a, m, b) durations.

A —8.8.11— B —9.15.15— C —6.8.10— D —4.7.10— E

Fig. MCQ. 95

What is the probable range of the total duration?
(a) 34.2 to 47.2
(b) 34.2 to 44.2
(c) 32.6 to 44.2
(d) 32.6 to 42.4

96. Which of the following is the correct sequence to analyse a project for implementation?
(a) Time-cost study, Network, WBS, Scheduling with resource allocation
(b) Network, Time-cost study, Scheduling with resource allocation, WBS
(c) WBS, Network, Scheduling with resource allocation, Time-cost study
(d) WBS, Time-cost study, Network, Scheduling with resource allocation

97. A bar chart of four activities indicating their scheduled start and finish "end of day" values and the resource requirement per day are given in Fig. MCQ 97.

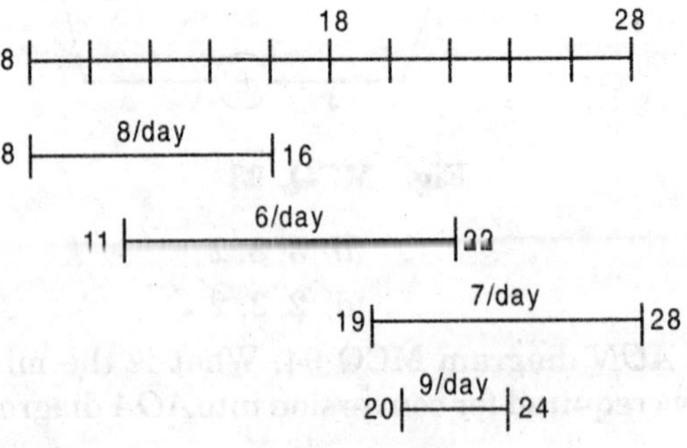

Fig. MCQ. 97

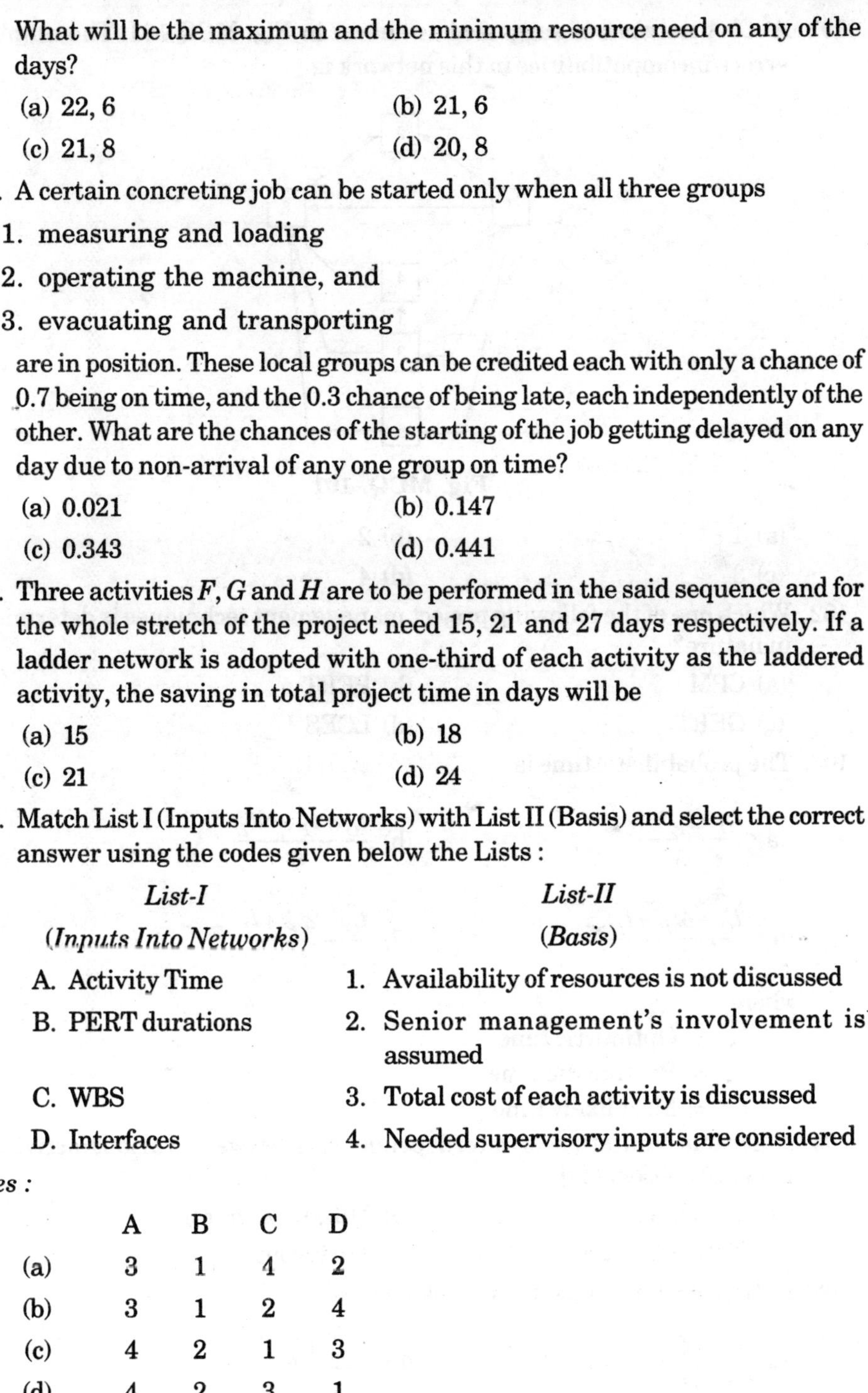

What will be the maximum and the minimum resource need on any of the days?

(a) 22, 6 (b) 21, 6

(c) 21, 8 (d) 20, 8

98. A certain concreting job can be started only when all three groups
 1. measuring and loading
 2. operating the machine, and
 3. evacuating and transporting

 are in position. These local groups can be credited each with only a chance of 0.7 being on time, and the 0.3 chance of being late, each independently of the other. What are the chances of the starting of the job getting delayed on any day due to non-arrival of any one group on time?

 (a) 0.021 (b) 0.147

 (c) 0.343 (d) 0.441

99. Three activities *F*, *G* and *H* are to be performed in the said sequence and for the whole stretch of the project need 15, 21 and 27 days respectively. If a ladder network is adopted with one-third of each activity as the laddered activity, the saving in total project time in days will be

 (a) 15 (b) 18

 (c) 21 (d) 24

100. Match List I (Inputs Into Networks) with List II (Basis) and select the correct answer using the codes given below the Lists :

List-I (*Inputs Into Networks*)	*List-II* (*Basis*)
A. Activity Time	1. Availability of resources is not discussed
B. PERT durations	2. Senior management's involvement is assumed
C. WBS	3. Total cost of each activity is discussed
D. Interfaces	4. Needed supervisory inputs are considered

Codes :

	A	B	C	D
(a)	3	1	4	2
(b)	3	1	2	4
(c)	4	2	1	3
(d)	4	2	3	1

101. *A–O–A* network is suggested as shown in Fig. MCQ 101. The number of errors/incompatibilities in this network is

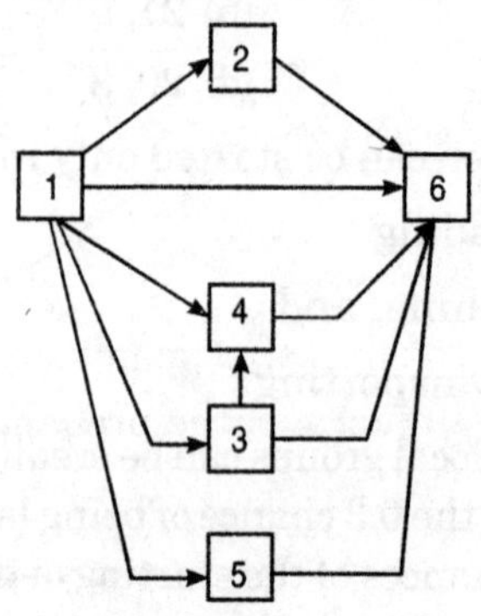

Fig. MCQ. 101

(a) 1 (b) 2

(c) 3 (d) 4

102. Which one of the following project management techniques is deterministic in nature?

(a) CPM (b) PERT

(c) GERT (d) LCES

103. The probabilistic time is

(a) $\dfrac{t_O + t_P + t_L}{3}$ (b) $\dfrac{t_O + t_P + 4t_L}{6}$

(c) $\dfrac{t_O + 4t_P + t_L}{6}$ (d) $\dfrac{t_O + 2t_P + t_L}{6}$

where

t_O = Optimistic time

t_P = Pessimistic time

t_L = Most likely time

104. A serious limitation of interdependencies between various activities is generally observed in

(a) Bar charts (b) Milestone charts

(c) Network analysis (d) Job layouts

105. In time-cost analysis, the cost slope C_s is

(a) $\dfrac{C_c - C_n}{t_c - t_n}$ (b) $\dfrac{C_c - C_n}{t_n - t_c}$

(c) $\frac{t_c - t_n}{C_c - C_n}$ (d) $\frac{C_n - C_c}{2(t_n - t_c)}$

where

C_c = Crash cost

C_n = Normal cost

t_c = Crash time

t_n = Normal time

106. The probability that the load on a scaffolding will exceed the design load of 3 tonnes is 0.15. At the same time, the probability that the strength of the scaffolding will be more than 3 tonnes is 0.85. The probability that the scaffolding will fail is

(a) 0.2775 (b) 0.1275

(c) 0.0225 (d) 0.0020

107. In the network shown in Fig. MCQ 107, the critical path of activities is

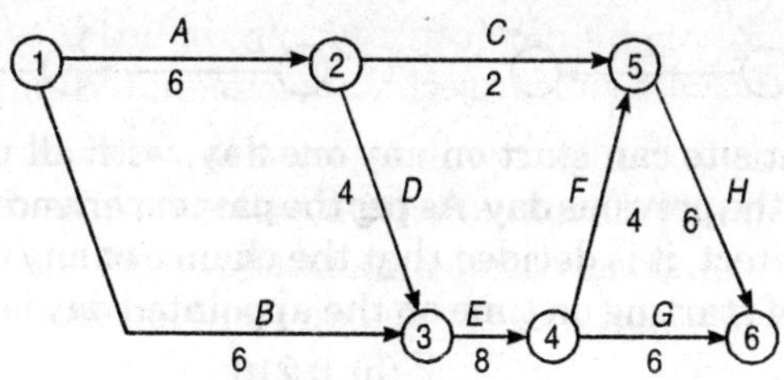

Fig. MCQ. 107

(a) *A–C–H* (b) *B–E–F–H*

(c) *A–D–E–F–H* (d) *A–D–E–G*

108. The optimum duration is the

(a) summation of normal durations of each activity in the project

(b) summation of the normal duration of activities on critical path

(c) one, which gives the minimum total cost for completing the project

(d) summation of crash-time of activities on critical path

109. In order to investigate a method of least-cost scheduling, which of the following assumptions are made?

1. The planned duration of an activity can be any whole day value between the normal and crash durations.
2. The direct cost of an activity is linear between the normal and crash direct costs.
3. The overhead cost is linear during the entire project.

Select the correct answer using the codes given below:

Codes:

(a) 1 and 2 (b) 1 and 3

(c) 2 and 3 (d) 1, 2 and 3

110. In PERT analysis, the time estimates of activities and probability of their occurrence follow

(a) Normal distribution curve (b) β-distribution curve

(c) Poisson's distribution curve (d) Binomial distribution curve

111. Activity *C* follows activity *A* and activity *D* follows activities *A* and *B*. The correct network for the project is

(a) 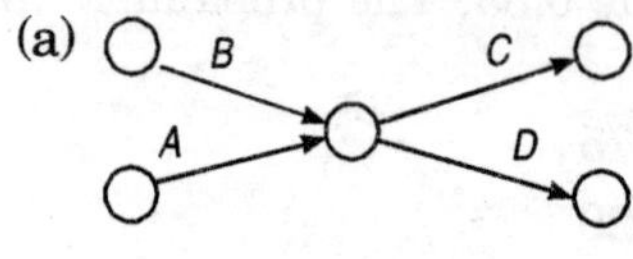

(b) 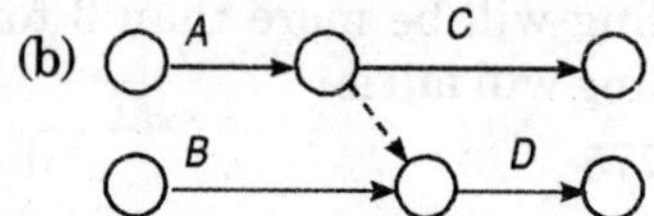

(c) 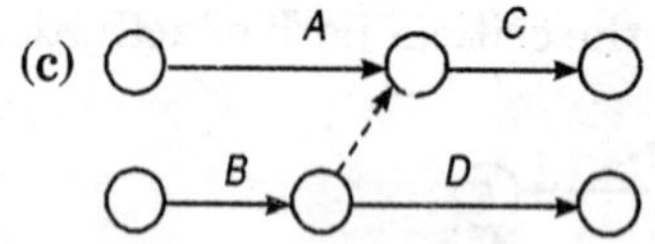

(d) 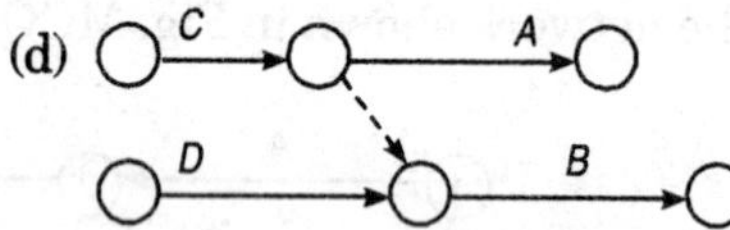

112. Concreting at site can start on any one day, with all preparations having been done on the previous day. As per the past experience of owner, contractor and the architect, it is decided that the chance of any one being late is 0.4. The chance of starting on time on the appointed day is

(a) 0.064 (b) 0.216

(c) 0.288 (d) 0.432

113. Consider the following statements regarding the curve shown in Fig. MCQ 113.

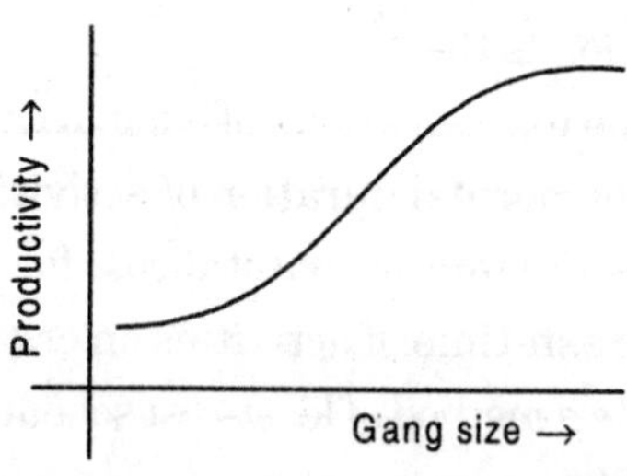

Fig. MCQ. 113

As the gang size increases,

1. **the out-turn rate of the gang will always increase irrespective of the number of gang.**
2. **the out-turn rate of the gang will decrease once it exceeds the optimal number.**
3. **beyond the optimal number, the inefficiency of the gang will increase.**

Which of these statements are correct?

(a) 1, 2 and 3 (b) 1 and 2

(c) 2 and 3 (d) 1 and 3

114. In the time-cost analysis, the cost slope is defined as

(a) $\dfrac{\text{Crash cost} - \text{Normal cost}}{\text{Crash time} - \text{Normal time}}$ (b) $\dfrac{\text{Crash time} - \text{Normal time}}{\text{Crash cost} - \text{Normal cost}}$

(c) $\dfrac{\text{Crash cost} - \text{Normal cost}}{\text{Normal time} - \text{Crash time}}$ (d) $\dfrac{\text{Normal cost} - \text{Crash cost}}{\text{Normal time} - \text{Crash time}}$

115. Which one of the following is the base for resource levelling?

(a) Delaying the completion of critical activities

(b) Delaying the start of non-critical activities

(c) Reducing completion time of critical activities

(d) Not delaying the completion of critical activities

116. The probability that the load on a scaffolding will exceed $2t$ is 0.15. The probability that the strength of the scaffolding will be more than $2t$ is 0.8. The probability of failure of the scaffolding will be

(a) 0.68 (b) 0.17

(c) 0.12 (d) 0.03

117. Every cu. m of excavation requires either 3 man-hours or 0.2 machine-hour. The respective rates are Rs. 8 per man-hour and Rs. 200 per machine-hour. A total quantity of 4000 cu. m of excavation is to be done. The possible minimum total cost for the complete job, by a suitable combination of manual and mechanical means of excavation will be

(a) Rs. 80,000 (b) Rs. 1,20,000

(c) Rs. 1,50,000 (d) Rs. 1,80,000

118. A, B and C are three activities to be executed in that order. Their total durations, in days, are 15, 24 and 18 respectively. However, for better estimation of overall total duration, they are put into a ladder network with 3 equal sub-parts of each. The modified total duration for total completion of all the activities will be

(a) 35 days (b) 37 days

(c) 39 days (d) 41 days

119. There are four cosecutive activities in a simple linear network, each with mean duration of T and each with k as the standard deviation of its duration. The overall project duration through these activities is likely to be in the range

(a) $4T \pm k$ (b) $4T \pm 2k$

(c) $4T \pm 4k$ (d) $4T \pm 6k$

120. A certain type of resource can be developed in a variable strength during parts of the duration of an activity. The following are the data in this context:
   1. Six weeks duration with 10 units of the resource in each week, or
   2. Four weeks duration with 10 units of the resource in each week followed by 5 weeks duration with 5 units in each week, or
   3. Eight weeks duration with 7 units in each week, or
   4. Four weeks duration with 7 units in each week followed by 3 weeks duration with 10 units in each week.

   For developing the CPM network involving this activity therein, the duration of this activity will be considered as

   (a) 9 weeks (b) 8 weeks
   (c) 7 weeks (d) 6 weeks

121. Consider the activity-on-arrow (*A-O-A*) network of a project shown in Fig. MCQ 121. (Activities are designated by alphabets and durations are shown around the stem of the arrow)

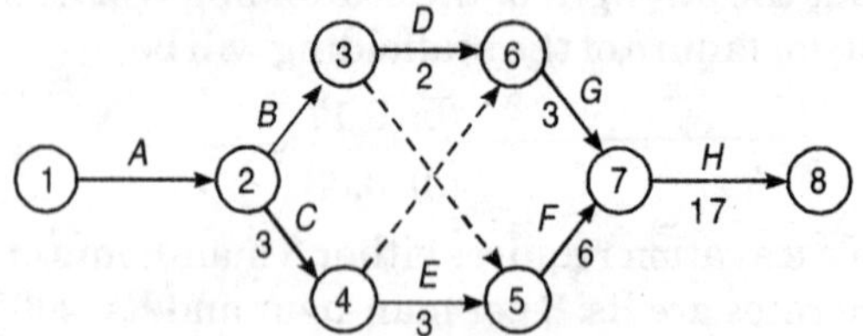

Fig. MCQ. 121

The critical path will be

(a) 1–2–3–6–7–8 (b) 1–2–3–5–7–8
(c) 1–2–4–5–7–8 (d) 1–2–4–6–7–8

122. Consider the following pairs:
   1. Difference between total float and free float : Interfering float
   2. Sum of independent float and tail slack : Free float
   3. Sum of independent float, tail slack and interfering float :Total float

   Which of these pairs are correctly matched?

   (a) 1, 2 and 3 (b) 1 and 2
   (c) 2 and 3 (d) 1 and 3

123. The earliest date and the latest date of events 3 and 10 are given in Fig. MCQ 123. Activity *E* is connecting both the events and its duration is 10 weeks.

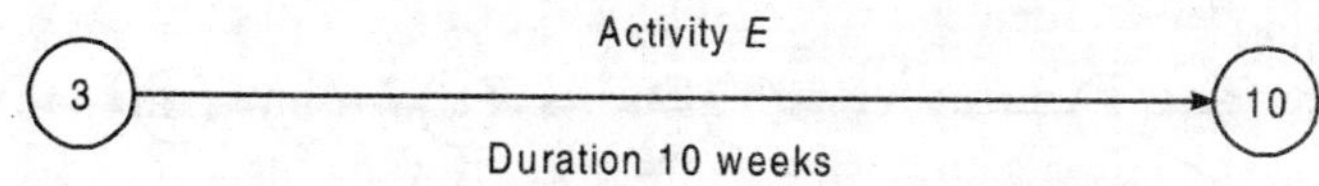

Fig. MCQ. 123

The independent float of the activity is

(a) 5 weeks (b) 10 weeks

(c) 15 weeks (d) 20 weeks

124. From the network shown in Fig. MCQ 124 (the number on each arrow denotes the time duration of activity in days), the earliest start time, in days for activity 5–6 is

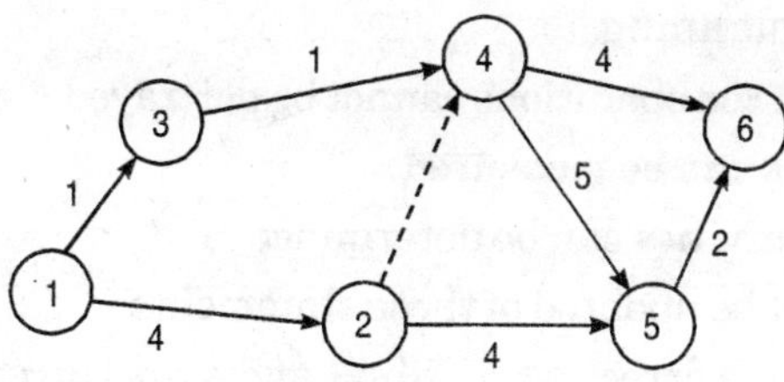

Fig. MCQ. 124

(a) 8 (b) 7

(c) 9 (d) 11

125. The figure given below shows the arrow diagram for a particular project.

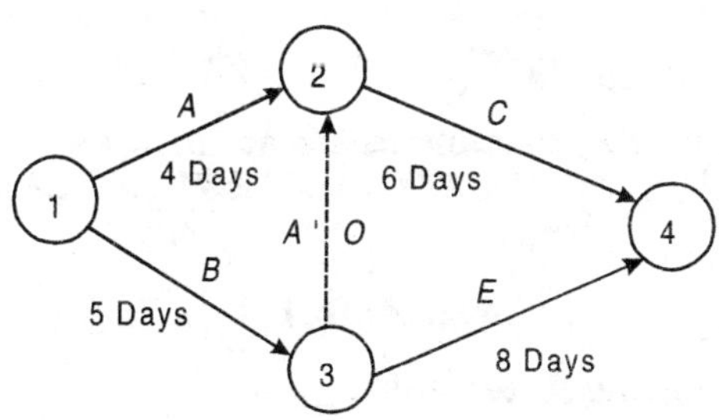

Fig. MCQ. 125

The arrow A´ is known as

(a) critical activity (b) logic arrow

(c) dummy activity (d) sub-critical activity

126. A 'merge event' is represented by

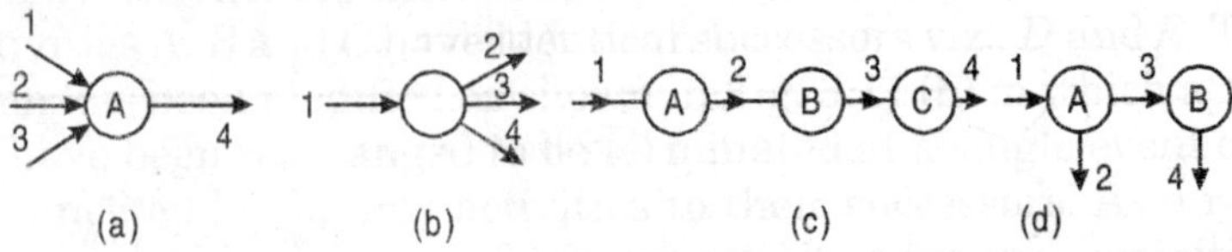

Fig. MCQ. 126

127. A tractor shovel has a purchase price of Rs. 4.7 lacs and could save the organization an amount of rupees on lac per year on operating costs. The salvage value after the amortization period is 10% of the purchase price. The capital recovery period will be

(a) 3.7 years (b) 4.23 years

(c) 5 years (d) 7.87 years

128. Consider the following statements :

In the bar chart planning

1. Independence of the operations cannot be portrayed
2. Progress of work can be measured
3. Spare time of activities can be determined
4. Schedule cannot be updated of these statements

(a) 1, 2 and 3 are correct (b) 1 and 4 are correct

(c) 2, 3 and 4 are correct (d) 1, 2 and 4 are correct

129. Activities *A* and *B* can be started independently. Activity *E* can be started only when *A* and *B* have been completed. Activity *D* follows *A* and precedes *F*. Activities *E* and *F* merge at the objective event. The network plan will be as in

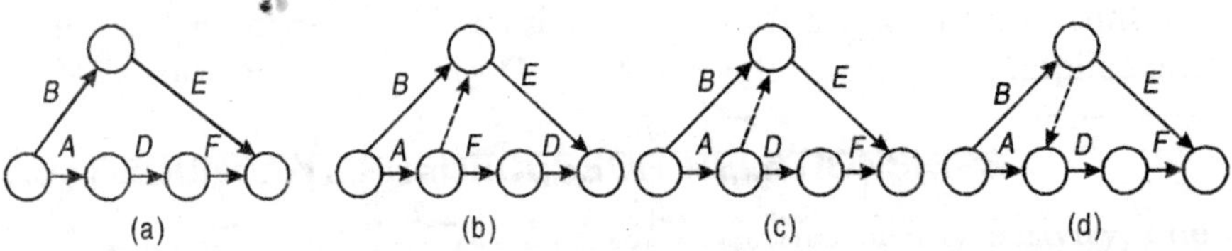

Fig. MCQ. 129

130. Consider the following statements :

In the critical method of construction planning Free float can be

1 greater than total float
2. greater than independent float
3. equal to total float
4. less than independent float of these statements

(a) 1 and 4 are correct (b) 2 and 3 are correct

(c) 3 and 4 are correct (d) 1 and 2 are correct

131. Which one of the following diagrams will be the correct one for deciding the most optimal cost and duration of a project ?

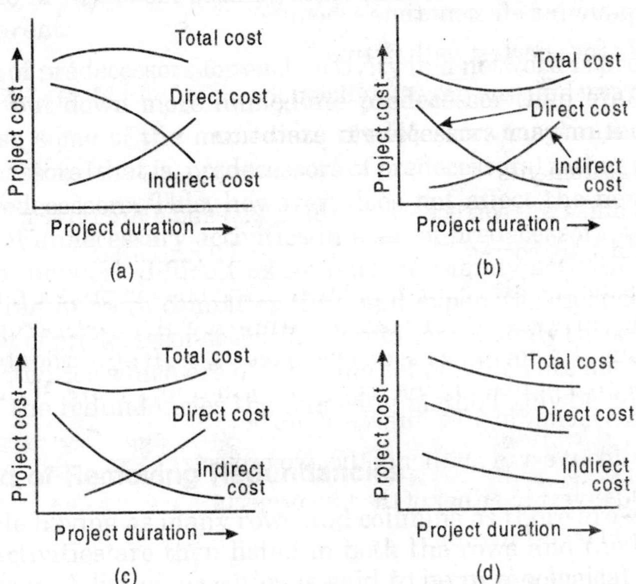

Fig. MCQ. 131

132. In time-cost optimisation of a project, crashing is done

(a) on all activities

(b) on all the activities lying on the critical path

(c) only on activities lying on the original critical path and having flatter cost slope

(d) on original critical activities and those that become critical at any stage of crashing in the order of ascending cost slope

133. For the path of a certain network shown in the figure given below the expected time and standard deviation will be respectively

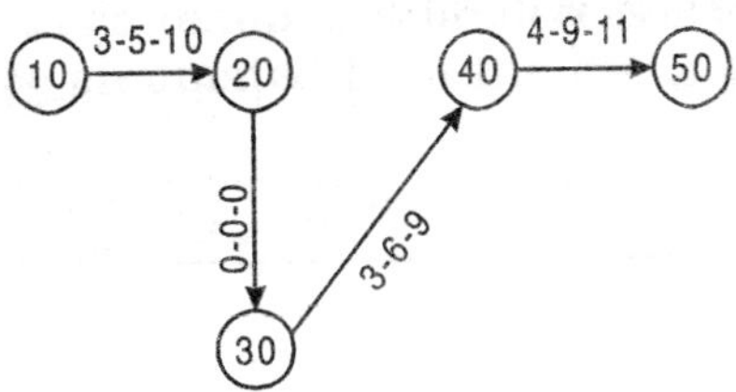

Fig. MCQ. 133

(a) 15 and 1.5 (b) 20 and 1.75

(c) 15 and 1.62 (d) 20 and 1.93

134. Consider the following statements

The critical path in a network plan of a project

1. help in planning efficient time schedule
2. indicates the shortest path in time
3. helps in crashing the project judiciously
4. helps in encouraging discipline in execution

of these statements

(a) 1, 3 and 4 are correct (b) 1, 2, 3 and 4 are correct

(c) 1 and 4 are correct (d) 2 and 3 are corect

135. A contractor has two option; I : Invest his money in project *A* or II : Invest his money in project *B*. If he decides to invest in *A*, for every rupee invested, he is assured of doubling his money in ten years. If he decides to invest in *B*, he is assured of making his money 1.5 times in 5 years. If the contractor values his money at 10% interest rate, he

(a) should invest in neither of the two projects

(b) could invest in either of the two projects

(c) should invest in project *A*

(d) should invest in project *B*

136. There are three parallel paths in a part of network between a bursting node and the next merging node with only one activity in each path. The minimium number of dummy arrows need will be

(a) Zero (b) 1

(c) 2 (d) 3

137. Match List I with List II and select the correct answer using the codes given below the Lists :

List-I (*Activity types*)	*List-II* (*Property of activity*)
A. Critical activity to be crashed first to reduce project duration	1. It has float
B. Critical activity	2. it has least cost slope
C. Dummy activity	3. It maintains logic of network
D. Subcritical activity	4. It has not float

Codes :

	A	B	C	D
(a)	1	2	4	3
(b)	3	1	2	4

(c)	2	4	3	1
(d)	4	3	1	2

138. The following figure indicates a project network, the number above each activity represents its normal duration in days

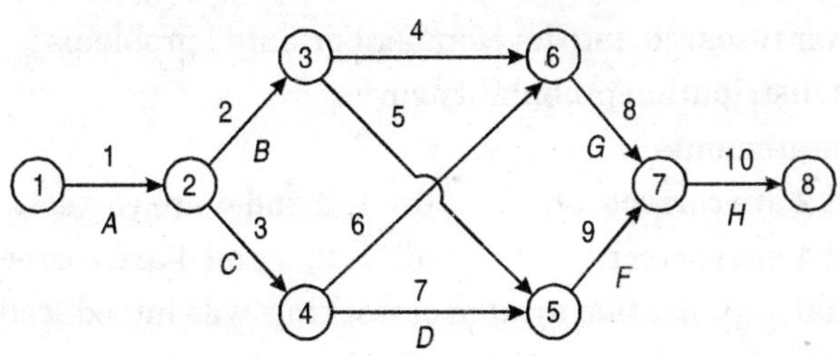

Fig. MCQ. 138

The critical path is along

(a) $1 \rightarrow 2 \rightarrow 3 \rightarrow 6 \rightarrow 7 \rightarrow 8$ (b) $1 \rightarrow 2 \rightarrow 4 \rightarrow 5 \rightarrow 7 \rightarrow 8$

(c) $1 \rightarrow 2 \rightarrow 3 \rightarrow 5 \rightarrow 7 \rightarrow 8$ (d) $1 \rightarrow 2 \rightarrow 4 \rightarrow 6 \rightarrow 7 \rightarrow 8$

139. For an activity i–j the early event times at i and j, and the late event times at i and j, respectively are 5, 24, 9 and 29. The activity duration is 6.

Match List I with List II and select the correct answer using the codes gives below the lists :

List-I	*List-II*
A. Free float	1. 5
B. Total float	2. 9
C. Inter ference	3. 13
D. Independent	4. 18

Codes :

	A	B	C	D
(a)	4	3	1	2
(b)	3	4	1	2
(c)	3	4	2	1
(d)	4	3	2	1

140. Consider the following statements :

CPM network helps an engineer to

1. concentrate his attention on critical activities
2. divert the resources from non-critical advanced activities to critical activities
3. be cautions in avoiding any delay in the critical activities in order to avoid delay of the whole project

of these statements

(a) 1 and 2 are correct (b) 2 and 3 are correct

(c) 1 and 3 are correct (d) 1, 2 and 3 are correct

141. Consider the following statements :
PERT
1. takes care of uncentainties in the completion time
2. requires single time estimate
3. is useful for research and development oriented problems
4. uses beta distribution probability curve

Of these statements
(a) 1 and 2 are correct (b) 1, 3 and 4 are correct
(c) 3 and 4 are correct (d) 1, 2, 3 and 4 are correct

142. 'Functional organization system of working' was introduced by
(a) F.W. Taylor (b) Henry Gnatt
(c) M.R. Walker (d) J.E. Kelley

143. In resources Levelling
(a) total duration of prject is reduced
(b) total duration of project is increased
(c) uniform demand of resources is achieved
(d) cost of project is controlled

144. The original cost of an equipment is Rs. 10,000. Its salvage value at the end of its total useful life of five years is Rs. 1000. Its book value at the end of two years of its useful life end of two years of its useful life (as per straight line method of evaluation of depreciation) will be
(a) Rs. 8,800 (b) Rs. 7,200
(c) Rs. 6,400 (d) Rs. 5,000

145. Given that
t = the duration of various jobs
t_m = mean time of different durations
n = number of observations
The standard deviation is given
(a) $\frac{\Sigma t}{n}$ (b) $t - t_m$
(c) $\frac{\Sigma(t - t_m)^2}{n}$ (d) $\frac{\sqrt{\Sigma(t - t_m^2)}}{n}$

146. Consider the following features/factors :
1. Project are the non-repetitive type
2. Time required need not be known
3. Time required is known precisely
4. Events have been established for planning

5. Emphasis given to activities of project
PERT is preferred for planning because of

(a) 1, 2 and 4 (b) 3, 4 and 5
(c) 1, 3 and 4 (d) 1, 2 and 5

147. Match List I with List II and select the correct answer using the codes given below the Lists :

List-I (*Description of activity floats*)	*List-II* (*Names of the floats*)
A. Earliest start time of successor activity minus earliest start time of activity in question minus the duration of the activity	1. Total
B. Maximum time available for an activity performance minus the duration of the activity	2. Free
C. Excess of minimum available time over the required activity duration	3. Interfering
D. Difference between total float and free float of an activity	4. Independent

Codes :

	A	B	C	D
(a)	1	2	3	4
(b)	1	2	4	3
(c)	2	1	3	4
(d)	2	1	4	3

148. The flow net of activities of a project is given in the following figure. The duration of activities are indicated along the arrows.

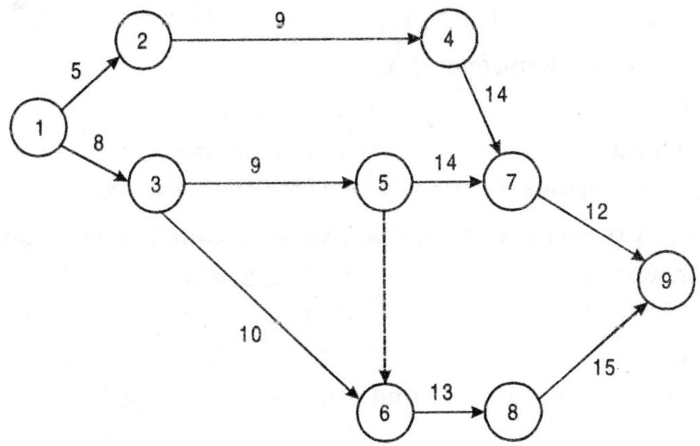

Fig. MCQ. 148

The critical path of the activities is along

(a) 1–2–4–7–9 (b) 1–3–5–7–9

(c) 1–3–6–8–9 (d) 1–3–5–6–8–9

149. Consider the following activities in a building construction :

1. Concreting of roof slabs.
2. Brick-jelly lime concrete terracing.
3. Erection of form work of slab.
4. Construction of parapet wall in terrace

The correct sequence of these activities

(a) 1, 3, 2, 4 (b) 3, 1, 4, 2

(c) 3, 1, 2, 4 (d) 1, 3, 4, 2

150. Match List I with List II and select the correct answer using the codes given below the Lists :

List-I (*Item*)	*List-II* (*Characteristic*)
A. Activity	1. Resourceless element
B. Event	2. Resource consuming element
C. Dummy	3. Spare time
D. Float	4. Instantaneous stage

Codes :

	A	B	C	D
(a)	1	4	3	2
(b)	2	1	4	3
(c)	2	4	1	3
(d)	3	1	4	2

151. Consider the following operations :

1. Drilling 2. Blasting
3. Mucking 4. Placing steel
5. Placing concrete

The correct sequence of these operations in tunnel construction :

(a) 1, 2, 4, 3, 5 (b) 1, 3, 2, 4, 5

(c) 1, 2, 3, 4, 5 (d) 1, 3, 4, 2, 5

152. For a given activity, the optimistic time, pessimistic time and the most probable estimates are 5, 17 and 8 days respectively. The expected time is

(a) 8 days (b) 9 days

(c) 10 days (d) 15 days

153. The following table contains data on four activities A, B, C and D :

Activity	*Startat : Week number*	*Ends with : Week number*	*Resource needed Per week*
A	9th	16th	6
B	11th	20th	4
C	15th	22nd	3
D	13th	24th	7

The maximum total resource load in any week will be

(a) 20 (b) 17

(c) 16 (d) 14

154. Three activities implementable in parallel, have the following time-cost relationships for direct cost components in each :

Activity A : 10 days-800 units 9 days-900 units 8 days-1000 units

Activity B : 11 days-1200 units 10 days-1350 units 9 days-1500 units

Activity C : 7 days-500 units 6 days-700 units 5 days-900 units

The feasible range of total direct cost component for the three activities together is

(a) 2500 to 3400 units (b) 2650 to 3200 units

(c) 2500 to 2900 units (d) 2600 to 3100 units

155. The following diagram shows the details necessary for the CPM network analysis :

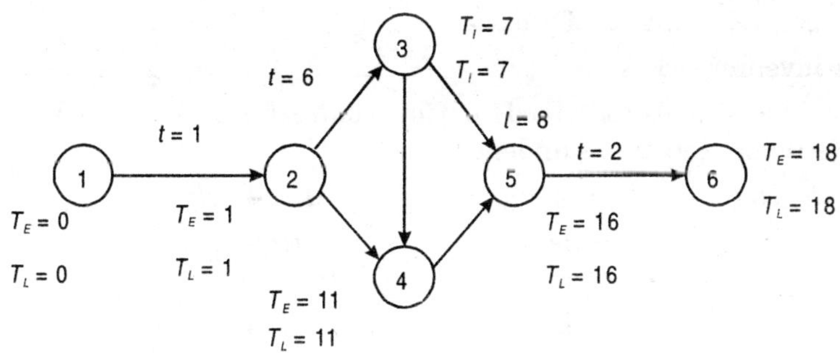

Fig. MCQ. 155

The critical path will be :

(a) 1–2–3–5–6 (b) 1–2–3–4–5–6

(c) 1–2–4–5–6 (d) 1–2–4–3–5–6

156. The profit and the associated probability of making the profits are given below in respect of four projects :

Project	*Profit*	*Probability of making the profit*
1	15%	0.5
2	10%	0.8
3	12%	0.7
4	11%	0.6

When the motive is maximisation of expected profit, the correct order of preference of these projects would be

(a) 1, 3, 4, 2 (b) 2, 3, 4, 1
(c) 3, 2, 1, 4 (d) 3, 4, 1, 2

157. Consider the following statements :
Resource levelling means
1. economical utilisation of resources.
2. gradual increase in resources.
3. adjustment of resources to have the least variations.
4. complete revamping of resources to suit the requirements.
5. validating network depending on resource constraints.
Of these statements
(a) 1 and 2 are correct (b) 2, 3 nd 4 are correct
(c) 3 and 5 are correct (d) 1, 2, 3, 4 and 5 are correct

158. Gantt charts indicate
(a) comparison of actual progress with the scheduled progress
(b) balance of worj to be done
(c) progressive costs of project
(d) inventory costs

159. The time estimates obtained from four contractors *P, Q, R* and *S* for executing a particular job are as under :

Contractor	*Optimistic time* t_o	*Most likely time* t_L	*Pessimistic time* t_p
P	5	10	13
Q	6	9	12
R	5	10	14
S	4	10	13

Which one of these contractors is more certain about completing the job in time ?
(a) P (b) Q
(c) R (d) S

160. The probability distribution taken to represent the completion time in PERT analysis is

(a) gamma distribution (b) normal distribution

(c) beta distribution (d) log-normal distribution

161. The network rules are common to all activity-on-arrow networking systems. The use of computers for making computations may impose certain rules. Which of the following basic rules of network logic are correct ?

1. Before an activity may begin, all the activities preceding it must be complete
2. Any two events may be directly connected by not more than one activity.
3. Event numbers must not be duplicated in a network.

Select the correct answer using the codes given below :

Codes :

(a) 1 and 2 (b) 2 and 3

(c) 1 and 3 (d) 1, 2 and 3

162. Consider the following statements :

Crashing a project in terms of its duration would result in

1. aqn increase in the indirect cost.
2. a decrease in the indirect cost.
3. a decrease in the direct cost.
4. an increase in the direct cost.

Of these statements

(a) 1 and 4 are correct (b) 2 and 3 are correct

(c) 1 and 3 are correct (d) 2 and 4 are correct

163. The flownet of the activities of a project are shown in the network given below indicating the dration of the activities along their arrows.

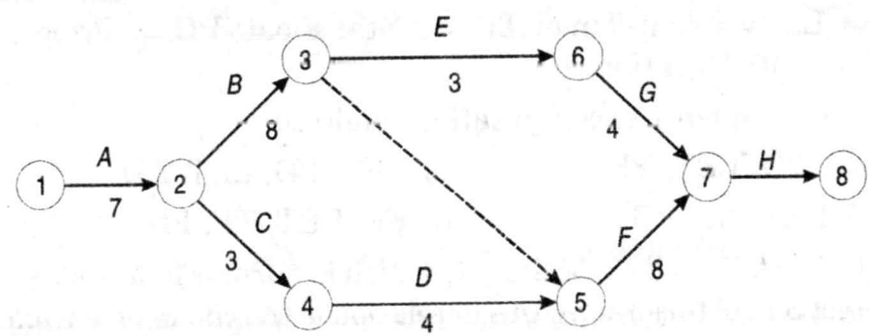

Fig. MCQ. 163

The critical path of the activities is along

(a) 1 → 2 → 4 → 5 → 7 → 8 (b) 1 → 2 → 3 → 6 → 7 → 8

(c) 1 → 2 → 3 → 5→ 7 → 8 (d) 1 → 2 → 4 → 5 → 6 → 7 → 8

164. Which of the following are the possible changes during the updating of the project network ?

1. Change in the duration of an activity
2. Addition or deletion of an activity
3. Change in the logical relationship among the activities.

Select the correct answer using the codes given below :

Codes :

(a) 1, 2 and 3 (b) 1 and 2
(c) 2 and 3 (d) 1 and 3

165. In time-cost optimization using CPM method for netwqork analysis, the crashing of the activities along the critical path is done starting with the activity having

(a) longest duration (b) highest cost slope
(c) least cost slope (d) shortest duration

166. Two events *K* and *L* can cause delay in a construction activity when occurring either each independetly or both together, but the two events are not statistically independent of each other. The prpbability that at least one of the envents occurs is 0.75 and the probability that each one occurs by itself is 0.45. The critical probability for occurrence of delay in the activity is

(a) $\dfrac{0.75}{0.75+0.45}$ (b) $\dfrac{0.75-0.45}{0.75}$

(c) $\dfrac{2\times 0.45-0.75}{0.75}$ (d) $\dfrac{2\times 0.45-0.75}{0.45}$

167. Consider the implicit details between, before and after successive steps in/within the order while doing time computations on a CPM network

(FP ⇒ Forward pass, BP ⇒ Backward Pass; LET ⇒ Late Event Time, EET ⇒ Early Event Time; TF ⇒ Total Float; PD ⇒ Project Duration; AD ⇒ Activity Duration)

The correct sequence of computation would be

(a) EFT, PD, LET, TF (b) EET, PD, LET, AD
(c) AD, EET, BP, PD (d) FP, EET, TF, PD

168. Activity *P* is followed by Activity *Q* which in turn, is followed by Activity *R*. The direct cost of these activities in relation to the choice of feasible durations table is given below :

	Activity P			*Activity Q*			*Activity R*		
Duration in days	7	6	5	8	7	6	9	8	7
Direct cost Rs. '000	12	14	15	20	23	27	40	42	45

For all the three activities taken together the minimum possible direct cost for a total duration of 21 days will be

(a) Rs. 81,000 (b) Rs. 79,000

(c) Rs. 78,000 (d) Rs. 77,000

169. A machine costs Rs. 16,000. By constant rate of declining balance method of depreciation, its salvage value after an expected life of 3 years is Rs. 2,000. The rate of depreciation is

(a) 0.25 (b) 0.30

(c) 0.40 (d) 0.50

ANSWERS

1. (d)	2. (d)	3. (c)	4. (b)	5. (a)	6. (b)	7. (d)
8. (c)	9. (a)	10. (c)	11. (d)	12. (b)	13. (d)	14. (c)
15. (d)	16. (a)	17. (c)	18. (a)	19. (b)	20. (d)	21. (a)
22. (b)	23. (c)	24. (d)	25. (a)	26. (c)	27. (d)	28. (c)
29. (b)	30. (a)	31. (b)	32. (a)	33. (c)	34. (a)	35. (b)
36. (c)	37. (d)	38. (a)	39. (c)	40. (b)	41. (d)	42. (b)
43. (b)	44. (c)	45. (b)	46. (a)	47. (b)	48. (a)	49. (c)
50. (a)	51. (c)	52. (a)	53. (c)	54. (d)	55. (a)	56. (c)
57. (d)	58. (b)	59. (c)	60. (b)	61. (a)	62. (b)	63. (c)
64. (d)	65. (c)	66. (b)	67. (c)	68. (a)	69. (b)	70. (d)
71. (a)	72. (b)	73. (c)	74. (a)	75. (b)	76. (c)	77. (b)
78. (a)	79. (d)	80. (c)	81. (b)	82. (b)	83. (c)	84. (c)
85. (b)	86. (b)	87. (c)	88. (d)	89. (b)	90. (a)	91. (b)
92. (a)	93. (c)	94. (a)	95. (c)	96. (c)	97. (a)	98. (b)
99. (c)	100. (b)	101. (a)	102. (a)	103. (b)	104. (a)	105. (b)
106. (c)	107. (c)	108. (c)	109. (b)	110. (b)	111. (b)	112. (b)
113. (c)	114. (c)	115. (b)	116. (d)	117. (b)	118. (c)	119. (b)
120. (a)	121. (c)	122. (a)	123. (a)	124. (d)	125. (c)	126. (a)
127. (b)	128. (b)	129. (c)	130. (b)	131. (b)	132. (c)	133. (d)
134. (a)	135. (b)	136. (c)	137. (c)	138. (b)	139. (b)	140. (d)
141. (c)	142. (a)	143. (c)	144. (c)	145. (d)	146. (c)	147. (d)
148. (c)	149. (c)	150. (c)	151. (c)	152. (b)	153. (a)	154. (a)
155. (b)	156. (c)	157. (c)	158. (a)	159. (b)	160. (c)	161. (c)
162. (d)	163. (c)	164. (b)	165. (c)	166. (a)	167. (c)	168. (d)
169. (d)						

Glossary

Activity Any definable and time-consuming task, operation, or function to be executed in a project.

Activity Description A condensed explanation of the nature of work to be performed.

Activity Duration The length of time from start to finish of an activity, estimated or actual, in working or calender time units.

Activity Times Time information generated through the CPM calculation that identifies the start and finish times for each in the network.

Activity Total Slack The latest allowable end time minus earliest allowable end time. The activity slack is always greater than or equal to the slack of the activity ending event.

Actual Costs The actual expenditures incurred for a programme or project.

AON Diagram or Activity-On-Node Diagram It is a network in which activities are denoted by nodes or circles and the immediate predecessor relationship between two activities is shown by an arrow connecting the two nodes.

Arrow The graphic representation of an activity in the CPM network. One arrow represents one activity. The arrow is not a vector quantity and it is not drawn to scale. It is uniquely defined by two event nodes.

Arrow Diagram A network on which the activities are represented by arrows between event nodes.

Beginning Event An event that signifies the beginning of an activity. Synonym : Predecessor event.

Beginning Network Event The event that signifies the beginning of a network. Synonym : Initial event.

Cost Control Utilises data on planned and actual expenditure by activity; provides reports on status of expenditure compared with those planned; predicts ultimate cost of project compared with planned cost; summarises data by accounting periods.

Cost Optimisation Utilises 'normal' and 'crash' cost estimates for each activity to make time-cost trade off computation ; provides list of alternative project durations and associated costs.

Cost Slope The additional cost to be incurred in reducing an activity time per unit time.

CPM Critical Path Method.

Crash Cost The increased cost of crashing an activity/project.

Crashing or Activity Compression The process of advancing the completion date of the project to suit a revised and reduced project duration by reducing the duration of one or more activities on the critical path.

Critical Activity An activity for which total float is equal to zero.

Critical Path A particular sequence of activities in a path that has the greatest negative or least positive slack ; therefore the longest path through the network.

Direct Cost Costs charged directly to an activity or work package in the contract.

Dummy Activity A zero time activity placed in the network merely to show a dependent relationship (Logical Restraint).

Dummy Activity (Dummy) An activity which represents only an interdependency and does not consume either resources or time.

Dummy Start Activity An activity entered into the network for the sole purpose of creating a start for the network.

Duration The Activity Duration.

Earliest Expected Time or Earliest Expected Date The earliest time or calender date on which an event can be expected to be completed, or on which the completion of an activity, work package or summary item occurs.

Earliest Event Time The earliest time at which an event may occur.

Earliest Finish Time The earliest time at which an activity can be completed.

Earliest Start Time The earliest time at which an activity can be started.

End Event An event with preceding activities but no succeeding activities. It marks the completion of the project. Synonym : Final Event.

Ending Event The event that signifies the completion of an activity. Synonym : Successor Event.

End Network Event The event that signifies the end of a network. Synonym : Final Event.

Estimate-to-Complete The estimated man hours, costs and time required to complete a work package or summary item (includes applicable overhead unless only direct costs are specified).

Event A specific accomplishment of an activity or activities at a recognizable point or time ; or a point in time representing the intersection of two or more arrows. Events do not consume time or resources.

Event Name An alphanumeric description of an event.

Event Number A numerical description of an event for computation and identification purposes.

Event Slack The difference between the latest allowable time T_L and the earliest expected time T_E for an event, i.e., $(T_L - T_E)$. Synonym : Slack or Slack Time.

Event Times Time information generated through the CPM calculation that identifies the start and finish times for each event in the network.

Expected Time or Expected Elapsed Time (t_E) A statistically weighted time estimate or a single knowledgeable estimate for activity duration. A weighted or mean time estimate incorporates an optimistic (t_O), most likely (t_L) and pessimistic (t_P) time estimates for the work to be accomplished.

Final Event An event which marks the completion of a project. Obviously it has preceding activities but no succeeding activities. Synonym : End Event.

Float The range within which the start time of an activity or its finish time may fluctuate without affecting the completion of the project. It is analogous to the term slack.

Free Float The difference between the earliest finish time for an activity and the earliest start time for its successor activity. Thus it is that portion of the total float which will not reduce the float for any succeeding activity.

Head Event An event at the termination point of an activity.

Independent Float The excess time that exists between finishing and starting of two activities if the preceding activity ends as late as possible and the succeeding activity starts as early as possible. Thus it is that portion of the total float within which the starting of an activity can be delayed without affecting the floats of the preceding activities.

Initial Event An event with which a project commences. It is an event with only succeeding activities and no preceding activities. Synonym : Start Event.

Interface Events The events which are common to two or more subnetworks.

Interfering Float The difference between the total float and free float of an activity.

Item A summary item on a work breakdown structure.

Lag A specified time interval between the start or completion of an activity and the start or completion of a successor activity.

Latest Event Time (T_L) The latest time by which an event must be completed to keep the project on schedule.

Latest Finish Time (LFT) The latest time at which an activity can be finished without delaying the completion of the project.

Latest Start Time (LST) The latest time by which an activity can be started without delaying the completion of the project.

Level The number of the level on the work breakdown structure (WBS) showing all the milestone and interface events.

Milestone A key network event that is of major significance in achieving the programme or project objectives.

Milestone Event An important or key event on a network which is of significance to the management.

Monitoring Following the progress of the work and indicating and highlighting the deviation from schedule.

Most Likely Time Estimate (t_L) This is the most realistic estimate of the time an activity might consume. When only one time estimate is given, this one is used. (PERT technology).

Multi Project Scheduling The use of the technique of resource allocation to schedule more than one project by considering all projects together and scheduling by activity priority within the constraints of available resources.

Network Analysis A group of techniques for presenting information relating time and resources so as to assist in the planning, scheduling and controlling of projects. The information usually represented by a network helps to determine the sequences, interdependencies, interrelationships and criticality of various activities of the project (This encompasses both PERT and CPM).

Negative Float The time by which an activity duration should be reduced for the project to be completed by the targeted date.

Normal Cost The cost of activity/project when it is performed under normal conditions.

Optimistic Time Estimate (t_O) The shortest possible time in which an activity can be completed under ideal conditions.

PERT Programme Evaluation and Review Technique.

Pessimistic Time Estimate (t_p) The maximum possible time that would be required to complete an activity.

Planning The establishment of the project activities and events, their logical relations and interrelations to each other and the sequence in which they are to be accomplished.

Predecessor Event An event that signifies the beginning of an activity in a network.

Project A scheme or a proposal of something intended to be constructed or devised.

Project Control The ability to determine project status as it relates to the selected time plan and schedule.

Project Time The time in which the project is planned to be completed. It must be consistent and is a net value (less holidays).

Required Completion Date The required date of completion assigned to a specific activity.

Resource Manpower, equipment, etc., required to implement the project.

Resource Aggregation (Resource Totalling) The totalling of resources required for concurrent activities having a commonality of such resources during a discrete portion of a project.

Resource Allocation The general technique of scheduling activities and the resources required by those activities so that predetermined constraints of resource availability and/or project time are not exceeded.

Resource Code The code for a particular manpower skill, material or equipment type.

Resource Levelling The rescheduling of activities such that as far as possible uniform demand for the resources is achieved but the maximum or peak demand for the resources does not exceed the available resources.

Resource Smoothing The rescheduling of the activities so that as far as possible a uniform demand for the resources is achieved within the scheduled, total project duration.

Resource Usage Profile or Histogram or Loading Chart A diagrammatic representation of the requirement of a particular type of resource for the various activities of a project.

Responsible Organisation The organisation responsible for management of a work package.

Schedule Completion Time (or Date) The time (or date) assigned for completion of a project which is also known as *contractual obligation time.*

Scheduled Event Time In PERT, an arbitrary schedule time that can be introduced at any event but is usually only used at certain milestones or the last event.

Scheduling Preparation of time bound programme for performance of activities as per agreed plan.

Slack or Slack Time The difference between the latest allowable time T_L and the earliest expected time T_E for an event, i.e., $(T_L - T_E)$. Synonym : Event Slack.

Slack Paths Those sequences of activities and events that do not lie on the critical path or paths.

Standard Deviation of Activity **(σ)** A measure of uncertainty calculated when using three time estimates. It is computed from the formula based on

Beta distribution : $\sigma = \left(\frac{t_P - t_O}{6}\right)$.

Standard Deviation of Activity Successor Event **or** ***Standard Deviation for the Project Network*** A measure of uncertainty about the event expected date. It is calculated by computing the square root of the sum of the squares of the activity standard deviations on the critical path or the longest path leading to the event under consideration.

Start Event An event with only succeeding activities and no preceding activities. Synonym : Initial Event.

Subcritical Activity An activity for which total float is positive.

Subcritical Path **or** ***Semi-critical Path*** A path with a least float next after the critical path.

Subnetwork A network which is part of a larger network, depicting details wherever necessary.

Supercritical Activity An activity for which total float is negative.

Total Float The difference between latest start time and earliest start time for an activity. This is given by the difference between the latest event time of the succeeding event minus the earliest event time of the preceding event and its duration time, i.e., $\left(T_L^j - T_E^i - t^{ij}\right)$.

Updating The process of periodic reviewing, reallocating the resources where necessary and redrafting the network when the project is in actual progress.

Variance of Activity The square of the activity standard deviation. Used in determining the standard deviation of an activity successor event.

Work Breakdown Schedule A pictorial representation of major and minor objectives of a project. It highlights the identifiable components of a project which needs to be completed to achieve the completion of the project.

REFERENCES

1. Ahuja, H.N., *Project Management*, Wiley–interscience.
2. Barrie, D.S., and Paulson Jr., B.C., *Professional Construction Management*, McGraw - Hill.
3. Chandra, D., Plan for Success the PERT Way, *National Productivity Council*.
4. Choudhury, S., *Project Scheduling and Monitoring in Practice*, South Asian Publishers.
5. Clough, R.H., *Construction Project Management*, Wiley–Interscience.
6. Federal Electric Corporation, *A Programmed Introduction to PERT*, John Wiley and Sons.
7. Hackney, J.W., *Control and Management of Capital Projects*, John Wiley and Sons.
8. Levin, R.I., and Kirkpatrick, C.A., *Planning and Control with PERT/CPM*, Tata McGraw-Hill Publishing Company Ltd.
9. Naik, B.M., *Project Management Scheduling and Monitoring by PERT/CPM*, Vani Educational Books.
10. Sinha, A.K., and Sinha, R., *Project Engineering and Management*, Vikas Publishing House Pvt., Ltd.
11. Srinath, L.S., *PERT and CPM Principles and Applications*, Affiliated East-West Press Pvt., Ltd.
12. Wiest, J.D., and Levy, F.K., *A Management Guide to PERT/CPM*, Prentice-Hall of India Pvt., Ltd.

Index